EXPLORING
THE
SCRIPTURES

THE JOHN PHILLIPS COMMENTARY SERIES

EXPLORING THE SCRIPTURES

An Overview of the Bible from Genesis to Revelation

JOHN PHILLIPS

KREGEL
PUBLICATIONS

Exploring the Scriptures: An Overview of the Bible from Genesis to Revelation

© 1965, 1970, 2022 by John Phillips

Published in 2001 by Kregel Publications, a division of Kregel Inc., 2450 Oak Industrial Dr. NE, Grand Rapids, MI 49505.

Library of Congress Cataloging-in-Publication Data
Phillips, John.
   Exploring the Scriptures: an overview of the Bible from Genesis to Revelation / by John Phillips.
      p.   cm.
   Originally published: Chicago: Moody Press, 1967.
   1. Bible—Introductions. I. Title.
BS475.3 .P48   2001   220.6'1—dc21   2001033770
                                      CIP

ISBN 978-0-8254-4515-6

Printed in the United States of America

1 2 3 4 5 / 29 28 27 26 25 24 23 22

Contents

Foreword

It gives me much pleasure to write a few words by way of commendation of this excellent and important book. My pleasure is intensified by the fact that I have known Mr. John Phillips as a dear friend and fellow worker for many years.

It was shortly after the second World War that our association became intimate and meaningful. Mr. Phillips was then a young man, just released from the Armed Forces—searching and questing for "the deep things of God." He became a member of a Young People's Fellowship in the British Isles, of which I was both leader and teacher. As I observed him at that time, I had the conviction that he would one day distinguish himself as an able student and Bible expositor. This he has done, under the good hand of God, the anointing of the Holy Spirit, and a systematic study of the Scriptures.

The Bible contains 3,566,480 letters, 810,697 words, 31,175 verses, 1,189 chapters, and 66 books. It is, therefore, a "divine library," and demands not only spiritual illumination but also the practical application of reverent and diligent study methods in order to master its diversified subjects, as well as its unified message.

The right approach to such an examination of the Bible is first to analyze and then to synthesize the contents. *Exploring the Scriptures* is concerned with the first aspect of this approach, or seeing the Book as a whole. To put it another way, we might say that before showing us the street maps of the great cities of the world, Mr. Phillips, like a good student of geography, takes us further back to see the countries to which these cities belong. In other words, he directs our attention to the fact that like the world, the Bible has two hemispheres, and within those hemispheres continents, seas, islands, rivers, mountain ranges, and many other features of inspired "doctrine, reproof, correction, and instruction in righteousness." With such a glorious perspective, the author thus prepares us for the exciting itinerary into God's world of unfolding truth.

Of one thing I am particularly thankful. Mr. Phillips does not attempt to entertain us with "Biblical objectivism." His book, though designed to aid our study of the Word of God, is also a call to holiness, prayerfulness and fruitfulness of life in Christ. We certainly need men and women who know and preach the Bible; but even more urgent is the need for men and women who LIVE the Bible! It is my earnest prayer that the Lord will use this exceedingly useful volume to help us all to learn, love and live THE SCRIPTURES.

Stephen F. Olford

1
Climbing the Heights

P roperly done, Bible study is an adventure-packed experience. It is a voyage of discovery for, as often as not, we find ourselves sooner or later in unknown parts. Like all explorers, the wise student of Scripture will climb the heights now and then to survey the lay of the land.

Going Places

In the Bible there are themes which wend their way like flowing rivers from Genesis to Revelation. There are towering ranges of prophetic truth and mighty peaks of revelation. These all need to be seen in their right relationship the one to the other. That is why Bible survey is such a basic and vital method of exploring the Book.

The topography of the Bible is varied indeed. The great foundation stones of the Pentateuch appear first. Then the undulating plains of Bible history can be seen. Next come the limpid lakes and rich pastures of Hebrew poetry. And behind these tower the beetling crags of the prophetic ranges. These are the mighty Himalayas of God's Word, challenging the vigorous student to come and plant his feet on higher ground.

Beyond Mount Malachi is a dark valley lying between two testaments. Then the Gospels appear, familiar territory to most, leading on into the great metropolis of the book of Acts. Next come the fertile fields of the epistles, the fragrant letter-lands of the New Testament. Then once again, and for the last time, the country slopes upward by way of mysterious Mount Revelation until finally, high and lifted up, we see the golden streets of the celestial city, the New Jerusalem.

Meeting People

The Bible is a book of people and places. One of the best ways to master it is deliberately to visit—in the study, that is—all the places it mentions. They are interesting places. Glance at them for a moment. Eden, the garden of God, man's first and most beautiful home. Ur of the Chaldees, where Abraham was born. Bethel, the house of God. Egypt, ancient land of the Nile. There is Canaan, the Promised Land, the focal point of all Bible geography. And who can think of Canaan without thinking of Jericho, Jerusalem, and Jordan, of Bethlehem and Beersheba, of Samaria, Shechem, and the Sea of Galilee? Then, beyond the borders of Canaan lie the great empires of antiquity: Assyria, Egypt, Babylon, Persia, Greece, and Rome—and the important cities of days gone by: Antioch, Corinth, Ephesus, Athens, and Rome.

And what of the multitudes of people who crowd the pages of the Bible? Adam and Eve, Cain and Abel, Enoch and Noah, Shem, Ham, and Japheth, Abraham, Isaac, and Jacob—these names, together with Joseph's, spell out the story of Genesis. Moses and Aaron tell us the story of Exodus. Then there is Joshua, followed by the judges; Samuel and the great seers of Israel; Saul and David, Solomon and the long line of Hebrew kings. Mingling with these are Isaiah and Jeremiah, Jonah and Joel, Hosea, Habakkuk, and Haggai, and the goodly company of the other prophets.

Passing from Malachi to Matthew we move from the old to the new and are ushered into the presence of Jesus of Nazareth, that Holy One of Israel, the Lamb of God, who bore our sins in His own body on the tree. He it is who dominates the Bible from cover to cover and around whom all history revolves.

The Gospels throng with people. They press in upon us—people just like ourselves with fears and frustrations, sins and sorrows, burdens and needs. Passing on into the book of Acts we meet members of the early church: Peter and Paul, James and John, Silas and Stephen, and multitudes from every nation, kindred, people, and tongue. Then, with John the Beloved, we are caught up in the Spirit to see that countless multitude on high awaking the echoes of the everlasting hills with the resounding praises of the Lamb.

The Proper Perspective

A certain copy of the Constitution of the United States was once executed in superb penmanship by the hand of an artist. In some places the words are all cramped together, while in others they are spaced far apart. Looking at the manuscript closely, there seems to be little reason for such a spacing of the words. Standing back, however, and looking at the production from a distance, the artist's purpose becomes clear. He not only wrote out the Constitution but also portrayed the face of George Washington, his cramped and spaced-out words forming lights and shadows on the page.

Thus it is with the Bible. The creation of the stars is covered in Genesis 1 in five short words: "He made the stars also." Yet the story of the tabernacle is spread over some fifty chapters of the Bible. All we know of the life of Jesus between His birth and His baptism is covered in a single page of Scripture. Yet page after page is devoted to genealogies which perhaps appear endless and pointless to us. We ask, "Why such an uneven choice of subject matter?" The answer becomes clear when we take a survey look at the Bible. Woven into *all* the Scripture is the perfect portrait of God's beloved Son.

Jesus Used the Survey Method

Long years ago, two sad and discouraged disciples of the crucified Christ were making their way back home across the hills of Judea. It had been a delightful dream while it lasted. They had known Christ well, had thrilled to His words and His works, had staked everything on Him. They had expected Him to sweep Jerusalem of its corruption, rid the Promised Land of the Romans, and extend His empire to the uttermost parts of the earth. It was all over now. Christ had been crucified on a Roman cross and had been buried in a Jerusalem tomb.

The dream was over! True, certain women were circulating a story of a resurrection and an empty tomb. There could be nothing to a tale like that! All they had left were memories, and dreams of what might have been. Then, on that weary road they were joined by Another. "Ought not Christ to have suffered?" He asked. Then, "beginning at Moses and all the prophets, he expounded unto them in all the Scriptures the things concerning himself." By giving them a *survey* of the Scriptures, He gave them back their proper perspective. They had thought only of a sovereign Messiah. He showed them also a suffering Messiah. From bias He wooed them back to balance. To their view of a Christ coming to reign He added a view of a Christ coming to redeem.

This is one of the supreme values of seeing the Bible as a whole. Not only can the parts of the Bible be held in proper perspective but the student, exploring any given part, can have a proper sense of direction. So then, let us climb the heights.

11

2
Genesis: The Book of Beginnings

It has well been said that Genesis tells us the beginning of everything except God. It is the seed-plot of the Bible. Almost every subject of major importance has its roots in Genesis. As the great, spreading oak tree once reposed in an acorn, so the vast ramifications of truth revealed in the Bible lie latent in Genesis.

An Analysis of Genesis

Genesis is an easy book to analyze. It can be summed up in eight words: Creation, Fall, Flood, Babel, Abraham, Isaac, Jacob, and Joseph.

   I. THE BEGINNINGS OF THE HUMAN RACE—PRIMEVAL HISTORY
      (1:1–11:9)
      A. The Creation
      B. The Fall
      C. The Flood
      D. The Tower of Babel
   II. THE BEGINNINGS OF THE HEBREW RACE—PATRIARCHAL HISTORY
      (11:10–50:26)
      A. Abraham

B. Isaac
C. Jacob
D. Joseph

The quickest way to demolish a building is to attack its foundation. If the foundation can be destroyed, the whole superstructure will fall. It is not surprising, therefore, that some of the heaviest attacks against the Bible have been leveled against its earlier chapters. If a person can be persuaded to pull out the first pages from his Bible, so to speak, it will not be long before the last pages will be falling out also.

The Creation

Harold Fortescue, when a junior reporter for a great London paper, handed in an embellished account of a social function he had been assigned to cover. Proud of his efforts, he awaited the editor's comments. "Cut it down to one sheet!" he was told. Protesting, Fortescue argued that this would be impossible. "Young man," said the editor, "you have evidently failed to observe that the story of the Creation is told in just ten words: 'In the beginning God created the heaven and the earth.'" Such is the wonder of the Word. At once it is both simple and sublime.

The Bible makes no attempt to prove that there is a God. It takes this fact as self-evident. Thirty-two times in thirty-one verses in Genesis 1 God is mentioned by name, and a further eleven times by use of personal pronouns. Genesis 1 is the most God-centered chapter in the Bible. The expression "and God said" occurs ten times. Here are God's first ten commandments addressed to the material world, all of which have been perfectly kept. They thus stand in marked contrast with His second set of ten commandments in Exodus 20, all of which have been continuously broken.

The Stages of Creation

THE FIRST PHASE	THE SECOND PHASE
1. Light established	4. The heavenly bodies ordained to function
2. The waters separated	5. Fish and fowl created
3. The continents raised from the sea and plant life established	6. Animals and man created

The expression "after its kind" occurs ten times in Genesis 1. This recognizes the principle that, while there may be mutation within a given "kind," there is no transmutation between the kinds.

The order of the Creation is interesting too. It begins with the coming of light, the separation of the "waters below" from the "waters above," and the emergence of the land masses from beneath the ocean waves. It continues with the creation of herbs, grasses, and trees, fish and fowl, cattle, creeping things, and beasts. It concludes with the creation of man.

The Fall

Man was made "in the image of God," a perfect being. Genesis 3 tells how he fell. Involved in the Fall of man were the animal kingdom (the temptation came through the serpent), the vegetable kingdom (the forbidden fruit was the object), and the human kingdom (both Adam and Eve were involved). It is important to observe that the serpent tempted Eve, and Eve tempted Adam. Eve was deceived, Adam was disobedient. The Lord Jesus believed about Adam and Eve (Matthew 19:4), and Romans 5 is built on the assumption that Genesis 3 is historically accurate.

Sin, sorrow, suffering, and death stemmed from the Fall. Adam's children were born in his own fallen image (Genesis 5:3). Man's first sin separated man from God; the second sin, as told in the story of Cain and Abel, separated man from man. Christ came to restore both these lost relationships through the work of the Cross.

The Flood

Genesis 4 lists the descendants of Cain and Genesis 5 the descendants of Seth. The history of Cain's descendants was one of worldly-mindedness which climaxed in the wickedness of Lamech, the seventh from Adam. The history of the Sethites was one of other-worldliness. In this line godliness climaxed in Enoch, likewise the seventh from Adam. In Genesis 6 the separation between the people of God and the children of the world disappears. Human apostasy reached to Heaven calling for judgment.

The Lord Jesus believed in a literal Noah, a literal ark, and a literal Flood. To question the historical accuracy of this event is to challenge the deity of Christ. The Flood was God's answer to man's unrepentant wickedness. It did not come, however, until the world had been well warned and provision made for salvation. The waters of the Flood did not fully abate for a whole year.

14

Adam's Immediate Descendants

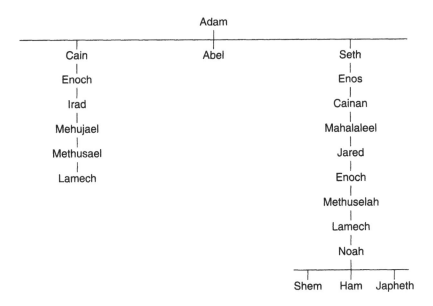

The Tower of Babel

Genesis 10 gives us the earliest table in existence of the origin of the nations. Shem, Ham, and Japheth, the sons of Noah, became the founders of the three great racial families of the earth. The Semitic tribes descended from Shem; the dark-skinned African and the Canaanite races descended from Ham; the other nations descended from Japheth.

The building of the Tower of Babel was an attempt by man to build a united world society from which God was to be excluded. It ended in judgment, the confounding of human speech, and the scattering of the human family to the ends of the earth.

Abraham

By the time of Abraham, idolatry had spread over the entire earth. Ur of the Chaldees, where Abraham was born, was a center of moon worship. Obeying the call of God, Abraham left Ur to become a pilgrim and stranger in the land of Canaan, the Land of Promise. God entered into a covenant with Abraham to give him and his seed this land forever.

Many testing experiences were brought into Abraham's life.

15

Hebrews 11 reminds us that he "died in faith, not having received the promises." His only actual territorial possession in Canaan was a tomb. Yet God had not failed. In the early days of Abraham's pilgrimage God told him that the promise would not be fulfilled until a future date. (See Genesis 15:13-21.)

Isaac

The covenant promises were confirmed to Isaac and later to Jacob. The word *overshadowed* gives us the clue to Isaac's history. The earlier part of it is incorporated into the story of Abraham, and the later part into the history of Jacob. In his unusual birth, in his "obedience unto death," and in his marriage, Isaac is one of the greatest illustrations of Christ in the Old Testament.

Jacob

Jacob's history can be summarized in three words: supplanter, servant, and saint. His deceitful conduct toward his twin brother Esau laid the foundations for the national enmity which existed later between the nations of Israel and Edom, and which continues today. At Peniel, where Jacob wrestled with the angel, it seems that both his name and his nature were changed. From Jacob ("supplanter") he became Israel ("he who strives with God," or "prince with God"). His sons became known as "the children of Israel" and were the founders of the twelve tribes. Their history occupies the greater part of the Old Testament. These sons were, in the order of their birth, Reuben, Simeon, Levi, Judah, Dan, Naphtali, Gad, Asher, Issachar, Zebulun, Joseph, and Benjamin.

Joseph

About one quarter of Genesis is taken up with the history of Joseph, Jacob's favorite son. Sold as a slave into Egypt through the jealousy of his brothers, Joseph was later falsely accused and imprisoned. Subsequently, because of his ability to interpret Pharaoh's dreams and because of his practical wisdom, he was promoted to the highest office in the land. A severe famine forced the Hebrew patriarchal family to seek food in Egypt. Joseph, now the "prime minister" of Egypt, recognized his brethren and so worked upon their consciences as to bring them to a voluntary confession of their sin in selling him as a slave. Then he made himself known to them and installed them and their families in the land of Goshen.

Before his death, Jacob adopted Ephraim and Manasseh, the two sons of Joseph, into the patriarchal line. In Genesis 49 we read how Jacob summoned his sons to his side to give them his dying blessing, and foretold their history to the end of time.

To give a visualization of the relationships which existed between the more important personages of Genesis, a simple "family tree" is given below.

Adam to the Twelve Tribes

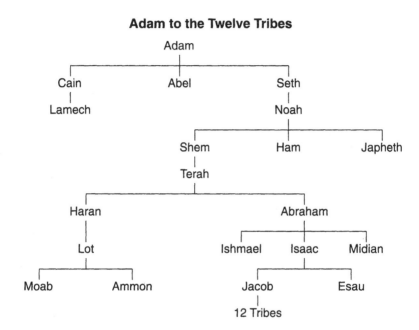

THE BACKGROUND
OF GENESIS

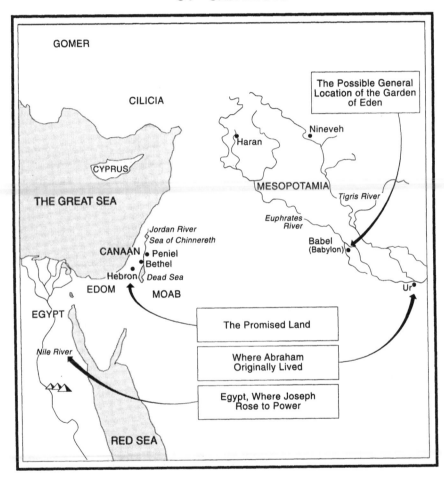

3
Exodus: The Way Out

E xodus is the book of redemption. Its first word, *now*, links it onto Genesis. Leviticus, Numbers, and Deuteronomy all begin with conjunctions also, making the Pentateuch one single book. Exodus begins with the expression "Now these are the names," for redemption ever has to do with names—names written by grace into the book of God. The word *exodus* comes from the Greek and means "the way out."

Between Genesis and Exodus the patriarchal family became a nation numbering between two and three million. In Genesis 15:13-16 God plainly told Abraham that at least 400 years would elapse between the *promise* of Canaan as an inheritance and the *possession* of Canaan as an inheritance.[1] He was also told in advance that his people would be afflicted in a strange land.

Outline of Exodus

There are three distinct movements in the drama of redemption as seen in Exodus:

    I. AN ENSLAVED PEOPLE ARE SAVED (1–12)
      A. God Develops His Man (1–4)
      B. God Displays His Might (5–11)
      C. God Declares His Mind (12)
    II. A SAVED PEOPLE ARE SEPARATED (13–18)

Redemption Begins with a Man

Throughout the Scriptures redemption is centered in a man, the Man Christ Jesus. Moses was a type of Christ, Egypt a type of the world, Pharaoh a type of Satan, and Israel a type of man, enslaved and needing to be redeemed. Israel in "the house of bondage" needed a kinsman-redeemer. He was found in Moses, who was an Israelite both by birth and by choice (Hebrews 11:24-26). Of his own free will he cast in his lot with an enslaved people in order to deliver them from bondage.

The Importance of Moses

Moses occupies a very prominent place on the pages of Scripture. He is one of the most important of all Bible characters, his name occurring about 720 times. Our Lord was a firm believer in a historical man named Moses. And Peter, Paul, Jude, and John all referred to him.

The record of his life presents a series of most interesting parallels to Christ. Like Christ, he was born with the jaws of death gaping for him. Like Christ, he was reared in obscurity. Between his birth and his call to redeem we get but one glimpse of Moses, as we get but one glimpse of Jesus in a similar period. In both cases the one glimpse is sufficient to show us the way the twig is bent and the way the tree will grow. Like Christ, Moses came to his own only to be scornfully rejected. Similarly, he took a "Gentile bride" during the days of his rejection. Finally he reappeared in Israel's darkest hour (as Christ yet will) and brought about the national salvation of Israel by acts of irresistible supernatural power. It is little wonder that in later years Moses deliberately likened himself to Christ. "The Lord thy God will raise up unto thee a Prophet from the midst of thee, of thy brethren, like unto me" (Deuteronomy 18:15).

Demonstrations of Divine Power

The Israelites could no more deliver themselves from Pharaoh than we today can deliver ourselves from the power of sin. Their case was hopeless. They were born in bondage and under the sentence of death. Then came Moses, armed with divine authority, with mighty demonstrations of power, and Pharaoh's kingdom was shaken to its foundations. The false gods of Egypt were exposed as impotent. Egypt was judged and its prince, its policies, and its pretenses humbled in the dust.

In all this Moses was a faint shadow on the scene of history of the coming Christ. Never, before or since, have demonstrations of divine power been seen such as Jesus displayed. Demons, disease, death, and disaster all fled at His word. From the cradle at Bethlehem to the cross at Calvary, the Lord Jesus went forth "conquering and to conquer." He could not be destroyed, deviated, nor deceived. Satan's wiles were employed against Him in vain. The citadel of His soul was impregnable. It could be taken neither by storm from without nor by seduction within. He could not be tempted to deliberate sin nor trapped into an accidental fall. He could not be crowded to a hasty decision, baited to speak a hasty word, nor pressured into a hasty act.

Jesus came to challenge Satan and to deliver his captives. He came with deeds that demonstrated Deity in humanity, words that were the sublimest ever spoken, and wisdom that awed even His foes. He came with the ultimatum, "Let my people go." He shattered Satan's power, destroyed his kingdom, and made a way of escape possible for all slaves of sin.

Redemption by Blood

In Exodus it is made crystal clear that redemption rests upon the shedding of the blood of the Paschal lamb. Each individual personally must shelter behind the blood. The lamb must be without spot or blemish. The date of its death was set by divine decree.

Long centuries afterward, John the Baptist pointed to Christ with the words, "Behold the Lamb of God, which taketh away the sin of the world" (John 1:29). God's terms of redemption are the same today as they were in the days of Moses. Israel looked forward by faith to Christ's atoning death on Calvary's cross, while we look back by faith to the same event.

Separation from Egypt

Even before the contest with Pharaoh was over, God instructed Moses to lead the people clear across the Red Sea. There was to be no going back to Egypt. The old way of life was to be left behind forever. In the waters of the Red Sea, Israel, as it were, died to Egypt, and Egypt's hold over Israel was completely broken. On the wilderness side of the sea, Moses lifted up his voice in song—the first song in Scripture. Only a redeemed people can truly sing. Salvation and song go together. When a person is saved and knows it, when he has learned that he has passed from death unto life, and is separated from the old way of life—then he can sing!

Not all the experiences which awaited Israel after their redemption were pleasant, but all were necessary. God intended to mature His people before bringing them into Canaan, where the sternest battles would have to be fought. Drinking water from the smitten rock, feasting on the manna, warring with Amalek—all these experiences were necessary. Israel often murmured at these experiences, betraying immaturity. But God patiently continued His wise dealings with them. Sometimes new Christians wonder why they are not exempt from the trials of life. Often the Christian life is much harder than life in the old days of slavery to sin. God is faithful, however, in molding and maturing His own. Notice also what an impact the testimony of redeemed Israel made on Jethro, Moses' father-in-law (Exodus 18). God expects that redeemed people will always make an impact on others.

The Law

At Mount Sinai Israel was given the law. Up to this point all had been of grace, but at Sinai Israel rashly undertook to keep the whole law of God. The law itself was given under the most solemn circumstances. Its chief purpose was to expose sin and paint in most vivid colors the fearful, blazing, dazzling holiness of God.

The law fell into two divisions, moral and ceremonial. The moral law revealed why holiness was important, and the ceremonial law revealed how holiness was to be imparted. The moral law reveals to saint and sinner alike that the human heart cannot produce holiness of itself. The ceremonial law with its many sacrifices and offerings points to Christ, who alone kept the moral law and whose blood alone can cleanse from sin.

The Tabernacle

A large part of Exodus is devoted to a description of the tabernacle. Actually some fifty chapters in the Bible relate to this important structure. The tabernacle was the focus of the national life of Israel in the wilderness, for the tribes encamped around it in an orderly fashion. The life of the nation was lived in direct relationship to the tabernacle, every part of which spoke of Christ, the true gathering center of His redeemed people (Matthew 18:20).

The tabernacle had three courts. The first of these was a large curtained enclosure with a wide gateway hung with curtains of gorgeous color. Just inside the gate was the brazen altar, on which the animal sacrifices were offered. Beyond that was the brazen laver containing water for the various washings demanded of the priests. The tabernacle itself was made of boards overlaid with gold. Draped over these boards were four different coverings of various materials. The tabernacle was divided into two parts by a magnificent drape called the veil.

In the outer part, called the Holy Place, were three pieces of furniture: the lampstand, the table of shewbread, and the golden altar of incense. Beyond the veil in the Holy of Holies was the sacred ark of God with its golden lid known as the mercy seat. Resting on the mercy seat was the Shekinah cloud, the visible token of God's presence among His people.

The book of Exodus ends with a description of the Shekinah glory filling the tabernacle. Despite the failures of even a redeemed people, God in His grace cannot be hindered from fulfilling His ultimate purposes in redemption. Exodus can be summarized in three words: life, law, and love—and the greatest of these is love.

---

1. Compare Galatians 3:17. The 430 years are from the time Jacob came to Egypt to the Exodus, and thus this Scripture refers to the covenant promises being renewed to Jacob as in Genesis 35:9ff. or 46:2ff. (Cf. Psalm 105:9f.)

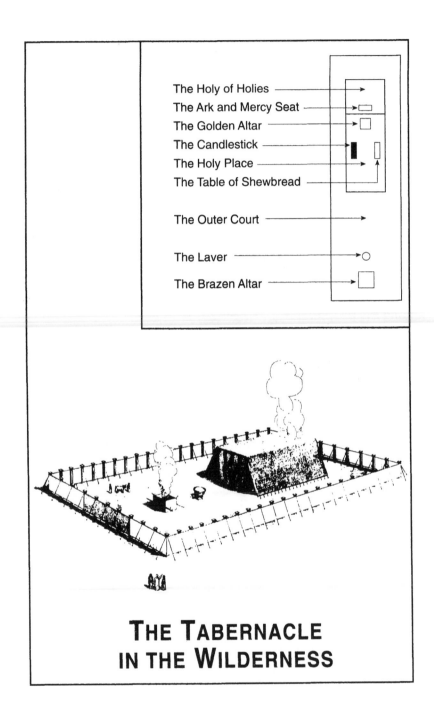

The Holy of Holies

The Ark and Mercy Seat

The Golden Altar

The Candlestick

The Holy Place

The Table of Shewbread

The Outer Court

The Laver

The Brazen Altar

THE TABERNACLE IN THE WILDERNESS

4

Leviticus: Provisions for Holy Living

In Exodus we see how God gets His people out of Egypt. In Leviticus we see how God gets "Egypt" out of His people. Exodus begins with sinners, Leviticus with saints. Exodus shows the way out from the land of bondage. Leviticus shows us the way into the sanctuary of God. Exodus is the book of deliverance, Leviticus is the book of dedication.

The book of Leviticus stands in relation to Exodus as the epistles stand in relation to the Gospels. In Exodus the Passover is introduced and appropriated by faith, making the *fact* of sacrifice clear. Leviticus goes into detail and gives the *doctrine* of sacrifice. The sinner needs only to know that the sacrifice has been made, but the saint needs to know much more. He needs to know the implications of the sacrifice.

The whole of Leviticus and the first ten chapters of Numbers (through 10:10) come between the first day of the first month and the twentieth day of the second month in the year following that of the exodus. Leviticus begins with God speaking to Moses "out of the tabernacle." This is in contrast with God's previous words to Moses in that mount which burned with fire and shook beneath the feet of God.

In Leviticus great spiritual truths are enshrined in vivid symbols. Much that Leviticus was intended to teach has already been fulfilled, as the Epistle to the Hebrews shows. There are, however, truths taught here in type which still await fulfillment at the second coming of Christ. This is especially so with the underlying teaching of the feasts.

Outline of Leviticus

    I. THE WAY TO GOD (1–10)
      A. The Sacrifices of the People (1–7)
        1. Requirements (1:1–6:7)
        2. Regulations (6:8–7:38)
      B. The Sanctity of the Priesthood (8–10)
        1. Consecration (8)
        2. Ministration (9)
        3. Violation (10)
    II. THE WALK WITH GOD (11–20)
      A. A Clean Life Selfward (11–15)
      B. A Clean Life Godward (16–17)
      C. A Clean Life Manward (18–20)
    III. THE WORSHIP OF GOD (21–24:9)
      A. The Family of the Priests (12–22)
        1. The Priest's Family (21:1-15)
          a. Mourning in the Family (21:1-6)
          b. Marriage in the Family (21:7-15)
        2. The Priest's Fellowship (21:16–22:16)
        3. The Priest's Function (22:17-33)
      B. The Feasts of the Lord (23)
      C. The Furniture of the Tabernacle (24:1-9)
    IV. THE WITNESS TO GOD (24:10–27:34)
      A. In the Sphere of Profession (24:10-23)
      B. In the Sphere of Possession (25–26)
        1. Times Connected with the Possession (25)
        2. Terms Connected with the Possession (26)
      C. In The Sphere of Promise (27)

The Offerings

There were five major offerings required under the law. These all set forth aspects of the sacrifice of Christ on the cross. Actually there were more than five offerings required under the Mosaic law, but the others were complementary to these five. These five offerings were divided into two main types. The first three were *sweet savor* offerings, that is, they were fragrant because they set forth Christ's willing devotedness to the divine will. The last two were *sin* offerings, that is, they typified what Christ has done to obtain forgiveness for men. They can be set forth thus:

1. The Preciousness of Christ's Sacrifice
   (The Sweet Savor Offerings—The Godward Side of Calvary)
   a. The Burnt Offering—The Fullness of Christ's Devotion
   b. The Meal Offering—The Flawlessness of Christ's Devotion
   c. The Peace Offering—The Fruitfulness of Christ's Devotion
2. The Purpose of Christ's Sacrifice
   (The Sin Offerings—The Manward Side of Calvary)
   a. The Sin Offering—Covering the Principle of Sin
   b. The Trespass Offering—Covering the Practice of Sin

The Jew of the Old Testament times probably only dimly apprehended the typical significance of these offerings. They were to him a very practical provision under the law for the problem of sin's guilt. From earliest times God had insisted on sacrifice as the ground upon which He was to be approached. Every Israelite knew this. Adam, Abel, Noah, and Abraham all had their altars. The time had now come for the sacrifices to be systematized and made an integral part of the Hebrew religion.

The burnt offering was used in worship, for all was for God. The variations allowed in the types of victim to be offered taught the people proportionate giving in worship, for God does not expect more than we have to give. Nor does He expect less.

The sin offering covered sins of error, weakness, and ignorance, not deliberate sin. Everything about this offering was designed to convey to the sinner the seriousness of his sin, his responsibility for it, and the cost of his atonement. Sin, he learned, is a radical disease and calls for a radical cure.

The trespass offering was always accompanied by a recompense paid both to God, who had been offended by the sin, and to the person who had been defrauded by it. This type of offering was to be made whenever a tithe or a duty had been neglected, whenever a divine command had been broken, and whenever someone had been defrauded.

The peace offering did not carry with it so much the ideas of presentation and atonement so conspicuous in the three offerings

27

mentioned above. The idea of this offering was that of communion, for the offerer and the priest sat down in the presence of God and feasted upon the sacrifice together. It was a kind of "Lord's Supper" in Old Testament times.

The meal offering was a gift to God and was not a means of atonement. It was always the product of human labor and gave the Israelite an opportunity to bring his service to God in a sacrificial way.

It is easy to visualize the conscience-smitten Israelite, faced with a broken law and fearing the wrath of God, bringing his lamb to the altar. There he stands, placing his hands upon the creature's head and confessing his sin. Now he stands back and watches as the lamb is slain, its blood shed, and its lifeless remains committed to the fire upon the altar, the flames of which were never to be extinguished. The sacrifice complete, the Israelite returns home conscious that he has availed himself of God's provision under the law for his sin. It is easy, too, to see the grateful Israelite worshiper bringing his ox to the altar as an expression of worship and thanks to God for all His bounty and care.

Provision was made under the Mosaic law for rich and poor. The wealthy could bring an ox, the poor could bring a dove. Solomon, at the dedication of the temple, offered twenty-two thousand oxen and one hundred and twenty thousand sheep (1 Kings 8:63) whereas Mary, the mother of the Lord, brought for her purification a pair of turtle-doves (Luke 2:24), the offering of the poor.

The epistle to the Hebrews reminds us that the sacrifices of the Old Testament were only a temporary provision for sin. In themselves they could not give the guilty conscience peace nor wash away the stain of sin. They had to be repeated over and over again because of their impotence to make the offerer perfect. But now "richer blood has flowed from nobler veins," and in the sacrifice of the Lord Jesus at Calvary we have the one perfect offering for sin. Actually both Old Testament and New Testament believers are saved by faith, the former by looking forward to Calvary, and the latter by looking back.

The Priesthood

It has been observed that "where priesthood is introduced as an office it is for a people already redeemed." There is no priesthood for the world. The priest's function was to represent the people of God. Of course, the Lord Jesus as Great High Priest alone does this to perfection. The priesthood connected with Aaron was a provisional measure to be abolished in due time by the better priesthood of Christ, as the book of Hebrews so fully explains.

Israel's first official priest was Aaron, the brother of Moses. Elaborate instructions were given concerning the consecration, robing, office, and functions of Israel's priests. Aaron and Moses were from the tribe of Levi, and the whole tribe was later set apart to minister to God in connection with the more secular aspects of the tabernacle service. Only Aaron's sons and descendants, however, could properly be priests. Since Israel's kings were to be from the tribe of Judah, it follows that no man in Israel could be both a king and a priest. Technically this would have excluded the Lord Himself from being a priest. Indeed, during His lifetime He made no attempt to intrude into the priestly office. Never once did He seek to enter into the Holy Place of the temple, still less into the Holy of Holies.

Centuries before the birth of Aaron there was a king-priest by the name of Melchizedek reigning in Jerusalem (Genesis 14:18-20). Christ's title to priesthood, like that of Melchizedek, has nothing to do with descent from Aaron. His priesthood is superior to that of Aaron in every way. He is a royal priest with an eternal, changeless, unique, and effective ministry. While the Aaronic priesthood is inferior to that of Melchizedek and, of course, to that of Christ, it does set forth many valuable lessons.

Whenever Aaron is considered alone, he sets forth the priestly ministry of the Lord Himself. Where he is considered in connection with his sons, he sets forth the priestly ministry of the church. Where he is considered in connection with the Levites, he sets forth the priestly ministry of each true believer today.

Cleanness of Life

The book of Leviticus sets before the redeemed people of Israel the emphatic need for personal cleanliness. The dietary laws of chapter 11 were not only medically sound; they also set forth many valuable spiritual lessons concerning the believer's walk. The same applies to the laws covering births, leprosy, and issues in chapters 12–15.

The Day of Atonement, described in chapter 16, was a great day in Israel. The ritual was most impressive. There were great searchings of heart, and sin was symbolically put away from the nation. On this day the high priest was permitted to enter the Holy of Holies in the tabernacle. He did so to sprinkle blood on the mercy seat of the ark of the covenant. The teaching connected with the Day of Atonement speaks of the finished work of Christ and of His present appearing in the presence of God for His people. In view of this great provision, Israel was expected to maintain the highest standards of holiness in all its conduct (17–20).

The Feasts of the Lord

Israel's religious festivals were great days. They were planned by God to constantly remind the people of the great epochs in their history. These festivals were intended to give public acknowledgment to the fact that all the land belonged to God. And they helped to bring about a sense of national unity—a fact which Jeroboam recognized when he set up the rival ten-tribe kingdom in revolt against the throne of David in Jerusalem in later years. One of Jeroboam's first acts was to organize a new religious calendar to break all ties with Jerusalem and the temple. The festivals commanded under the law were also to serve as object lessons to the children, and were to be the occasion of giving religious instruction to the little ones.

The annual feasts and fasts were seven in number. Four of them were celebrated in rapid succession at the beginning of the year. The other three took place in succession in the seventh month. The first four were all literally fulfilled through Christ by His first coming. The remaining three will be just as literally fulfilled by Christ at His second coming. The interval between the feasts in Israel's religious calendar illustrates the time gap between the first and second comings of the Lord.

The Passover

This feast commemorated the deliverance of Israel from Egypt in the days of Moses as recorded in the book of Exodus. It speaks of redemption, and typically it stands for "Christ our passover . . . sacrificed for us" (1 Corinthians 5:7).

The Unleavened Bread

This feast was closely associated with the Passover. In the Bible leaven is invariably a symbol of evil, especially evil doctrine. The Israelites were to put all leaven out of the house and for seven days they were to eat unleavened bread. First comes redemption and then a separated walk.

The Firstfruits

This feast was a consecration of the harvest and marked the beginning of the grain harvest in the land. A sheaf of barley was taken from the field and waved before the Lord. The feast took place on the first day of the week and is typical of the resurrection of Christ.

The Feasts of Israel

MONTH				FESTIVAL	
Sacred Year	Civil Year	Jewish	Christian	Day	Event
1	7	Nisan (Abib)	March-April	14	Passover
1	7	Nisan (Abib)	March-April	15-21	Unleavened Bread
1	7	Nisan (Abib)	March-April	16	Firstfruits (barley harvest)
3	9	Sivan	May-June	6	Pentecost
7	1	Tishri (Ethanim)	Sept.-Oct.	1	Trumpets
7	1	Tishri (Ethanim)	Sept.-Oct.	10	Day of Atonement
7	1	Tishri (Ethanim)	Sept.-Oct.	15-21	Tabernacles

Pentecost

Fifty days after the presentation of the wave sheaf, two loaves were presented and waved before the Lord, marking the completion of the grain harvest. In type, of course, Pentecost looked forward to the day when Pentecost would be *fully* come (Acts 2:1) and the Holy Spirit would descend to bring the Church into being.

Trumpets

A long interval elapsed between the Feast of Pentecost and the Feast of Trumpets. The trumpets represented Jehovah's call to Israel to regather in preparation for the two great events to follow almost immediately.

Atonement

The Day of Atonement marked the most solemn occasion in Israel's religious calendar. It was called a day of affliction and was a time when the nation's sins were called to remembrance. On this day only in the whole year the high priest was permitted to pass into the Holy of Holies in the tabernacle. Two goats were taken, and one, chosen by lot, bore away the sins of the nation into "a land not inhabited," while the other was slain and its blood sprinkled by the high priest on the mercy seat in the Holy of Holies. This festival anticipates the time when Israel will be smitten with remorse for the crucifixion of Christ and will nationally repent and turn to Him.

31

Tabernacles

This feast was always connected in Israel's history with periods of joy. The people gathered together for eight days, dwelling in booths and rejoicing in the goodness of God. The firstfruits of the oil and the wine were brought in, and a final thanksgiving was made for the year's crops. Commemorated also were the wanderings of Israel in the wilderness after the exodus from Egypt (Leviticus 23:39-43). This feast looks forward to a future era of peace and prosperity when Jesus shall reign.

In the Old Testament these feasts were called "feasts of Jehovah," but in the New Testament they had so deteriorated in the thinking of the people that they were labeled "feasts of the Jews" (John 5:1; 6:4).

Times and Seasons

Just as the people of Israel were to observe a weekly Sabbath so they were to observe a Sabbath of years, for every seventh year was to be a year of rest for the land. In addition to this they were to observe what was called "the year of jubilee." After forty-nine years (7 times 7) the fiftieth year was to be a time of celebration of a special nature. All debts were to be canceled by law, and all property was to revert to the original owner. Thus God would teach His people to avoid covetousness, and wean them away from a materialistic philosophy of life. Israel was also taught in this way that the Promised Land belonged to God and not to them. Their terms of occupancy were clearly spelled out by Him. It was because of their failure to keep these Sabbatical years, together with their other sins, that they were expelled from the land (2 Chronicles 36:21).

The book of Leviticus closes with the laws governing vows made to God. We are warned that promises to God are to be kept. Throughout the book can be traced the admonition that God's people are to be holy. At home or on the highway, in work or worship, in private life and in public life, at all times and in all places a redeemed people must maintain in conduct and conversation the highest standards of holiness. This is the message of Leviticus.

5

Numbers: The Book
of Pilgrimage

B etween the last chapter of Exodus and the first chapter of
Numbers a month elapses and the book of Leviticus intervenes.
The events covered in Numbers occupy a period of about thirty-
eight years. The book gets its name from the two numberings recorded in its pages. It is important to bear in mind that the generation
numbered at the beginning of the book is not the same as that
numbered at the end of the book. The tragic failure of Israel at Kadesh-
barnea to press on into Canaan and possess the Promised Land occurs
between, and the disbelieving generation is condemned to wander in
the wilderness until all are dead. Only two men, Joshua and Caleb,
escape this judgment.

The lessons of the book of Numbers are full of interest and are of
a very practical nature. Leviticus deals with the believer's worship,
Numbers with the believer's walk. Purity dominates Leviticus, whereas
pilgrimage dominates Numbers.

Outline of Numbers

It should be remembered that the wanderings in the wilderness which occupy our attention in this book were brought on by

disobedience. God had a way through the wilderness which would have brought Israel into immediate possession of Canaan. Unbelief ever robs us of the present enjoyment of salvation.

I. ISRAEL IN THE WILDERNESS—THE OLD GENERATION (1–19)
   A. Discipline in the Wilderness (1:1–9:14)
      1. The People Counted (1)
      2. The People Camped (2–4)
      3. The People Cleansed (5)
      4. The People Consecrated (6:1–9:14)
   B. Direction in the Wilderness (9:15–10:36)
      1. The Instruments of This Direction (9:15–10:10)
         a. The Vision of the Cloud (9:15-23)
         b. The Voice of the Trumpet (10:1-10)
      2. The Incident of This Direction (10:11-28)
      3. The Influence of This Direction (10:29-32)
      4. The Invocation of This Direction (10:33-36)
   C. Discontent in the Wilderness (11–13)
     Criticizing:
      1. The Present Life of Faith (11:1-9, 31-35)
      2. The Perfect Love of God (11:10-25)
      3. The Prophetic Light of Others (11:26-30)
      4. The Personal Leadership of Moses (12)
      5. The Promised Land of Canaan (13)
   D. Death in the Wilderness (14–16)
   E. Despair in the Wilderness (17–19)
II. ISRAEL ON THE WAY—THE NEW GENERATION (20–36)
   A. Recalling the Past (20)
   B. Redeeming the Present (21:1–27:11)
   C. Reviewing the Future (27:12–36:13)
      1. The Leadership of Israel (27:12-23)
      2. The Laws of Israel (28–30)
      3. The Land of Israel (31–36)

One simple way of remembering the content of the book of Numbers is to memorize the geographical movements it describes. The three main movements are:

1. From Sinai to Kadesh-barnea (1–12)
2. From Kadesh-barnea through the various wilderness wanderings and back to Kadesh-barnea (13–19)
3. From Kadesh-barnea to Jordan (20–36)

THE CAMP OF ISRAEL

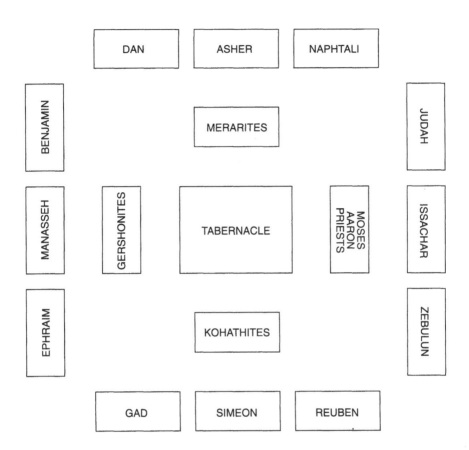

Preparation for the March

God is a God of order. One of the things which impresses itself on our minds as we read through Numbers is that Israel, a nation of two or three million people, was no mob in the wilderness. Israel comprised an orderly camp spread out according to divine decree around the tabernacle. Each person had his proper place among the people of God. All things were done decently and in order.

First the fighting men were counted. Pedigree was the determining factor in this. Only true Israelites were allowed to fight the battles of the Lord. Next the Levites were counted. There were three families of Levites: the Gershonites, Kohathites, and Merarites, each family being descended from one of the sons of Levi. The handling of the tabernacle and its furniture was entrusted to these Levites. When the princes of Israel gave their dedicatory offerings of wagons and oxen for the transportation of the tabernacle, an unusual division of these was made by Moses. He did not divide the six wagons and twelve oxen equally between the three families of Levi. The Kohathites received none at all. The reason becomes clear when it is seen that to them God entrusted the transportation of the ark, the table, the candlestick, the altar, and the vessels of the sanctuary. These sacred objects were to be carried by hand.

The People's Complaint

Someone has suggested that a better title for Numbers would be "The Book of Murmurings." From the time the people left Egypt till the time they finally forfeited their right to enter Canaan, they complained. They complained about the manna. They criticized when the prophetic gift was manifested by others. Aaron and Miriam criticized Moses for his marriage to a foreign woman. Finally the people criticized the Promised Land itself.

Kadesh-barnea

This is a significant place in Hebrew history. At Kadesh-barnea the people who had come up out of Egypt by an act of faith so thoroughly disbelieved God as to make their entry into the land an impossibility. They trusted God to bring them out of Egypt but failed to trust Him to bring them into Canaan. The report of the spies concerning the giants and the walled cities undermined their faith. The passionate pleadings of Joshua and Caleb went unheeded. Unbelief won the day. There is a solemn and practical lesson for us all in this. How many there are who can, it seems, trust God to save them from the penalty of sin, yet fail to trust Him to save them from the power of sin. All their lives they live in defeat and discouragement, never entering into their "Canaan" of peace, prosperity, and power. All their days they wander, as it were, in the wilderness, coming short of God's best for their lives.

At Kadesh-barnea the people wept and murmured against Moses and Aaron. "Would God that we had died in the land of Egypt, or would God we had died in this wilderness," they cried in their dread of the Canaanite giants. And, solemn thought, God answered their prayer. "Your carcasses shall fall in this wilderness" was His sobering judgment (Numbers 14:29).

THE JOURNEYS AND WANDERINGS OF ISRAEL

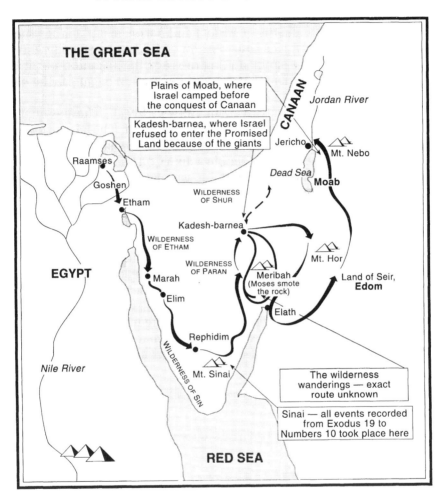

More Rebellion

Korah was the first cousin of Moses and Aaron. Soon after the judgment at Kadesh-barnea, Korah led a rebellion against the leadership of Moses and the priesthood of Aaron. He and his fellow conspirators were exposed and executed in a most startling way. The earth yawned open to swallow up the rebels. And Aaron's rod miraculously budded to vindicate his right to the priesthood.

The New Generation

It is important to observe that a gap of thirty-seven and one-half years occurs between chapters 19 and 20 of Numbers. The second section of the book begins by recalling the past. This is vividly seen in the account of the deaths of Miriam and Aaron, sister and brother of Moses. Moses, too, was told that he could not personally enter Canaan because of his sin in smiting the rock the second time. It is interesting to observe also that the new generation began, as the old one ended, by criticizing Moses.

But the wanderings were over and the wars began. The foes on the wilderness side of Jordan were met and conquered. The false prophet Balaam, hired by Balak, king of Moab, to curse the Israelites, discovered that he could not curse a people whom God had blessed. His evil counsel to Balak that he corrupt them was all too successful, but the success was short-lived. The offenders were judged, and Israel continued on its victorious way. At last Balaam, seeking refuge among the Midianites, fell before the sword of Joshua.

Once more the people were numbered and given final instructions in view of the coming conquest of Canaan. Joshua was ordained as Moses' successor. The two and a half tribes (Reuben, Gad, and half tribe of Manasseh) pleaded that their inheritance in the land might be on the wilderness side of Jordan. The actual territorial extent of the land they were to possess was given and arrangements made, in faith, for its division. The book of Numbers ends on a note of expectation. At last the people were about to enter the Promised Land.

6

Deuteronomy: The Book of Remembrance

J ohn Bunyan, in the second part of *Pilgrim's Progress*, tells how
Christiana and her boys, having belatedly set off to follow Christian on his pilgrimage to the Celestial City, come within sight of
that dreadful valley where, some time before, Christian had so desper-
ately fought with the fiend Apollyon. Responding to a question put by
young Samuel, Mr. Greatheart, the companion of Christiana and her
boys, replies:

> Your father had that battle with Apollyon at a place yonder
> before us, in a narrow passage just beyond Forgetful Green. And
> indeed, that place is the most dangerous place in all these parts.

In one of his books, F. W. Boreham relates this incident to the book
of Deuteronomy and suggests that, in view of the nature of
Deuteronomy, a better title would be "The Dangers of Forgetful
Green." For the book of Deuteronomy consists of a series of addresses
by Moses warning the Israelites, whom he was soon to leave, of the
dangers of forgetfulness. "Beware lest ye forget," he said again and
again. "Thou shalt remember." These two warnings run like a refrain
from page to page of Deuteronomy.

"Take heed to thyself, and keep thy soul diligently, lest thou forget the things which thine eyes have seen" (4:9). "Take heed unto yourselves, lest ye forget the covenant of the Lord your God" (4:23). "And remember that thou wast a servant in the land of Egypt" (5:15). "Then beware lest thou forget the Lord, which brought thee forth out of the land of Egypt, from the house of bondage" (6:12). "And thou shalt remember all the way which the Lord thy God led thee these forty years in the wilderness" (8:2). "Beware that thou forget not the Lord thy God, in not keeping his commandments" (8:11). "But thou shalt remember the Lord thy God: for it is he that giveth thee power to get wealth" (8:18). "Remember, and forget not, how thou provokedst the Lord thy God to wrath in the wilderness" (9:7). "Remember what the Lord thy God did unto Miriam" (24:9). "Remember what Amalek did unto thee by the way" (25:17).

Outline of Deuteronomy

The generation which experienced the redemption from Egypt was dead. Joshua, Caleb, and Moses alone remained, and Moses himself was soon to die. A new generation stood on the frontiers of the Promised Land, a new leader stood ready to conquer Canaan. New challenges loomed ahead, new dangers, new prospects. In a series of ten sermons Moses sought to prepare the people of God for the future by reminding them of the past. There are four looks in the book: the backward look, the inward look, the forward look, and the upward look.

    I. THE HISTORY OF ISRAEL—THE BACKWARD LOOK (1–3)
        A. The Journey Reviewed—Horeb to Kadesh (1)
           1. Trekking to Kadesh (1:1-19)
           2. Trembling at Kadesh (1:20-45)
           3. Tarrying at Kadesh (1:46)
        B. The Journey Resumed—Kadesh to Beth-peor (2–3)
           1. Conquering the Land East of Jordan (2:1–3:17)
              a. Victory over the Giants Possible (2:1-23)
              b. Victory over the Giants Proven (2:2–3:17)
            2. Contemplating the Land West of Jordan (3:18-29)
              a. Moses Speaks to Israel (3:18-20)
              b. Moses Sees the Inheritance (3:21-29)
    II. THE HOLINESS OF ISRAEL—THE INWARD LOOK (4–11)
        A. Moses Speaks about the Law (4–6)
        B. Moses Speaks about the Lord (7–8)
        C. Moses Speaks about the Land (9–11)

III. THE HERITAGE OF ISRAEL—THE FORWARD LOOK (12–30)
Laws concerning:
A. Purity in the Land (12–14)
B. Property in the Land (15)
C. Piety in the Land (16:1-17)
D. Positions in the Land (16:18–18:22)
E. Protection in the Land (19–20)
F. Persons in the Land (21–25)
G. Priorities in the Land (26)
H. Permanence in the Land (27–30)
IV. THE HERO OF ISRAEL—THE UPWARD LOOK (31–34)
A. Moses the Statesman (31)
B. Moses the Singer (32)
C. Moses the Seer (33)
D. Moses the Saint (34)

Looking Backward

As W. Graham Scroggie has said, Deuteronomy "stands in relation to the four preceding books much as John's Gospel does to the Synoptic Records." They Synoptic Gospels give us certain historical facts, and John shows the spiritual significance of these facts. In like manner the spiritual significance of the other books is given in Deuteronomy. Genesis to Numbers gives us the facts of Israel's history, and Deuteronomy gives us the philosophy of it.

At Kadesh-barnea, Israel first heard about the giants. The fear of the giants of Canaan brought spiritual paralysis and a death sentence in the wilderness. Now the shadow of the giants loomed again. And Moses, mindful of the past, wanted to make sure that history did not repeat itself. With tact and skill he reminded Israel that other nations had met and mastered those giants. Indeed the foes of Canaan were no more terrible than Sihon the Amorite and Og, the king of Bashan, whose territory they now possessed.

Looking Within

The source of all national greatness lies in a right relationship to God. This is so with all peoples but especially so with Israel, since God's purpose in granting them nationhood was that they might be a witness for Him to all mankind. Moses therefore warned Israel against forgetting the law of the Lord. In few books of the Bible are the blessings of a proper relationship to God and the curses of forgetting Him more graphically portrayed than in Deuteronomy. Reminding the people that their tenure of the Promised Land hinged on their giving God His proper place, Moses set before them blessings and curses. They were solemnly warned that they were to be recited when once the land was theirs—the blessings on Mount Gerizim and the curses on Mount Ebal. All Israel, gathered by their tribes, were to say "Amen" as these injunctions and invocations were read. It is interesting to see in Deuteronomy how the divine goodness and the divine severity are interwoven. Law and love, goodness and grace, wooings and warnings go hand in hand.

Looking over Jordan

"These are the statutes and judgments which ye shall observe to do in the land." Some nineteen chapters of Deuteronomy set forth principles and precepts that have to do with the occupancy of Canaan. Urgently Moses warned the people against making leagues with the Canaanites and falling into the snare of idolatry. The practices of the pagans were to be avoided like the plague. It was for these abominations that Israel, as God's scourge, was to annihilate them. The moral and religious pollutions of Canaan were a loathsome cancer on the society of mankind and must be removed by the surgery of the sword. This was not cruelty but kindness. Israel must beware of compromise, of committing the very sins that called for the extermination of the Canaanites. They were to be a holy people, a living witness to all mankind, a testimony to the world of the one and only true God.

Looking Up

The last four chapters show Moses looking over a darker Jordan, the river of death. His last words to Israel, his prophetic vision, his song, and his strange burial by the hand of God on some unknown slope of Nebo are full of interest. Deuteronomy closes with Joshua standing in the shoes of Moses on the threshold of the Promised Land.

7
Joshua: From Victory to Victory

J oshua had been born a slave and had experienced the glorious redemption of Israel from "the house of bondage." He had lived through the experiences in the wilderness. He had sat at the feet of Moses and had led the armies of Israel. With Caleb and ten others he had spied out the Promised Land. His had been the glowing account of the land that "flowed with milk and honey." Upon Joshua's shoulders the mantle of Moses fell. He was now the leader of Israel, and his was the task of bringing the people of God into the promised rest of Canaan.

The book of Joshua occupies a strategic place in the Old Testament. It is the link between Israel out of the land and Israel in the land. It corresponds positionally with the book of Acts and spiritually with the book of Ephesians. In Deuteronomy, Israel had the prospects of Canaan. In Joshua, Israel took possession of Canaan. In Deuteronomy, Moses set before Israel the vision of faith. In Joshua, the Israelites were led upon the venture of faith.

The Exodus from Egypt could have taken place about the year 1440 B.C. It is possible that Hatshepsut, daughter of Thutmose I, was the royal Egyptian princess who adopted Moses. She was certainly a strong enough personality to defy the edict of Pharaoh which called for the death of the baby in the Nile. Thutmose III may have been the

Pharaoh of the oppression. He was one of the greatest of the empire-building Pharaohs, extending Egypt's influence to the Euphrates. In doing so he smashed the Hittites and Amorites, and this would have made Joshua's subsequent conquest of Canaan easier, humanly speaking.

Outline of Joshua

     I. CLAIMING THE LAND (1–5)
       A. Faith Believes the Bible (1)
       B. Faith Counts the Cost (2)
       C. Faith Makes a Move (3)
       D. Faith Strengthens Its Stand (4)
       E. Faith Pays the Price (5)
    II. CONQUERING THE LAND (6–11)
       A. Overcoming the Word—at Jericho (6)
       B. Confidence in the Flesh—at Ai (7–8)
       C. Facing the Wiles of the Devil (9–11)
         The Devil will:
         1. Seek an Agreement through the Gibeonites (9)
         2. Seize the Advantage through the Southern Alliance (10)
         3. Stage His Attack through the Northern Threat (11)
   III. COLONIZING THE LAND (12–24)
       A. Declaring the Spoils of Victory (12)
       B. Dividing the Spoils of Victory (13–21)
         1. Statutes of Liberty (13–19)
         2. Statements of Equality (20)
         3. Standards of Justice (21)
       C. Dedicating the Spoils of Victory (22)
       D. Defending the Spoils of Victory (23–24)

"Moses My Servant Is Dead"

A sense of inadequacy must have swept over Joshua when he was left alone to bear the burden Moses had carried for forty years. Israel was camped on the eastern side of Jordan. Canaan with its giants and walled cities lay before them. The tribes of Israel were unseasoned in war and had already played the coward when faced with the conquest of Canaan. The first chapter of Joshua tells how God in sovereign grace spoke personally to Joshua and encouraged him. He fixed Joshua's attention on the written Word, the fact of the divine Presence, and the certainty of the divine promise. Joshua, encouraged and strengthened, believed.

THE CONQUEST AND SETTLEMENT OF CANAAN

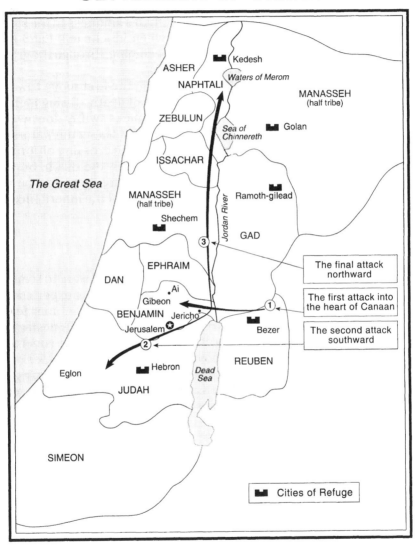

Rahab the Harlot

Two spies were sent into Jericho, the great Canaanite stronghold which must first be subdued if the invasion was to have any hope of success. Israel must again count the cost of possessing the inheritance. Finding shelter in the house of a harlot, the two spies learned that Jericho was already as good as theirs. The fear of God had fallen upon the people, and Rahab herself was already more than half a believer in the God of Israel. Because of Rahab's kindness to the spies and because of her faith, she was spared when Jericho fell. Later she married into one of the families of Judah, becoming, through the grace of God, an ancestress of David and of Christ.

Crossing the Jordan by faith, Israel made the first move toward victory in the land. The river Jordan speaks of death. Rising high in the mountains north of Canaan, this river plunges swiftly downward and is named "The Descender." It buries itself at last in the waters of the Dead Sea, from which there is no outlet. The crossing of Jordan symbolizes the identification of the believer with the death, burial, and resurrection of Christ. Without this crossing there can be no conquest of Canaan for Israel and no possessing of the inheritance in Christ for the believer today.

Gilgal

The monuments reared when Jordan was crossed were to remind all future generations of that crossing. The wilderness experiences were over and the manna would fall no more. Instead, Israel must feast on "the old corn of the land." The rite of circumcision, sadly neglected over the years, was enforced, for it was the symbol of the covenant relationship existing between Jehovah and Israel. For us it speaks of the cutting off of the flesh, an experience vital to us if we are going to gain any victories for God. The Passover was kept and Joshua was required to yield up his sword to the true Captain of the Lord's hosts. By these deliberate steps of faith the land was claimed and the victory assured.

The Central Campaign

By attacking Jericho and Ai, Joshua drove a wedge into the heart of Canaan making it impossible for the powerful coalitions to the north and the south to unite. The secrets of victory were faith, courage, and obedience. Jericho soon fell as Israel obeyed God, but Ai's conquest was hindered by sin in the camp and Joshua's trust in his own carnal reasoning. The story of Achan shows what a vital relationship exists between believers and how the sin of one can hold up victory for the entire body of God's people.

After subduing Ai, Joshua made one of his serious mistakes. He made a league with the Gibeonites, forgetting the injunction of 1:8 and the warning of Deuteronomy 7:1-2. The crafty Gibeonites outwitted Joshua and Israel because of Joshua's prayerlessness and self-confidence.

The Southern Campaign

After making the league with Gibeon, the Israelites retired to Gilgal only to receive a hasty summons from their new allies. A powerful southern coalition, headed by Adoni-zedek, king of Jerusalem, had attacked Gibeon. A forced march from Gilgal brought Joshua and his army to the scene. Their foes were crushed, scattered, and mopped up one by one. Once more Israel returned to Gilgal. The sudden attack on Gibeon illustrates how swiftly Satan exploits any advantage he can gain in our lives.

The Northern Campaign

A new alliance in the North against Joshua initiated the final campaign which centered around the waters of Merom. The strength of this alliance struck fear into Joshua's heart, calling forth the divine admonition, "Be not afraid because of them" (11:6). Satan sometimes seeks to overwhelm us with his terrors, but we need not tremble for he is a defeated foe. Joshua attacked before the alliance could be properly cemented and totally defeated his foes. Joshua's final crusades were against the mountain foes, some of whom were giants. All his glorious victories were attributed to God.

The Land Divided

The land was divided among the tribes of Israel by lot. Other factors entered into the division, such as the capacity of the holder, rights of conquest, request, faithfulness. Most space in the narrative is devoted to the inheritances of Judah, Ephraim, and Manasseh. The cities of refuge, required under the law, were set apart. And the Levites, who had no actual tribal inheritance, were given cities among the tribes. In this way the religious influence of this tribe could be felt throughout the entire nation. Forty-eight cities in all were given to the Levites.

The fighting over, the two and a half tribes which had chosen their inheritance east of Jordan were allowed to return home. They built an altar which almost brought about civil war until they hastily explained that it was intended to signify their solidarity with the other tribes. Joshua's last words in chapter 24 are filled with significance in view of the failure which followed, as recorded in the book of Judges.

8
Judges: The Folly of Forsaking God

I n those days there was no king in Israel: every man did that which was right in his own eyes." Mark that expression well. It is the last sentence in the book of Judges. It gives us not only the key to the book but the key to human nature as well. Observe that every man did that which was *right* in his own eyes, not that which was wrong. The tragedy is that man's idea of what is right and what is wrong is often exactly opposite to God's. This becomes evident when we realize that one of the constantly recurring expressions in Judges is "And the children of Israel did evil in the sight of the Lord."

The book of Judges is a sad sequel to the book of Joshua. In Joshua the "heavenlies" are typified, in Judges the "earthlies." Joshua rings with the shout of victory; Judges echoes with the sobs of defeat. In Judges we go round and round—rebellion, retribution, repentance, and restoration. Then the same cycle all over again, some six or seven times.

Analysis of Judges

The book of Ruth, together with the last five chapters of Judges, forms a kind of appendix to the book of Judges, high-lighting the moral and spiritual conditions of the whole period.

I. ISRAEL'S WARS (1:1–2:5)
   A. The Tribe of Judah (1:1-21)
      1. The Promise of Initial Victory (1:1-18)
      2. The Peril of Incomplete Victory (1:19-21)
   B. The House of Joseph (1:22–2:5)
      1. The Promise of Initial Victory (1:22-26)
      2. The Peril of Incomplete Victory (1:27–2:5)
II. ISRAEL'S WOES (2:6–16:31)
   Subjection to:
   A. The Mesopotamians (3:8-11)
   B. The Moabites, Ammonites, and Amalekites (3:12-30)
   C. The Canaanites (4)
   D. The Midianites (6–7)
   E. The Ammonites (10:6–12:15)
   F. The Philistines (13–16)
III. ISRAEL'S WAYS (17—21)
   A. Religious Perversion (17–18)
   B. Moral Pollution (19–21)

To get a better picture of the period of the Judges, see the chart on page 52. Some of the periods probably overlapped.

Israel's Prevailing Sin

Solemnly and repeatedly Israel had been warned in the law to make no league with the inhabitants of Canaan. The iniquity of the Amorites was full. Their religious, moral, and social habits were utterly vile. They had polluted the land with their abominations. Their gods were demons and their religious practices filthy. The worship of Ashtaroth was the special sin of the Canaanite nations. It entailed idolatry of the most revolting form in which immorality was elevated to an act of worship. All virtue was surrendered. "To go a whoring" was far more than a figure of speech.

Israel was instructed to remove this moral cancer from the land. In its place they were to set up the pure worship of Jehovah and be a witness to all mankind of the true and living God. Instead they "forsook the Lord God of their fathers, which brought them out of the land of Egypt, and followed other gods, the gods of the people that were round about them, and bowed down themselves unto them and provoked the Lord to anger."

Sowing and Reaping

The early victories of Israel were not carried through to final triumph. The "iron age" was dawning in Canaan, and the Israelites felt themselves unable to cope with the military machinery of their foes. Forgotten was the fact that "the Lord of Hosts" was the true Captain of their salvation. Israel surrendered. Soon compromise ended in complicity, and Israel sank to the level of the nations she had been destined to replace.

Baal and Asherah, the gods of Syria, Zidon, Moab, and Ammon, and Dagon, the god of the Philistines—all these Israel served in turn. Behind the grotesque idols of wood and stone were the real gods of Canaan—evil spirits. Idolatry in any form is inspired by demons (Leviticus 17:7; Deuteronomy 32:17; 1 Corinthians 10:19-22) and invariably results in degradation.

Again and again God allowed Israel to taste the bitter fruits of idolatry. Cruel, evil, and ruthless tyrants oppressed Israel. The nations Israel had failed to drive out grew stronger and subdued them. Terrible times of hardship, privation, and woe followed hard upon each period of national apostasy. First the Mesopotamians oppressed Israel until, finally, when the people cried to the Lord, God raised up Othniel to be their deliverer. Othniel was the younger brother of Caleb.

Then Eglon, fat and repulsive king of Moab, joined with the Ammonites and Amalekites to subdue Israel. God used left-handed Ehud to bring deliverance. It is interesting to see how God used the "weak thing" to bring deliverance in the book of Judges: the left hand, an oxgoad, a woman, a nail, a piece of millstone, a pitcher and trumpet, and the jawbone of an ass. (See 1 Corinthians 1:27 and 2 Corinthians 12:9.)

After Eglon came Jabin, king of the Canaanites, whose armed forces were led by Sisera. Sisera had nine hundred of those iron chariots Israel dreaded so much. God raised up Deborah as a prophetess, Jael as a heroine, and Barak as a deliverer, and proved to Israel that God is not impressed by iron chariots.

Next came the Midianites, whose raids upon Israel brought the nation to extreme straits of famine. Gideon with his noble three hundred was given a miraculous victory in spite of great numerical odds. Gideon refused to be crowned as king by grateful Israel but foolishly sowed the seeds of future idolatry by making an "ephod." Israel actually worshiped this sacred garment. Gideon's son, Abimelech, took steps to have himself crowned king after his father's death. He was an unscrupulous man, described as a "bramble" by his youngest brother Jotham. He came to a sudden and ignominious end.

Of five of the judges we know very little. Tola, Jair, Ibzan, Elon, and Abdon are all dismissed with a few words in the narrative. The next great deliverer was Jephthah, a man rejected by his brethren but raised up by God to redeem Israel out of the hands of the Ammonites.

The story of Samson's exploits makes interesting reading. It may be observed that despite his sins of the flesh, the Spirit of God is mentioned more in connection with Samson than with any of the other judges. The Philistines were the great oppressors of Israel during his days. Samson began the work of ridding the land of them but failed to carry it through to completion, and it was not until David came that the Philistines finally met their match.

The Moral Climate of the Period

The last five chapters of Judges give examples of the prevailing apostasy of the times. The story of Micah, his theft of money from his mother, the way he restored this money only to make an idol of silver from part of it, makes strange reading. Micah set up a false religion of his own based on the worship of his idol, and persuaded a passing Levite to act as priest of this new religion. His idol was stolen from him by some passing adventurers from the tribe of Dan, and the Levite, a true opportunist, became "priest" to a tribe instead of to a single man. This Levite's name was Jonathan and he was a grandson of Moses. (The Authorized Version gives the grandfather's name as Manasseh, but the Masoretic Text in Hebrew has a textual problem and the Greek and Latin versions give the name of Moses. See Judges 18:30.)

The next story details the vile happenings in Gibeah, a town in the territory of Benjamin. What happened was so horrible that, even in those days of moral decay, the other tribes felt action must be taken. Civil war followed, with the result that almost the whole tribe of Benjamin was wiped out. A grandson of Aaron, Phinehas by name, is mentioned in the context of the story. This is of interest because it is the only time the true high priest of Israel is mentioned in the whole book (20:28).

It is interesting to observe how frequently during the days of the Judges God used people and things of no account, humanly speaking. Othniel was a younger brother, Ehud was a left-handed man, Barak had to be urged to be a man by Deborah, Gideon went to war with a lamp and a pitcher, Shamgar had an oxgoad, Jephthah was an outlaw, Samson used the jawbone of an ass.

Truly, "God hath chosen the foolish things of the world to confound the wise; and God hath chosen the weak things of the world to confound the things which are mighty; and base things of the world, and things which are despised hath God chosen, yea and things which are not, to bring to nought things that are: that no flesh should glory in his presence" (1 Corinthians 1:27-29).

51

The Period of the Judges

THE ENEMY	SUBJECTION	DELIVERER	PEACE
Mesopotamians	8 years	Othniel	40 years
Moabites Ammonites Amalekites	18 years	Ehud Shamgar	80 years
Canaanites	20 years	Deborah Barak	40 years
Midianites	7 years	Gideon Abimelech, the usurper Tola Jair	40 years 3 years 23 years 22 years
Ammonites	18 years	Jephthah Ibzan Elon Abdon	6 years 7 years 10 years 8 years
Philistines	40 years	Samson	(20 years)
Totals	111 years		279 years*

*This total does not include Samson's twenty years, which overlapped with the forty-year Philistine oppression. In addressing the Sanhedrin, Stephen summarized this period as follows: "And after that he gave unto them judges about the space of four hundred and fifty years, until Samuel the prophet" (Acts 13:20). We can arrive at that figure thus:

Years of subjection	111 years
Years of rest	279 years
The ministry of Eli	40 years
The ministry of Samuel	20 years
Total	450 years

9
Ruth:
The Virtuous Woman

W ho can find a virtuous woman?" wrote king Lemuel, "for her price is far above rubies" (Proverbs 31:10). "All the city of my people doth know that thou art a virtuous woman" said the noble Boaz to Ruth the alien woman from the land of Moab (Ruth 3:11).

The setting of the book of Ruth is in the book of Judges. It shows that despite the prevailing apostasy of the nation there were individuals living godly lives, seeking to rule their lives by the law of Moses and free from the corruption around them. The character, integrity and piety of Boaz are outstanding. His familiarity with the Mosaic law and his personal knowledge of Jehovah are in marked contrast with the general ignorance, immorality, indifference and idolatry of the times. God never leaves Himself without a witness.

The book of Ruth is one of the most beautiful stories ever told. The climax towards which the whole book moves is the birth of a baby in Bethlehem. It provides the vital link between the days of the Judges and the coming of David. Yet the whole romance is woven around the story of a prodigal family and a kinsman-redeemer, around a Gentile woman and a high-born Hebrew of the princely line of Judah.

The book of Ruth is the story of redemption. It tells how one who was a stranger to the commonwealth and covenants of Israel, dwelling afar off in heathen darkness was introduced to one who became her kinsman-redeemer and her lord.

The book divides into three parts.

I. How She Was Sought
II. How She Was Taught
III. How She Was Bought

When the story opens Ruth was a pagan. She was a member of a hostile race and cut off from any knowledge of the living God. In fact, as a Moabitess, she was not only without God but she was without hope for the law of Moses legislated with particular severity against her people (Deuteronomy 23:3-4). Yet, in spite of this, we see God setting in motion a chain of events which brought her at last to Boaz. Yes, and lifted her into the royal line and gave her a living link with the Christ Himself (Matthew 1:5).

The first link in the chain that brought her to Boaz was a *famine* (1:1), a providential act of God over which she had no control and about which she probably knew nothing and cared less. For the famine was not even in Moab, it was in Judea. Yet it was the beginning of things for Ruth although she did not know it.

The second link in the chain was a *family*. There moved into her life a family from Bethlehem. Although they were away from God and although they were in a place where they had no right to be and although their testimony must have been dim indeed, yet Ruth first heard of Jehovah through this family. She married into this family and had a first-hand opportunity to see and to hear for herself their devotion to their God. For despite their backslidden condition there must have been much about the family of Elimelech which spoke to her heart.

The third link in the chain was a *funeral*. In fact there were three funerals one after another. Her own husband died. It was a tragedy at the time, perhaps, but she could never have come to know Boaz as God intended her to know him without that funeral. God is too loving to be unkind and too wise to make any mistakes.

The fourth link in the chain was a *fear*. Her mother-in-law, Naomi, announced one day that she was leaving Moab. The only light Ruth had, and a dim, poor light it was, was going out. She feared to be left in the dark and she voiced her resolution to get to know Naomi's God in one of the most forthright statements of purpose in Scripture (1:16-17).

The final link in the chain was a *field*. For when she arrived at Bethlehem and sought some means to support herself and Naomi she went out to glean "And," says the Spirit of God, "her hap was to light on a part of the field belonging to Boaz" (2:3). That's how she was sought. God overruled the affairs of her life until she was brought face to face with the one who was to become her redeemer.

From this point on the story moves swiftly. She was taught by Naomi to put herself at the feet of Boaz and ask to be redeemed, ask to be put into his family. Then she was bought by Boaz, according to the redemption laws of Israel, and made his very own.

One does not have to look very far to see how all this pictures our own redemption. First, God takes the initiative and begins to move behind the scenes to bring us into the presence of His Son and under the sound of His word. He teaches us the simple plan of redemption and makes us willing to ask the Lord Jesus to become ours and to make us His. Then He shows us how the redemption price has been paid at Calvary and, unworthy as we are, He lifts us up and makes us His very own.

Had Ruth known the glad Gospel song so familiar to us she surely would have sung

> I bless the hand that guided
> I bless the heart that planned,
> Now throned where glory dwelleth
> In Immanuel's land.

10
1 and 2 Samuel: Israel Comes of Age

I t was God's intention to give Israel a king. As far back as Genesis 49, Jacob had prophesied, "The sceptre shall not depart from Judah, nor a lawgiver from beneath his feet, until Shiloh come; and unto him shall the gathering of the people be." The great sin of Israel in 1 Samuel was that of anticipating the purpose of God and insisting on the king of their choice instead of waiting for God's king.

In the books of Samuel the long period of national disorder ends. Samuel has been called "the last of the judges and the first of the prophets." He crowned two of Israel's kings—Saul, the people's choice, and David, God's choice.

Analysis of 1 Samuel

First Samuel is the story of four men: Eli, Samuel, Saul, and David. Their stories are interwoven so that the story of Eli overlaps that of Samuel, the story of Samuel overlaps that of Saul, and the story of Saul overlaps that of David. There is a note of failure which runs through 1 Samuel. The office of the priests sank to a low ebb during the days of Eli and his evil sons. Saul and David, representatives of Israel's kings, both failed. Saul, however, failed more than David. Samuel was a prophet and, as such, stood apart from both kings and priests and exercised authority over both. The appearance of a prophet in Bible times always signified failure. But Samuel, great as he was, also failed, for his sons failed to walk in his ways and this, as much as anything, gave rise to the popular clamor for a king. The failures of these four men only make all the brighter the luster of the Lord Jesus, who, as Prophet, Priest, and King, alone brought perfection to each of the offices.

    I. THE FAILURE OF THE PRIESTLY OFFICE—ELI
        A. Eli's Failure as a Priest (1:9, 13; 2:27-36)
        B. Eli's Failure as a Parent (2:12-17, 22-25)
    II. THE FORMING OF THE PROPHETIC OFFICE—SAMUEL
        A. Samuel as a Person
            1. His Birth (1:1-8, 10-28; 2:1-10)
            2. His Boyhood (2:11, 18-21, 26; 3:1-21)
        B. Samuel as a Prophet
            1. Teaching the People (4:1–7:14)
                a. To Wait (4–6)
                b. To War (7:1-14)
             2. Reaching the People (7:15-17)
    III. THE FOUNDING OF THE PRINCELY OFFICE—SAUL, DAVID
        A. The Tragedy of Saul (8–15)
            1. The Finding of Saul (8–10)
            2. The Fitness of Saul (11–12)
            3. The Failure of Saul (13–15)
        B. The Training of David (16–31)
            1. As a Lover of God (his years as a shepherd)
            2. As a Lord over Self (his years as a courtier)
            3. As a Leader of Men (his years as an outlaw)

Eli

Samuel was born in dark days. The priesthood in Israel was represented by a feeble old man, Eli by name, whose sons' behavior was a public scandal. The civil, religious, and moral confusion of the days of the judges, the neglect of the tabernacle, the demoralization of the people, and the impiety and immorality of even the priests had all left their mark.

The family of Elkanah was another of those little lighthouses in the land, for Elkanah was a godly man. His favorite wife, Hannah, was a woman of great piety. Through prevailing prayer she overcame her barrenness and was given a child, Samuel.

It is a commentary on Eli's spiritual condition that he failed to discern between a drunken woman and a devout worshiper (1 Samuel 1:12-17). It is a commentary on the faith and spiritual strength of Hannah that she could trust her precious little Samuel to Eli's upbringing when he had already proved his parental incompetence in the lack of discipline of his own family.

Samuel

At a very tender age Samuel learned to hear and recognize the voice of God. His first message was one of judgment on Eli and his house. Samuel's influence on Israel was profound. He did much to dispel the dark clouds of the previous centuries. Under his leadership the Philistines, hereditary foes of Israel, began to receive intimation that their domination over the people of God was drawing to a close.

Samuel made regular itineraries from his home in Ramah to teach the people the Word of God. He founded a school at Ramah and trained young men to read and write, and fostered the growth of a system of national education. It was Samuel who laid the foundation of the national culture and who lifted Israel from its mental and moral torpor. It was Samuel who guided the first steps of the monarchy, speaking fearlessly with the voice of divine authority as occasion demanded. Samuel was one of God's giants.

Saul (1043 B.C. - 1011 B.C.)

Saul was Israel's first king. Born of the tribe of Benjamin, the smallest of all Israel's tribes, little in his own eyes in his early days, standing head and shoulders above the people physically, sadly ignorant of God's will, impulsive, given to fits of insane jealousy and, at last, completely under the control of an evil spirit, Saul was a bundle of contradictions.

Saul showed early promise. His beginnings couldn't have been better. He had wise and godly counsel from Samuel, and his initial victories over Israel's foes were glorious. His two sins which cost him the kingdom were presumption (1 Samuel 13:5-15) and incomplete obedience (1 Samuel 15:1-23).

Saul's insane jealousy of David, when he discovered that David was to replace him on the throne, knew no bounds. On nine distinct occasions he attempted to murder David. Saul's son Jonathan was of a different mold. Ever a lover of David, he sought to compensate David in many ways for the bitter hostility of Saul. The love of David and Jonathan is one of the great stories of 1 Samuel.

David (1011 B.C. - 971 B.C.)

David was God's choice for Israel's king. Generous, brave, compassionate, thoughtful, a born leader of men and, above all, a mature believer, David is one of the greatest men of history. From David came a race of kings. The Lord Jesus traced His own human rights to Israel's throne back to David, as Matthew shows.

David appears before us in 1 Samuel as a shepherd, a courtier, and a fugitive. In each of these experiences God taught His man new lessons, fitting him for the kingdom. The experiences of David on the Judean hills made him a lover of God. And his long days and nights of meditation, harp in hand, gave birth to many of the psalms. His secret victories over the wild beasts of the forest prepared him for his famous fight with the giant Goliath of Gath. His wise conduct when a courtier won him the hearts of the men of Israel and inflamed still more the fears and jealousies of Saul. His many experiences as an outlaw taught him how to command men. The noble band of "mighty men" he gathered around him in the caves and hideouts of Judea became the core of his army and government when he came to power. David was a thoroughly human person, and in those early days no praise of him could be too high. Truly he was "a man after God's own heart."

Analysis of 2 Samuel

    I. THE PATIENT YEARS (1–4)
       A. The Lament for Saul (1)
       B. The House of Saul (2–4)
    II. THE PROSPEROUS YEARS (5–12)
       A. David's Coronation (5)
       B. David's Convictions (6)
       C. David's Covenant (7)
       D. David's Conquests (8)
       E. David's Compassion (9)
       F. David's Critics (10)
       G. David's Crime (11)
    III. THE PERILOUS YEARS (13–24)
       A. Trouble with His Kinsmen (13–19)
       B. Trouble with His Kingdom (20–24)

David's Rise

Upon the death of Saul the tribe of Judah crowned David king. However the other tribes, led by Ish-bosheth, Saul's son, clung to the tattered remnants of Saul's regal robe with the result that for some seven years there was desultory civil war. Eventually Ish-bosheth was murdered, as had been his general, Abner, a little earlier. David was innocent of both these murders and was swept on a wave of popular enthusiasm to supreme power over a united nation.

David's Reign

David was a wise and generous king. He cleared Jerusalem of the last remnants of the Jebusites, who had held that stronghold in defiance of Israel for centuries, and made the city his capital. He founded a lasting dynasty, for God entered into solemn covenant with David to establish his house forever. He began preparations for the building of the temple which for many centuries was to be the center of Jewish national life. He led a sweeping renaissance in Jewish cultural life and a great revival in Jewish religion. He appointed court recorders and scribes so that the national records could be systematically kept. And he conquered all of Israel's foes, pushing the frontiers of the Promised Land to their fullest extent.

David's Sin

At the zenith of his power, David sinned in a scandalous way. He committed adultery with Bathsheba, wife of Uriah the Hittite, one of his most faithful officers and one of his mighty men. He then had Uriah murdered and sought to cover his crime, living for months in hypocrisy. Then God sent Nathan the prophet to David with a message of judgment.

Nathan's ministry was successful. Tender in conscience, David wept bitter tears of repentance, but the turning point had come in his fortunes. From then on David had trouble, first with his own family and then on a national scale. Absalom, his favorite son, led a rebellion which was almost successful, for it drove David temporarily from the throne. David's closing years were spoiled by troubles of various sorts, the consequences of his sin haunting him down the years.

David left the kingdom to Solomon knowing that this wise son of his, under God's guidance, would be able to restore Israel again to greatness and power. The story of David reminds us that there is no respect of persons with God.

11
1 and 2 Kings:
Israel Faces the Sunset

T he two books of Kings record the meridian splendor of Solomon's reign and the slowly lengthening shadows which crept across the monarchical phase of Hebrew history. For one hundred and twenty years the twelve tribes were united and were ruled from a single throne, Saul, David, and Solomon each reigning forty years. With the death of Solomon ten tribes broke away from the throne of David to set up an independent kingdom to the north. This kingdom, known as Israel, was eventually ruled from Samaria by various dynasties, all the kings of which were bad, although some were worse than others. The tribe of Benjamin remained true to Judah and the throne of David. Combined, these two tribes comprised the southern kingdom, known as Judah. This kingdom was ruled from Jerusalem by the heirs and successors of David. Some of Judah's kings were good, but most were bad.

Analysis of 1 and 2 Kings

In the Biblical account of the kings of Judah and Israel, the narrative alternates between the two kingdoms. It should be observed that the ministries of many of the prophets fall within this period, although these will not be dealt with particularly until later.

Solomon (971 B.C. - 931 B.C.)

Solomon rose to tremendous heights and fell to appalling depths. Twice God appeared to him after his succession to the throne of David his father. Solomon was given supernatural wisdom and wealth beyond dreams of avarice. His reign was one of peace and prosperity. His greatest achievement was the building of the temple in Jerusalem, one of the most magnificent structures ever built by man. His fame reached to the four corners of the earth.

Solomon's supreme mistake was in making political marriages. To strengthen his kingdom, as he thought, Solomon married many women from the surrounding nations. These alliances were disastrous, for his pagan wives brought their heathen religions with them. In his old age, Solomon forsook the Lord to serve the idols imported by his wives. He thus allowed idolatry to be reintroduced into Israel, and for this sin the united kingdom was rent. Upon Solomon's death, his son Rehoboam acted like a fool and brought to a head the smoldering resentment of the other tribes against the tribe of Judah.

The Northern Kingdom

1. *Jeroboam* (931 B.C. - 910 B.C.) The first king of the northern kingdom of Israel was Jeroboam, who is usually described as "the son of Nebat who made Israel to sin." Jeroboam, formerly an officer under Solomon, and with an ax to grind against the king, was a natural champion for the rebellious tribesmen. His first act on being proclaimed king by the ten tribes of Israel was to sever all religious connections with Jerusalem. Afraid that the annual pilgrimages of the people of Israel to Jerusalem to worship would undermine his authority, Jeroboam introduced an innovation. He set up a golden calf at

Bethel and another at Dan, and instructed his people to worship these. He ordained puppet priests and introduced a new religious calendar. Though solemnly warned that he would be visited with judgment if he persisted in this idolatry, Jeroboam refused to change his ways.

2. *Ahab* (874 B.C. - 853 B.C.) The most wicked of Israel's kings was Ahab. Jeroboam led Israel into a perverted worship of Jehovah. But Ahab with Jezebel, his wife, established the vile worship of Baal. At this time the prophet Elijah appeared on the scene with his solemn warnings and denunciations. Jezebel persecuted the true people of God and defied the prophet. Ahab and Jezebel both met violent deaths.

3. *Jehu* (841 B.C. - 814 B.C.) The evil dynasty of Omri, which came to its head under Ahab and Jezebel, was terminated by Jehu. Feigning great zeal for God, Jehu ruthlessly exterminated all of Ahab's family and put a temporary end to Baal worship in Israel. He was, however, an ungodly man and did not depart from the sins of Jeroboam, the son of Nebat.

4. *Jeroboam II* (793 B.C. - 753 B.C.) The only other king of real importance in Israel was Jeroboam II. For years Israel had been checkmated by her northern neighbor, Syria. Jeroboam II was able to throw off the Syrian oppressors and restore Israel to its former political greatness. His reign, however, was marked by widespread injustice and immorality. With the death of Jeroboam II the fortunes of Israel rapidly declined. A new and ominous power, Assyria, reappeared on the scene. The westward advance of this mighty expansionist empire finally engulfed Israel. The northern ten tribes were carried away into captivity. The warnings of the prophets had gone unheeded, and the long-suspended sentence of divine judgment was at last executed.

The Southern Kingdom

1. *Rehoboam* (931 B.C. - 913 B.C.) *and Asa* (911 B.C. - 870 B.C.) Rehoboam, the son of Solomon, was a weak and bad king. So was his son Abijam, but his grandson Asa was a good king, who sought to bring Judah back to God. It is interesting to observe how often, with the kings of Judah, the names of the mothers are mentioned. Asa's mother was an evil woman, and one of his first acts as king was to remove her from a position of influence.

2. *Jehoshaphat* (873 B.C. - 848 B.C.) *and Athaliah* (841 B.C. - 835 B.C.) Asa was followed by Jehoshaphat, another good king. Jehoshaphat made the grave mistake, however, of allowing himself to be drawn into

an alliance with Ahab, even going so far as to marry his son to the daughter of Jezebel. It was not long before this measure had the disastrous effect of introducing utter paganism into Judah. Athaliah, the daughter of Jezebel, was one of the most wicked women of history. She almost succeeded in stamping out the royal line of David.

3. *Jehoash* (835 B.C. - 796 B.C.) The royal line was preserved by God despite Athaliah's murderous policies. An heir to the throne was rescued and secretly raised by Jehoiada the priest in the temple. When the time was ripe, Athaliah, who had usurped the throne of David, was overthrown, and Jehoash, the boy king, was crowned in her stead. He was only seven years old. As long as he had Jehoiada to guide him, Jehoash ruled well. But, on the death of this good man, he turned to evil ways and was eventually assassinated.

4. *Amaziah* (796 B.C. - 767 B.C.) *and Uzziah* (790 B.C. - 739 B.C.) Amaziah, who succeeded Jehoash to the throne, was a good king. And so was Uzziah (sometimes called Azariah), his son. Uzziah reigned for fifty-two years and was a powerful ruler. At the peak of his power Uzziah unfortunately allowed pride to get the better of him and he sought to unite in his own person the offices of king and priest. For this presumption God smote Uzziah with leprosy. His son, Jotham, also a good king, followed him to the throne.

5. *Ahaz* (735 B.C. - 715 B.C.) The next king of Judah was Ahaz. At this time the Assyrians were expanding westward and Ahaz, very fearful of the Assyrians, made sweeping concessions to them. He plunged Judah into deep apostasy. With him Judah began the final downward plunge into the night which was already engulfing her sister nation Israel.

6. *Hezekiah* (715 B.C. - 686 B.C.) Hezekiah was one of Judah's greatest kings. Under the guidance of Isaiah he successfully resisted the Assyrians, of whom his father had been so fearful. God gave Judah a most miraculous deliverance from the hands of this foe. Hezekiah instituted great religious reforms, but all these good measures were soon swept away by his son Manasseh.

7. *Manasseh* (695 B.C. - 642 B.C.) *and Josiah* (640 B.C. - 609 B.C.) Of all Judah's kings, Manasseh reigned longest. He was one of the worst, reveling in idolatry. He covered the nation with shame and dragged his people to practices which were completely vile. At last he was carried into captivity by the Assyrians. He repented of his sins, was forgiven by God and restored to his throne. His son Amon was as wicked as Manasseh had been. But Manasseh's grandson, Josiah, led the last of Judah's religious revivals before the night settled down. However it was too late. The untiring efforts of this noble king struck no deep response in the hearts of the people or the princes. Upon

Josiah's death he was succeeded by four kings, all bad, who came increasingly under the power of Babylon.

The Final Plunge

The last days of Judah were characterized by international intrigues. The weepings and warnings of Jeremiah were ignored. In their desperation the kings of Judah looked for alliances which might save them from destruction. But Assyria was no more and Egypt was a broken reed. The Babylonians were coming to full power. In 605 B.C., the first Babylonian invasion took place, and another followed early in the year 597. Nebuchadnezzar, the Babylonian king, installed Zedekiah as a puppet king and retired from the scene. Ignoring Jeremiah and listening instead to evil counsel, Zedekiah rebelled against his master. Back came Nebuchadnezzar to sack Jerusalem, burn the temple in 586 B.C., deport much of the population of Judah to Babylon, and thus bring an end to the monarchy.

The times of the Gentiles had begun. From that day to this, Jerusalem has been almost entirely under Gentile control and will remain so until Jesus comes to reign.

The Kings of Judah and Israel

DATES	HEBREW HISTORY		REFERENCE	OTHER EVENTS
	THE UNITED KINGDOM			
1051-1011	Saul		1 Sam. 11:15	
1011-971	David		2 Sam. 5:4	
971-931	Solomon		1 Kings 2:12	
	JUDAH	ISRAEL		
931-913	Rehoboam		1 Kings 12:1	
931-910		Jeroboam I	1 Kings 12:19	
913-911	Abijam		1 Kings 15:1	
911-873	**Asa**		1 Kings 15:9	
910-909		Nadab	1 Kings 15:25	
909-886		Baasha	1 Kings 15:27	
886		Elah	1 Kings 16:8	
885		Zimri	1 Kings 16:9	
(885-880)		Tibni	1 Kings 16:21	
885-874		Omri	1 Kings 16:22	
874-853		Ahab	1 Kings 16:29	
? -852			(Elijah)	
873-848	**Jehoshaphat**		1 Kings 22:41	
853-852		Ahaziah	1 Kings 22:40	
852-841		Jehoram	2 Kings 3:1	
			(Elisha)	
848-841	Jehoram (called Joram)		1 Kings 22:50	
841	Ahaziah		2 Kings 8:24	Married
841-835	Athaliah		2 Kings 11:1	Athaliah—
841-814		Jehu	2 Kings 9:2	daughter of Ahab
835-796	**Jehoash** (called Joash)		2 Kings 11:4	and Jezebel
?830-815?			(Joel)	
814-798		Jehoahaz	2 Kings 13:1	
798-782		Jehoash	2 Kings 13:10	
792-767	**Amaziah**		2 Kings 14:1	
(793-782)		(Jeroboam II regent with Jehoash)		
(790-767)	**(Uzziah** regent with Amaziah)			

Good Kings in Bold

DATES	HEBREW HISTORY		REFERENCE	OTHER EVENTS
	JUDAH	ISRAEL		
785-775			(Jonah)	
782-753		Jeroboam II	2 Kings 14:16	
767-739	Uzziah		2 Kings 15:1	
	(called Azariah)			
765-755			(Amos)	
755-715			(Hosea)	
753-752		Zachariah	2 Kings 14:29	
752		Shallum	2 Kings 15:10	
752-742		Menahem	2 Kings 15:14	
(750-739)	(Jotham regent			
	with Uzziah)			
745-727				Tiglath-Pileser III
742-740		Pekahiah	2 Kings 15:22	
740-732		Pekah	2 Kings 15:25	
739-731	Jotham		2 Kings 15:32	
739-690?			(Isaiah)	
736-700			(Micah)	
(735-731)	(Ahaz regent			
	with Jotham)			
732-722		Hoshea	2 Kings 15:30	
731-715	Ahaz		2 Kings 15:38	
727-722				Shalmaneser V
722		FALL OF SAMARIA	2 Kings 17:6	ASSYRIAN CAPTIVITY
722-705				Sargon II
715-686	Hezekiah		2 Kings 18:1	
705-681				Sennacherib
(695-686)	(Manasseh			
	regent with			
	Hezekiah)			
686-642	Manasseh		2 Kings 21:1	
645-620?			(Nahum)	
642-640	Amon		2 Kings 21:19	
640-609	Josiah		2 Kings 22:1	
635-625?			(Zephaniah)	
627-575			(Jeremiah)	
620-610			(Habakkuk)	
612				Fall of Nineveh
609	Jehoahaz		2 Kings 23:31	
609-597	Jehoiakim		2 Kings 23:36	

Good Kings in Bold

DATES	HEBREW HISTORY		REFERENCE	OTHER EVENTS
	JUDAH	ISRAEL		
?609-585?			(Obadiah)	
605				Battle of Carchemish
605-562				Nebuchadnezzar
605-536			(Daniel)	
597	Jehoiachin		2 Kings 24:6	
597-586	Zedekiah		2 Kings 24:17	
593-558?			(Ezekiel)	
586	FALL OF JERUSALEM		2 Kings 25:1	BABYLONIAN CAPTIVITY
550-530				Cyrus
539				Fall of Babylon
	EVENTS IN JUDAH AFTER CAPTIVITY			
538	Decree of Cyrus			
538-512?	Zerubbabel			
536	Temple begun			
530-521				Cambyses
521				Smesdis
521-486				Darius I Hystaspes
520-496			(Zechariah)	
520-516			(Haggai)	
520	Temple resumed			
516	Temple finished			
486-464				Xerxes
478	Esther becomes queen			
473	Feast of Purim			
464-423				Artaxerxes
458-443	Ezra			
445-415?	Nehemiah			
435-415			(Malachi)	
423-404				Darius II

Note: Dates are based on *The Chart of Old Testament Kings and Prophets*, by John C. Whitcomb. Some of the dates of regencies and prophets are uncertain.

12

The Powers That Be Are Ordained of God

he history of Israel cannot be properly understood apart from some knowledge of the surrounding world empires. The family became a nation in Egypt. The northern kingdom was, in its later years, under constant threat from Assyria. This cruel nation was a terror to all its neighbors and eventually was permitted by God to bring judgment on Israel, carrying the ten tribes into captivity. The southern kingdom had Babylon to fear, and eventually Judah, too, tasted servitude. The Babylonian empire was succeeded by the Persians under whom the captivity came to an end. Later the Persians fell before the Greeks under Alexander the Great, and in time the Romans mastered the known world. Before considering the decline of the Hebrew monarchy some consideration must be given to Assyria, Babylon, and Persia. This will be done by giving a brief summary of the various kings of each of these empires, showing how they relate to the Bible story.

Assyria

1. *Tiglath-pileser III* (745-727 B.C.) About the time of the death of Jeroboam II of Israel, this famous king came to the throne of Assyria. He lifted Assyria from its decline which had made the ambitions of Jeroboam II possible, and made Assyria the foremost empire of the day. Early in his reign he was proclaimed king of Babylon. His Babylonian name was Pulu, and it is as Pul that he is known in the Bible

(2 Kings 15:19). His westward advances overshadowed the reigns of Pekahiah, Pekah, and Hoshea of Israel and the reigns of Uzziah, Jotham, and Ahaz of Judah. It was this emperor to whom Ahaz, king of Judah, foolishly appealed for help against the Syro-Israel league which plagued him. Israel was put under heavy tribute, her kings being little more than puppets of Assyria. Ahaz of Judah aped his Assyrian "protector" and dragged his people low.

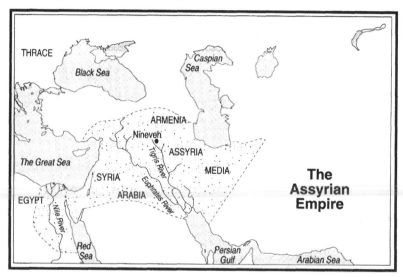

The Assyrian Empire

2. *Shalmaneser V* (727-722) Hoshea, the last king of Israel, listening to vain Egyptian promises of help, failed to pay tribute to this king, Tiglath-pileser's successor, thereby bringing about the siege of Samaria.

3. *Sargon II* (722-705) Samaria held out for three years and was finally overthrown by Sargon II in 722 B.C. The terrible deportation of the Israelites followed. Hezekiah of Judah also felt the weight of Sargon's hand. Having raised Assyria to new heights of prestige, Sargon fell in battle. Isaiah walked the streets of Jerusalem "naked and barefoot" as a sign that Assyria would conquer Egypt and Ethiopia and as a warning to any who might be tempted to look in that direction for help (Isaiah 20:2-6).

4. *Sennacherib* (705-681) Revolts broke out against Assyria on the death of Sargon II. Judah, under Hezekiah, threw off the Assyrian yoke completely. At this time, too, Merodach-baladan, pretending to congratulate Hezekiah on the recovery from his sickness, sought to win Judah into a great confederacy secretly formed against Assyria (Isaiah 39). Isaiah the prophet sharply rebuked Hezekiah for showing his treasures to the Babylonian envoys. Hezekiah's revolt against Assyria is described three times in the Bible (2 Kings 18:13–19:37;

2 Chronicles 32:1-21; Isaiah 36–37). Sennacherib was a fiendishly cruel and inhuman ruler, given to incredible atrocities. He had a violent death at the hands of his own sons.

5. *Esar-haddon* (681-669) One of the greatest of the Assyrian kings, this monarch extended Assyrian power to Egypt and was the first Assyrian king to bear the title "king of the kings of Egypt." He is mentioned prophetically in Isaiah 19:4. Ezra also speaks of him (Ezra 4:2). This was the king who carried Manasseh of Judah into captivity (2 Chronicles 33:11).

6. *Ashurbanipal* (669-633) This king continued his father's policies and resumed the unfinished task of subjugating Egypt. He is referred to in Nahum 3:8-10. The restoration of Manasseh to the throne of Judah was probably in line with the Assyrian policy of keeping the road to Egypt open. However the handwriting was on the wall for Assyria. Already the Medes were gathering their strength, and by 625 B.C. the Babylonians had joined the Medes. The Assyrians were driven out of Babylonia in 625 B.C. by Nabopolassar, father of Nebuchadnezzar. In 614 B.C., he joined with the Medes to capture Asshur, and in 612 B.C., he destroyed Nineveh. The slackening of the Assyrian hold made possible the reforms of King Josiah of Judah.

Babylon

1. *Nebuchadnezzar* (605-562) Nebuchadnezzar was a strong military leader. In one of the most important battles of history he destroyed the armies of Egypt at Carchemish on the Euphrates in 605 B.C. Having driven Pharaoh Necho out of Asia, Nebuchadnezzar returned to Babylon to take over the throne upon the death of his father. He invaded Judah and besieged Jerusalem three times, subjugated the last three kings of Judah, and terminated the Hebrew monarchy. Jerusalem was given over to Gentile domination. In 586 B.C., Nebuchadnezzar besieged Tyre, the siege lasting thirteen years. The Babylonians failed to get any spoil from the city, however, for the citizens withdrew to an island half a mile from shore, leaving the invader with the ruined remains of the old city. Ezekiel foretold this siege of Tyre (26:7-12) and then, after its fall, he recorded the fact that Nebuchadnezzar's army obtained no spoil, and promised that Egypt would be given to Nebuchadnezzar in payment (Ezekiel 29:18-20). The book of Ezekiel should be read against the background of Nebuchadnezzar's various military campaigns.

2. *Evil-merodach* (562-560) This king is known principally for his kindness to Jehoiachin in the thirty-seventh year of his captivity (2 Kings 25:27-30). He was murdered by his brothers in a palace plot.

3. *Neriglisar* (560-556) No important events took place in this

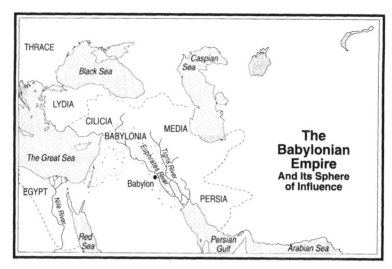

king's reign. He campaigned in Cilicia in an attempt to stem the rising power of the Lydians.

4. *Labashi-Marduk* (556) Only a boy when he came to the throne, he had reigned only nine months, when he was murdered and power passed to a new dynasty.

5. *Nabonidus* (556-539) This king was a very superstitious man and neither a great statesman nor a good general. During much of his reign he did not even live in Babylon. His son Belshazzar acted as regent in Babylon while Nabonidus was campaigning in Syria and northern Arabia. After the death of Nebuchadnezzar, the Babylonian alliance with the Medes was broken off. Nabonidus had many enemies, and revolts broke out in various parts of the empire. He stirred up the animosity of many Babylonians who resented his reforms.

6. *Belshazzar* (553-539) During this weak king's dissolute regency the Babylonian empire fell before the Medes and Persians. The Babylonian empire had lasted about seventy years, approximating the time of the seventy-year captivity of the Jews.

Persia

1. *Cyrus the Great* (550-530) Until 550 B.C. the Persians were subject to the Medes. Cyrus the Great succeeded his father as king of the small Persian kingdom of Anshan in 559 B.C. Soon afterward he rebelled against the Medes and in 550 united the Medes and Persians under his rule. He conquered Babylon in 539, and made Persia a world power which eventually stretched from east to west for three thousand miles. He permitted the Jews to return to Palestine, a fulfillment of Isaiah 45:1-7, and to rebuild the temple.

2. *Darius the Mede* (539-525) Darius was made king over Chaldea after the capture of Babylon by the army of Cyrus the Great (Daniel 5:31; 9:1). He reigned part of one year, at least, before Cyrus (Daniel 6:28). Probably he held the kingdom in trust for Cyrus, who was still campaigning in other parts.

3. *Cambyses II* (530-521)

4. *Smerdis (Gaumata)* This king reigned for only seven months. He is thought to be the Artaxerxes of Ezra 4:7. .

5. *Darius I (Hystaspes,* 521-486) The building of the temple in Jerusalem had come to a standstill when he came to the throne, but Darius permitted the work to go on (Ezra 5–6). The prophets Haggai and Zechariah prophesied during his reign, and the temple was completed.

6. *Xerxes* (486-464) This king, Ahasuerus, married Esther who became queen in 478 B.C. He was a cruel, vindictive, sensual, and fickle man, famous for his wars with Greece. He was roundly defeated at sea by a much smaller Grecian fleet at the famous battle of Salamis. A year later the Greeks defeated the land forces of this Persian tyrant. He was murdered eventually by a courtier.

7. *Artaxerxes I (Longimanus,* 464-423) This king was very favorably disposed toward the Jews, even allowing Nehemiah to go up to Jerusalem to rebuild its walls. He is mentioned in Ezra 7:1, Nehemiah 2:1 and 5:14. Later still, he permitted Nehemiah to become governor of Jerusalem (Nehemiah 5:14; 13:6).

8. *Darius III (Codomanus,* 336-331) This last king of Persia was defeated by Alexander the Great, first at Issus in 333 B.C., and then at Arbela in 331 B.C. He was murdered by his servants. The scepter of world empire passed from Asia to Europe.

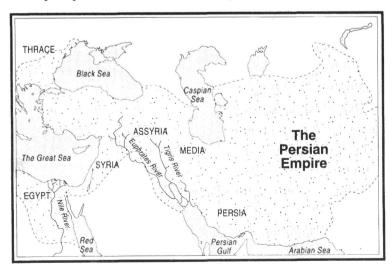

13

1 and 2 Chronicles: Second Thoughts

The books of Chronicles are not a mere repetition of the books of Kings. The books of Kings give us history from the viewpoint of the prophets, Chronicles from the viewpoint of the priests. The books of Kings give us history from the human standpoint, Chronicles from the divine standpoint. The first show man ruling, the others show God overruling. The revival under Hezekiah, for example, is given in three verses in Kings and in three chapters in Chronicles.

The Companion Bible has this helpful comment on the books of 1 and 2 Chronicles: "These books belong to quite another part of the Old Testament, and do not follow in sequence on the books of Kings. They are, according to the Hebrew Canon, the conclusion of the Old Testament; and the genealogies here lead up to that of Matthew 1:1 and the commencement of the New Testament. They end with the ending of the kingdom; and the question of Cyrus, 'Who is there?' (2 Chronicles 36:23), is followed by the answer, 'Where is he?' (Matthew 2:2), and the proclamation of the kingdom by the rightful King and His forerunner. It begins with the first Adam and leads on to the 'last Adam.' It deals with the kingdom of Judah because Christ was proclaimed as the successor of David."

Differences in Kings and Chronicles

KINGS	CHRONICLES
• Was written before the Captivity • Was written from the standpoint of the Prophets • Embraces the history of the Northern Kingdom • Is compulsive—was written in the dust and din and distraction of the time and place	• Was written after the Captivity • Was written from the standpoint of the Priests • Ignores the history of the Northern Kingdom • Is contemplative—was written in the quiet and calm of a library, far from the sounds and scenes involved

Analysis of 1 and 2 Chronicles

These books were originally one in the Hebrew Bible. For purpose of analysis they are taken together. The kings listed are from the tribe of Judah.

    I. THE CHRONOLOGY OF JUDAH'S KINGS (1 Chronicles 1–9)
       A. The Royal Line
          1. Adam to Noah (1:1-4)
          2. Shem to Abraham (1:24-28)
          3. Abraham to Israel (1:34)
          4. Israel to Jesse (2:1-12)
          5. David to Zedekiah (3:1-24)
       B. The Related Lines
          1. Japheth to Ham (1:5-23)
          2. Ishmael (1:29-33)
          3. Esau and Edom (1:35-54)
          4. Jesse and Caleb (2:13-55)
          5. Other Tribes (4:1–9:44)
    II. THE CHRONICLES OF JUDAH'S KINGS
       (1 Chronicles 10–2 Chronicles 36)
       A. The Throne of David (1 Chronicles 10–29)
       B. The Temple of Solomon (2 Chronicles 1–9)
       C. The Testimony of History (2 Chronicles 10–36)

The Purpose of the Writer

The books of Chronicles were written after the captivity in Babylon was over. The returned remnant found themselves back in the Land of Promise with a monumental task before them. Their cities were heaps of rubble, their temple was gone, the land was desolate and in ruins. Ancient enemies were hostile still, and many Jewish people were indifferent to their emancipation. They preferred a life of luxury in Babylonia and Persia to the rigors of pioneering under these conditions.

Most devastating of all, the throne of David was gone. The returning remnant under Zerubbabel had a commission to build a temple, not a throne. The books of Chronicles were written to interpret to the people the meaning of their history in the light of the present and the future.

The Things That Remained

First, although the *throne* of David was gone, the *line* of David was still in existence. From Adam to Zedekiah, as the chronicles proved, God had never allowed that line to become tangled, broken, or lost. Through all the long ages God had pursued His purpose. Through days bright with promise and days dark with apostasy God had remained true to His plan. It was inconceivable that the thread could be broken now. The throne of David was a divine institution. The line of David had never become extinct and never would until at last the Messiah Himself, so long promised by the prophets, should come.

Second, a new temple had been raised on the ruins of the old. The writer of Chronicles shows that the temple had occupied an important place in the history of the people of God. If David had given Judah a scepter, Solomon had given Judah a sanctuary. The one was as important as the other. Tenderly the writer of Chronicles keeps in mind the fortunes of the temple. Conceived in the mind of David, constructed under the guidance of Solomon, contaminated by some of the kings, and cleansed by others, and at last consumed in the fires that demolished Jerusalem, the temple is never far from the center of the story.

Third, the writer of Chronicles proves that all Israel's troubles stemmed from apostasy. Skillfully he gives the testimony of history. Looking back over the past, the people of God could see, in the sharp perspective of history, exactly where apostasy had brought the nation. The book of Chronicles is a philosophy of Hebrew history from the divine viewpoint. It is a clear warning to the people never again to forsake the temple and the worship of the living God.

The Scope of Chronicles

Beginning with Adam and ending with the decree of Cyrus, the book of Chronicles covers the longest period of any of the books of the

Bible. Beginning with David and going through to Zedekiah, it relates the history of twenty-one kings and also the inglorious reign of Queen Athaliah, the usurper. The kings of Israel are mentioned only occasionally in passing. There were the same number of kings on the throne of Israel, however the kingdom of Judah lasted 136 years longer than the kingdom of Israel. This was one effect which the half dozen God-fearing kings of Judah had on the history of their nation.

Israel and the World Powers

During the period covered by the Hebrew history of the Old Testament, Israel came into conflict with four world powers: Egypt, Assyria, Babylon, and Persia. Later they came into conflict with Greece and Rome as well.

Egypt, with its long, colorful, and brilliant history, was used of God during the formative years. In Egypt Israel grew up. Long after the exodus, Egypt periodically exercised an influence on Hebrew history. Solomon's queen was an Egyptian. Several of the Pharaohs invaded the land or brought Palestine into subjection. The imperial interests of Egypt were bound to clash with the interests of the tiny Hebrew nation.

Assyria was an implacable foe of Israel. Fierce, ruthless, cruel, and proud, the Assyrians were the scourge and terror of their neighbors. As has been seen, they finally brought to an end the nationhood of the northern ten tribes.

When the Babylonians succeeded the Assyrians on the world scene, the scattered ten tribes were absorbed into the Babylonian empire. With Nebuchadnezzar's conquests of Judea and Jerusalem the Hebrew monarchy ceased to exist. In Babylon, the home of idolatry, the Jews were cured of idolatry, their prevailing sin.

With the fall of Babylon, the Persians fell heir to "the Jewish problem." Cyrus wisely solved that problem by giving the Jews permission to return to their homeland. The last three books of Old Testament history and the last three books of Old Testament prophecy cover this event.

Against this changing panorama of world empire, God wrote Hebrew history. Overruling the passions and powers of men, immutable in His counsels, invincible in His purposes, from generation to generation pursuing His eternal purposes all down the years, God cannot be dethroned. This is the message of Chronicles, and it is as valid today as when it was written.

14

Ezra, Nehemiah, and Esther: Return of the Remnant

The captivity of Judah took place in three stages. In 605 B.C., Nebuchadnezzar first invaded the land and took away Jehoiakim and the leading nobles including Daniel. In 597 B.C., a second Babylonian invasion took place, and King Jehoiachin was carried away into captivity together with most of the people of importance including Ezekiel and the ancestors of Mordecai. In 586 B.C., the final destruction of Jerusalem took place. Zedekiah, the king of Judah, breaking his oath of allegiance to Nebuchadnezzar, had entered into an alliance with Egypt to throw off the Babylonian yoke. The Babylonians besieged Jerusalem and terrible scenes took place. At last the city was sacked, the temple burned, and the final deportation effected. The land began to make up for its neglected Sabbaths.

The deportations took place in three stages. The return of the remnant at the end of the captivity had a threefold movement to it as well. About the year 538 B.C., Cyrus the Persian issued the decree which gave the Jews liberty to return to Jerusalem and rebuild the temple. Led by Zerubbabel, a small group responded. In 458 B.C., a further group returned under the leadership of Ezra. This return was a whole generation later than the first. Then in the year 445 B.C., Nehemiah, a high official in the Persian court, was given permission to return to rebuild the walls of Jerusalem.

The observant student will note that there were two "exodus" movements in Old Testament history. The first was from Egypt and the second from Babylon, with almost a millennium lying between the two events. Both these exiles and returns were subjects of prophecy, the first in Genesis 15:13-14, and the second in Jeremiah 25:11-12; 29:10-11.

Before looking at the books which deal with the return of the remnant it will be helpful to see the entire period as a whole.

Cyrus the Great entered Babylon on October 29, 539 B.C. Following his policy of state, he encouraged the Jews to return to Palestine and rebuild their temple (2 Chronicles 36:22-23; Ezra 1:1-4). The first movement back to the homeland was led by Zerubbabel, the son of Shealtiel (his Babylonian name was Sheshbazzar). As the firstborn of the exiled king Jehoiachin, Zerubbabel gives us an important Messianic link between David and Joseph (Matthew 1).

Zerubbabel's contingent returned in 538 B.C. Included among the pioneers were Joshua the high priest and a goodly number of the priests, Levites and heads of the tribes of Judah and Benjamin. Their first concern was to build an altar to the Lord on its old site and to restore the daily sacrifices (Ezra 2:1–3:3). Next they laid the foundations of the new temple in April or May 536 B.C. This work was helped by financial aid given by the Persian king. There was great rejoicing as the foundations of the temple were laid although some of the older ones wept at the vanished glory of Solomon's temple (Ezekiel 3:8-13).

Work on the temple had not proceeded far before the Samaritans asked to have a share in the work. They were refused and henceforth did everything in their power to hinder and harass the builders. In their spite the Samaritans hired lawyers to misrepresent the Jews at the Persian court. This resulted in a halt to the work so that no further progress was made during the remainder of the reign of Cyrus nor during the reigns of Cambyses and Smerdis (Ezra 4:1-24).

Zerubbabel does not seem to be entirely blameless in this stoppage for the difficulties could have been surmounted and during the long sixteen-year suspension the settlers had no hesitation about building elaborate houses for themselves (Haggai 1:2-4).

On August 29, 520 B.C. Haggai began to exhort the Jews to resume work on the temple. His ministry was so effective that the Jews, under Zerubbabel and Joshua, began to work again on the temple. At this time, too, Zechariah began his ministry. As the work on the temple proceeded Tattenai, a Persian governor, wrote to Darius I to challenge it. Darius made a search of the state records and found the decree of Cyrus in the library at Ecbatana and at once ordered the governor Tattenai to help the Jews in every way and to give them financial support.

Chronology of the Rebuilding of the Temple

KINGS OF PERSIA	IMPORTANT EVENTS	PROPHETS	WORK ON TEMPLE
Cyrus 550-530	Entered Babylon 539 Cyrus' Decree 538 Zerubbabel 538		Temple foundation laid 536
Cambyses 530-521			
Smerdis 521			
Darius I Hystaspes 521-486	Joshua priest 519	Haggai 520 Zechariah 520	Work resumed 520 Work finished 516
Xerxes 486-464	Deposed Vashti 483 Married Esther 478		
Artaxerxes 464-423	Ezra returns 458 Nehemiah leaves Persia 445 Nehemiah arrives in Jerusalem 444		

In 519 Joshua the high priest was crowned by the prophet Zechariah in a highly symbolic ceremony looking forward to the day when the Messiah would unite the offices of priest and king in His own person (Zechariah 6:9-15).

In 518 B.C. a delegation of Jews came down from Bethel to Jerusalem to ask the priests and prophets if it was needful to continue mourning and fasting over the destruction of Jerusalem. This became the occasion for an important message from the Lord through Zechariah (7–8).

Work on the temple had now advanced to its completion and it was dedicated with much rejoicing in 516 in the sixth year of Darius.

From the time the temple was finished in 516 until the time Ezra appears in 458 some fifty-eight years elapsed. The long and prosperous reign of the mighty Darius I Hystapses had come to an end. He had ruled the mightiest empire the world had ever seen from the Grecian Archipelago in the west to Persia in the east. It comprised some two million square miles, Judah being an insignificant province.

Darius died in 486 B.C. and was followed on the throne by Xerxes, the king who deposed Vashti and then in the year 478 married Esther. In 464 B.C. Xerxes was succeeded by Artaxerxes I in whose reign Ezra and Nehemiah led more Jewish colonists back to the land of their fathers.

In 458 Ezra, under mandate from Artaxerxes, led the second group of exiles back. It should be remembered that since the book of Ezra describes both the return under Zerubbabel (Ezra 1–6) and the return under Ezra (chapters 7–10) a period of fifty-eight years divides the two sections of the book. In other words, there is a period of fifty-eight years between Ezra six and seven and a period of eighty years between Ezra one and seven.

Twelve years after Ezra's expedition, Nehemiah was also given permission by Artaxerxes to go to Jerusalem. His commission, in 445 B.C. was to rebuild the walls of Jerusalem. He was given a cavalry escort for the journey and letters of introduction to the various Persian governors along the way. He was also appointed governor of Judea. He arrived in Jerusalem in 444 B.C. in the twentieth year of Artaxerxes' reign and threw himself into the work with tireless energy. Despite the discouragements that faced him and the determined opposition of his enemies he was able to complete his monumental task in just fifty-two days.

The wall being built, attention was next given to the instruction of the people and a great religious revival followed. After governing Jerusalem for twelve years, Nehemiah returned to Persia about the year 433. Later he asked for a further leave of absence (13:6) and returned to Jerusalem where he seems to have ended his days.

Analysis of Ezra

It should be noted that some eighty years separate part one of Ezra from part two.

    I. REBUILDING THE TEMPLE WALLS (1–6)
       Under Zerubbabel (20 years)
       A. The Restoration (1)
       B. The Registration (2)

Building the Temple Walls

Zerubbabel was a descendant of David and the only royal person to return at this time. He was the political head of the remnant. Joshua, the high priest, was the religious leader. Cyrus gave to the returning remnant the vast treasure looted from the original temple by Nebuchadnezzar. The return journey was slow and perilous and, once the land was reached, the remnant had to face opposition from the mixed races which had settled there. The first act was to build the altar, for all true revival must begin with that concept of the cross which the altar symbolized. Then the foundation of the temple was laid. Due to the bitter hostility of the Samaritans, who had been refused permission to help in the work, it was fifteen long years before the temple was finished. During this period Haggai and Zechariah were raised up to urge forward the completion of the task with their stirring prophecies. The temple was finished twenty years after the return.

The Ministry of Ezra

Between the first and the second returns something like eighty years elapsed. In other words almost sixty years passed between the completion of the temple and the visit of Ezra. They were momentous years in secular history, but were silently passed over by the Spirit of God.

The leader of the second remnant was a priest of the tribe of Levi, of the house of Aaron. This was in contrast with Zerubbabel, who had been a prince of the tribe of Judah, of the house of David. Ezra was a godly man who left a permanent mark on the nation. He called himself a scribe and made it his task to teach the people thoroughly the Word of God and to bring about important reforms. Ezra especially insisted that the remnant vigorously separate themselves from all alliances with the surrounding peoples.

Outline of Nehemiah

Zerubbabel came to build the temple of Jerusalem. Nehemiah came to build the city walls. He arrived twelve years after Ezra.

I. THE WORK OF CONSTRUCTION   (1–7)
   A. The Prayer (1)
   B. The Place (2)
   C. The Plan (3)
   D. The Problems (4–5)
   E. The Prize (6)
   F. The Poll (7)
II. THE WORK OF CONSECRATION   (8–10)
   A. The Conviction (8)
   B. The Confession (9)
   C. The Covenant (10)
III. THE WORK OF CONSOLIDATION (11–13)
   A. How It Was Commenced (11–12:26)
      1. The Distribution of the Population (11)
      2. The Descendants of the Priests (12:1-26)
   B. How It Was Completed (12:27–13:21) (12 years later?)
      1. A Formal Dedication of the City (12:27-47)
      2. A Fundamental Dealing with Sin (13)

The Coming of Nehemiah

Nehemiah was appointed by Artaxerxes, king of Persia, to be the governor of Jerusalem and received his permission to rebuild the walls of the city. His book is a sequel to the book of Ezra. Arriving at Jerusalem, Nehemiah made a secret survey of the task before him and then attacked it with energy, scorn for opposition, practical wisdom, and determination. In spite of fierce opposition the monumental task was completed in seven weeks! How Nehemiah overcame the ridicule and rage, the greed and guile of his adversaries makes thrilling reading.

A Noble Pair

Ezra and Nehemiah stood shoulder to shoulder in the great work of consecration and consolidation which followed upon the completion of the wall. First Jerusalem had to be populated; thus one in ten of the population outside the city were chosen by lot to live within the city. Then followed a great religious revival, which brought the people back to the Bible, to times of heart-searching and confession, and to a renewal of the covenant. It would seem that the dedication of the walls of the city did not take place immediately but a number of years later, after Nehemiah's temporary absence from the city. Upon his return he found that old sins had reasserted themselves and had to be vigorously dealt with. Characteristically he lost no time in dealing as thoroughly and as drastically with the problem of wickedness as he had dealt with the problem of the walls.

Esther

The book of Esther is one of the two books in the Bible named after women. Ruth was a Gentile woman who married a Jew. Esther was a Jewish woman who married a Gentile. The events recorded in the book of Esther took place between the books of Ezra and Nehemiah.

Outline of Esther

The story of Esther is that of a plot to exterminate the entire Jewish race.

    I. HOW THE PLOT WAS FORMED (1–3)
       A. The Might of Ahasuerus (1–3)
       B. The Marriage of Esther (2:1-20)
       C. The Ministry of Mordecai (2:21-23)
       D. The Malice of Haman (3)
    II. HOW THE PLOT WAS FOUGHT (4–5)
       A. The Cry of Israel (4:1-3)
       B. The Convictions of Mordecai (4:1-14)
       C. The Courage of Esther (4:15–5:8)
       D. The Confidence of Haman (5:9-14)
   III. HOW THE PLOT WAS FOILED (6–10)
       A. The Death of Haman (6–7)
          1. He Was Publicly Humbled (6)
          2. He Was Publicly Hanged (7)
       B. The Decree of Ahasuerus (8)
       C. The Deliverance of Israel (9:1-18)
       D. The Day of Purim (9:19-32)
       E. The Dignity of Mordecai (10)

The book of Esther describes events which took place at Susa, the principal Persian capital. The actors are either Persians or Jews of the dispersion. No mention is made of Palestine, Jerusalem, the temple, the law of Moses, or general Hebrew history. The Persian king is mentioned 190 times in the book, but God is not mentioned at all. None of the titles for God in general use among the Jews are to be found, neither Elohim nor Jehovah nor Shaddai nor Adonai. One reason suggested for the absence of God's name is that some half century before, the Persian King Cyrus had issued a proclamation permitting the Jews to return to Palestine. This proclamation was a direct fulfillment of prophecy (Jeremiah 29:10; 25:11-12; Isaiah 44:28). Not a Jew should have remained in Persia, "not a hoof should have been left behind." Yet many Jews were far too comfortable in the land of their exile to want to face the rigors of pioneering in Palestine. They elected to stay where they were, and God simply did not allow His name to be linked with them in this book, although in grace He did care for and protect them.

The Story of Esther

The book itself contains a crisis which arose in Hebrew history in the days of the mighty Xerxes. This king is known to history as a tyrannical despot, imperious in temper, ruthless in the exercise of his power, grandiose in his schemes and ambitions, abandoned in his sensuality. During his reign the Jews of the dispersion were threatened with total extermination through the machinations of Haman, one of the emperor's chief ministers of state. Haman was angered because a Jew named Mordecai refused to pay him the homage of bowing to him as he passed by. In revenge Haman plotted the public execution of Mordecai on a special gallows and planned a sweeping purge of all the Jews in the vast Persian domain. His plot almost succeeded.

Haman's anti-Semitic bloodlust is by no means unique in history. Pharaoh attempted to stamp out the Jewish people when they were in bondage in Egypt in the days of Moses. In more recent times Hitler sought to do the same thing in Europe. But God has His hand upon the Jewish people and He has His own high purposes to work out with them. Satan's attempts to thwart the birth of Christ by annihilating the Jews failed. His subsequent attempts to wreak his vengeance on them have been terrible, but he has never succeeded in eradicating them. The Jews remain a gulf stream in the ocean of mankind, being neither assimilated or exterminated. They will yet occupy that lofty place in world affairs which God has planned for them.

In Esther we have no miraculous intervention by God to prevent Haman's plot from coming to fruition. Instead we have an outworking of events by natural sequence, God behind the scenes checkmating each of Haman's moves. God does not have to work miracles in order to bring to nought the schemes of men. Look at what happens. Esther becomes queen. Mordecai renders the king a great service, which goes unnoticed at the time although worthy of great reward. The king cannot resist the beauty, courage, and pleas of Esther. On the most critical night in the story the king cannot sleep and learns of Mordecai's service. Haman is forced to play the part of a slave to Mordecai in a public exhibition of the king's regard for this Jew. The archplotter is trapped at Esther's banquet and hanged on the very gallows he made for Mordecai. The Jews throughout the empire are delivered from their plight. The timing and sequence of the events are no less remarkable than the events themselves. To this very day the Jews annually keep the Feast of Purim in remembrance of the deliverance Esther wrought from the plot of Haman the Agagite.

With the book of Esther the historical portion of the Old Testament comes to a close. Looking back over the unfolding of this history, we see divine Providence overruling in the affairs of men, even in their darkest hours. Behind the scenes God rules. James Russell Lowell puts it thus:

> Careless seems the great Avenger; history's pages but record
> One death-grapple in the darkness 'twixt old systems and the Word.
> Truth forever on the scaffold, Wrong forever on the throne—
> Yet that scaffold sways the future and, behind the dim unknown,
> Standeth God within the shadow, keeping watch above His own.

It is against this background of history that the remaining poetical and prophetical books of the Old Testament should be read.

15
Hebrew Poetry: Music of the Heart

Dirge, drama, elegy, epic, idyll, lyric, and ode are some of the forms of poetry, and many of these are represented in the poetical sections of Scripture. The book of Lamentations is a dirge, a song of terrible grief. Psalm 22 is an example of lyrical poetry in which the deep feelings of the heart are bared rather than some outward incident described. Psalms 78, 105, 106, and 136 are odes.

In the Western world we generally expect poetry to have rhyme and rhythm and a definite swing to it although, of course, not all English poetry meets these demands. The blank verse so characteristic of Shakespeare is an example of poetry which does not altogether depend on rhyme. Hebrew poetry depends on parallelism of thought rather than on the phonetic coupling of words. An idea is stated one way and then repeated in another, and this is done in one of three ways:

Synonymous Parallelism

In this type of poetry the second half of the verse repeats the content of the first half only in different words as in the following examples:

He that sitteth in the heavens shall laugh;
The Lord shall have them in derision.

Psalm 2:4

Deliver me, O Lord, from the evil man;
Preserve me from the violent man.

Psalm 140:1

Antithetic Parallelism

In this poetic arrangement a thought is stated in the first verse only to be set out in contrast, or antithesis, in the second like this:

The young lions do lack, and suffer hunger:
But they that seek the LORD shall not want any good thing.

Psalm 34:10

A righteous man regardeth the life of his beast:
But the tender mercies of the wicked are cruel.

Proverbs 12:10

Synthetic Parallelism

In this type of poem a thought is given and then expanded in succeeding lines, each line building on the first as follows:

And he shall be like a tree planted by the rivers of water,
That bringeth forth his fruit in his season;
His leaf also shall not wither;
And whatsoever he doeth shall prosper.

Psalm 1:3

Wisdom hath builded her house,
She hath hewn out her seven pillars:
She hath killed her beasts;
She hath mingled her wine;
She hath also furnished her table.

Proverbs 9:1-2

Synthetic parallelism appears in various forms in Hebrew poetry. Introversion and alternation can be clearly traced with these features, sometimes extending over more than one psalm where, for example, two psalms go together as a pair. The following examples are taken from the Companion Bible, one showing an instance of introversion and the other a sample of alternation. See Psalm 135.

> A. The idols (v.15)
> > B. Their fabrication (v.15)
> > > C. Mouth without speech (singular) (v.16)
> > > > D. Eyes without sight (plural) (v.16)
> > > > D. Ears without hearing (plural) (v.17)
> > > C. Mouth without breath (singular) (v.17)
> > B. Their fabricators (v.18)
> A. The idolaters (v.18)[1]

In the next example not only is an illustration of extended alternation given but this parallelism illustrates how closely united in thought are Psalms 135 and 136.

> Psalm 135
> A. Exhortation to praise (vv. 1-5)
> > B. Creative wonders (vv. 6-7)
> > > C. Deliverance from Egypt (vv. 8-9)
> > > > D. Deliverance on journey (vv. 12-13)
> > > > > E. Gift of the land (v. 14)
> > > > > > F. Goodness to His people (v. 14)
> > > > > > > G. False gods (v. 15-18)
> > > > > > > > H. Praise (vv. 19-21)

> Psalm 136
> A. Exhortation to praise (vv. 1-3)
> > B. Creative wonders (vv. 4-9)
> > > C. Deliverance from Egypt (vv. 10-15)
> > > > D. Deliverance on journey (vv. 16-20)
> > > > > E. Gift of the land (vv. 21-22)
> > > > > > F. Goodness to His people (vv. 23-24)
> > > > > > > G. The true God (v. 25)
> > > > > > > > H. Praise (v.26)[2]

Acrostics were favorites of Hebrew poets who sometimes built their poems, each verse beginning with a separate letter of the Hebrew alphabet. The book of Lamentations is built on this principle and so are Psalms 111, 112, and 119.

Poetry can be found in all parts of the Bible. However, when we speak of the "Poetical Books" we generally mean the books of Job, Psalms, Proverbs, Ecclesiastes, and the Song of Solomon. It has often been observed that the teaching of these five books is progressive. As has been said, "Spiritually, these books present the experiences of the renewed heart from the hour self is revealed in all its unattractiveness (Job 42:5-6) until Christ becomes all in all (Song of Solomon 5:16)." The subject matter of these books may be summarized in this way:

Job	- The Problem of Pain
Psalms	- The Way to Pray
Proverbs	- The Behavior of the Believer
Ecclesiastes	- The Folly of Forgetting God
Song of Solomon	- The Art of Adoration

---

1. *The Companion Bible* (London: Oxford, 1885), p. 852.
2. *Op. cit.*, p. 853.

16
Job: The Problem of Pain

The Book of Job is believed to be the oldest in the world. He himself was a historical figure and is mentioned as such both in the Old Testament and the New (Ezekiel 14:20; James 5:11). Almost certainly he lived before the giving of the law, and some claim he lived before Abraham, placing the book between Genesis 11 and 12. Others have suggested he was one of the sons of Issachar (Genesis 46:13).

The book of Job consists of a prologue, a dialogue, and an epilogue, the dialogue being in poetry and the other parts in prose. Its subject is the problem of pain, especially as it bears upon the life of a believer. Job should be read in the light of Psalms 37 and 73, and Hebrews 12. Why do the godly suffer, and why is God silent? Job and his friends wrestle with these problems but arrive at no satisfactory conclusion. It is not until God speaks that the true answer is found, for in such matters human reasoning must ever bow before the superiority of divine revelation.

Outline of Job

 I. THE DISASTERS OF JOB (1–2)
  A. The Explanation of His Troubles
   These are traced to:
   1. The Majestic Purposes of God
   2. The Malignant Purposes of Satan
  B. The Extent of His Troubles

Satan was permitted to:
1. Take Job's Fortune
2. Touch Job's Family
3. Torture Job's Flesh
4. Turn Job's Friends
II. THE DEBATES OF JOB (3:1–42:6)
   A. Job's Cry (3)
   B. Job's Critics (4–31)
   C. Job's Comforter (32–37)
   D. Job's Creator (38:1–42:6)
III. THE DELIVERANCE OF JOB (42:7-17)
   A. The Reconciliation
   B. The Restoration

The Missing Link

Neither Job nor his friends possessed all the facts, being ignorant of those behind-the-scenes events unfolded in the prologue of the book. Job had no means of knowing why he suffered, nor what the outcome would be. This adds to the value of the book, for we, too, are often ignorant of many of the reasons behind our sufferings.

Job and his critics debate, often fiercely, the reason for Job's sufferings, but each one is arguing from incomplete data. Since none has all the factors in the equation, none can arrive at a proper solution to the problem. For a wise purpose, not revealed to Job, God permitted the tragedies to fall and, all unknown to His servant, held the tempest in perfect control. "Thus far," He said to the surging seas of sorrow, "and no farther, and here shall thy proud waves be stayed."

Like Job, we have to rest in the faithfulness of God, knowing that God is too wise to make mistakes, too loving to be unkind, and too powerful to be thwarted in His purposes. Sidlow Baxter well says, "*Behind* all the suffering of the godly is a high purpose of God, and *beyond* it all is an 'afterwards' of glorious enrichment."

The Great Controversy

The controversy began with Job's great and exceedingly bitter cry as, stripped of family, friends, wealth, and health for no apparent purpose, he at last gave way to his grief. For seven long days and nights his friends Eliphaz, Bildad, and Zophar had sat before him in silence, smitten dumb by the awfulness of what had happened to Job. These friends came indeed to sympathize but, like other well-meaning people today, they stayed on to sermonize.

The verbal duel between Job and his friends is recorded in three well-defined triads. Eliphaz, Bildad, and Zophar each advanced theories to account for Job's sufferings, each being vigorously rebutted by Job. Then came a second round in the same order, only hotter and fiercer than the first. Last of all Eliphaz and Bildad spoke again, being refuted as usual by Job. This time Zophar was silent, having nothing more to say. The arguments ended in a deadlock.

Eliphaz had a hypothesis to offer as his explanation of Job's sufferings. He *suggested* that Job had sinned. Bildad had an inference, for he *supposed* Job to be a sinner; and Zophar had an assumption, actually *saying* that sin was the cause of Job's calamities. Then another voice was added, that of Elihu, a younger man, who came nearer to the truth than any of the others, urging Job to humble himself, have patience, and submit to God's will. He believed there was something remedial about Job's sufferings, and he rebuked Job for unjustly accusing God.

All were wrong. Satan made the mistake of thinking that Job served God simply for material gain. Job's wife urged him to "curse God and die" and made the mistake of thinking that the loss of wealth meant the loss of everything. Job's friends made the mistake of thinking that Job was suffering for some hideous secret sin. Elihu made the mistake of thinking that he alone had the answer to Job's problem. Job made the mistake of accusing God of injustice.

Some More Unanswerable Questions

Finally God answered Job (38:1), and this answer came in a series of questions about God's government of the natural world, none of which Job could answer. The clear implication was that if Job could not understand God's government in the *natural* realm, how much less could he understand the principles of God's government in the *moral* and *spiritual* realms. Job was not meant to know the purpose of his sufferings. Moreover, God had a deep interest in Job's affairs, and Job had to see his own littleness and God's greatness. He was thus brought to an end of himself and to a confession of personal vileness.

Job's life had been a stage upon which a titanic struggle had been enacted. The struggle ended in the complete triumph of God and the overthrow of Satan. Job was instructed to pray for his friends who had so callously rubbed the salt of their hard words into the deep wounds of his soul. When Job did so, God gave him double for all that he had lost. Such is our God!

17

The Psalms:
Hymns of the Hebrews

T he book of Psalms was the Hebrew hymnbook. Actually, there
are five books of psalms, each one ending with a doxology; and
these have more than an accidental correspondence to the five
books of Moses.

Psalms 1–41, the first book, reflect the book of Genesis, the key
thought being man and God's counsels concerning him. Psalms 42–72
comprise the second book, the key thought of which is Israel. This
book begins with Israel's cry for deliverance and ends with Israel's
king reigning over the redeemed nation. Many of the psalms in this
group reflect the teaching of Exodus. Psalms 73–89, the third book,
have the sanctuary for their dominant note and therefore parallel
Leviticus. Psalms 90–106 clearly correspond to Numbers, the fourth
book of Moses. This group of psalms begins with one written by Moses
and ends with one which recounts Israel's rebellions in the wilderness. Psalms 107–150, the fifth book, are linked with Deuteronomy,
the prevailing thought being God's Word. The great Psalm 119 occurs
in this section, a psalm devoted to the exalting of God's Word.

It has been suggested that the first group of psalms, mostly written
by David, was collected by Solomon; that the second group was
collected by the Levites descended from Korah; that the third group
was collected by Hezekiah; and that the remaining two groups were

collected by Ezra and Nehemiah. If this is so, then the collection and arrangement of the Psalms took half a millennium to be completed.

The Value of the Psalms

Many of the Psalms were composed for private and public worship; others were born out of deep experiences of the soul. They include meditations, historical recitals, formal instructions, and passionate entreaties. They are a treasury of thought from which to draw when approaching God in prayer whether congregationally or privately, for in the Psalms man's soul is bared. Sin, sorrow, shame, repentance, hope, faith, and love are all expressed, and these things are universal in scope, timeless in nature, and the very stuff of which prayer is made.

The Authors

Of the one hundred and fifty psalms, one hundred are attributed to various authors, and fifty are anonymous. David is credited with seventy-three, and Asaph, one of David's choir leaders, with twelve. David's era was one of remarkable renaissance in Israel, much like the Elizabethan era in English history. Israel's enemies had been subdued, Jerusalem had become the nation's capital, the ark of God was in its place, Israel's influence was being felt abroad, prosperity had come to the nation, and plans were in hand to build a magnificent temple. These things left their mark on the cultural and religious life of the nation, and more than half the psalms were written in this period.

It is worth noting that all but thirty-four psalms have titles. Many of the psalms have roots deep in Hebrew history, and one good way to study them is to observe the circumstances which gave them birth. The following table will serve as a guide.

Psalm 3—2 Samuel 15–18	Psalm 56—1 Samuel 21:10; 27:4; 29:2-11
Psalm 30—2 Samuel 5:11-12	Psalm 57—1 Samuel 22
Psalm 34—1 Samuel 21:10–22:1	Psalm 59—1 Samuel 19
Psalm 51—2 Samuel 11–12	Psalm 60—2 Samuel 8:13-14
Psalm 52—1 Samuel 21–22	Psalm 63—1 Samuel 22:5; 23:14-16
Psalm 54—1 Samuel 23:19; 26:1	Psalm 142—1 Samuel 22:1 or 24:3

The Songs of Degrees

In this same connection the history of Hezekiah sheds light on the fifteen psalms entitled "Song of Degrees" (Psalms 120–134). The only other mention of degrees in Scripture is when the shadow on the sundial of Ahaz went back ten degrees as a miraculous sign to Hezekiah that he would recover from his sickness. The fact that there are fifteen psalms in this group suggests the fifteen years added to King Hezekiah's life. Ten of these psalms are not named (the other five are attributed to David and Solomon) and this could probably refer to the ten degrees on the sundial. Hezekiah would not need to name these if they were the songs he calls "my songs" in Isaiah 38:20. The historical record is in 2 Kings 20:8-11.

Classification of the Psalms

Many of the psalms lend themselves to classification under various titles relating to their general subject matter. Messianic, penitential, natural, historical, experiential, millennial, didactic, devotional, prophetic, imprecatory, and hallelujah psalms can all be studied. Examples of these are listed on page 98.

Experience the Psalms

The Lord Jesus went to death with the psalms upon His lips. At the Last Supper He sang the "Hallel" (Psalms 113-118). They were on His lips after He rose from the dead, for on the Emmaus road He turned to them, along with other Scriptures, in His talk with two of His disciples. Since these great songs of Israel were so precious to the Lord Himself when He sojourned here below, surely they should be precious to us as well. They should be to us a vast treasury of spiritual wealth upon which to draw for all the circumstances of life.

The Psalms Devotionally

The Psalms are an excellent source of devotional material, both for reading and meditation. One example will perhaps be sufficient to whet the reader's appetite for a more thorough exploration of these inspirational poems. Let us consider the well-known Twenty-third Psalm.

In its setting, this psalm is one of three, for in Psalm 22 Christ is seen as Substitute, in Psalm 23 He is seen as Shepherd, and in Psalm 24 He appears as Sovereign. These psalms deal with the past, the present, and the future. In the past we have the Cross, in the present we have the table and in the future awaits the crown.

Psalm 23 gives us the secret of a happy life (23:1-3); the secret of a happy death (23:4); and the secret of a happy eternity (23:5-6). It is the "He and me" psalm, these two great personal pronouns running through it from beginning to end. It is heartwarming also to see how the personal pronouns for the Shepherd change from the third person ("he") to the second person ("thou") in those verses which speak of danger and death, as if to suggest that the Lord is especially near His own at such times.

Many of the great Jehovah titles are embedded in Psalm 23. A careful reading of the psalm will discover Him there as:

Jehovah-Jireh, "the Lord will provide" (Genesis 22:14)
Jehovah-Nissi, "the Lord is my banner" (Exodus 17:15)
Jehovah-Rophi, "the Lord that healeth" (Exodus 15:26)
Jehovah-Shalom, "the Lord send peace" (Judges 6:24)
Jehovah-Tsidkenu, "THE LORD OUR RIGHTEOUSNESS"
  (Jeremiah 23:6)
Jehovah-Shammah, "the Lord is there" (Ezekiel 48:35)

Blessed indeed are those who can say, "The Lord is *my* shepherd."

Classification of the Psalms

Untitled	111 112 113 114 115 116 117 118 119 135 136 137 146 147 148 149 150 1 2 10 33 43 71 91 93 94 95 96 97 99 104 105 106 107
Songs of Degrees	120 121 122 123 124 125 126 127 128 129 130 131 132 133 134
Hallelujah	106 111 112 113 117 135 146 147 148 149 150
Imprecatory	35 58 59 69 83 109 137
Prophetic	2 16 22 40 45 68 69 72 97 110 118
Devotional	3 16 28 41 54 61 67 70 86 122 144
Didactic	1 5 7 15 17 50 73 94 101
Millennial	46 72 89
Experiential	3 7 18 30 34 51 52 54 56 57 59 60 63 142
Historical	78 105 106
Natural	8 19 29 33 104
Penitential	6 32 38 51 102 130 143
Messianic	2 8 16 22 23 24 31 40 41 45 68 69 102 110 118

18

Proverbs, Ecclesiastes, and the Song of Solomon: Books of Learning and Love

Solomon wrote 3,000 proverbs and 1,005 songs (1 Kings 4:32). He was wiser than all the fabled philosophers of his day, for his wisdom was a direct gift from God (1 Kings 3:12). He wrote three of the books of the Bible. And, while we do not know for sure the order in which they were written, presumably he wrote the Song of Solomon when he was young and in love, Proverbs when he was middle-aged and his intellectual powers were at their zenith, and Ecclesiastes when he was old, disappointed, and disillusioned with the carnality of much of his life.

Picture the background against which Solomon wrote his books. The wealth and wisdom of Solomon were the talk of every kingdom and tribe of his day. His great Tarshish ships plied the trade lanes of the Mediterranean and also found their way down the coastline of East Africa to Arabia and India, so that into Jerusalem flowed the exotic traffic of the East. Great caravans of camels crossed the deserts, bearing back riches for the king and spreading his fame far and wide.

From all over the East men came to hear the wisdom of Solomon. They talked with bated breath of the Godlike judgment which had suggested carving up a living child to share him half and half with two women, each claiming him as her own, thus revealing the true mother.

His fame reached far south to Ethiopia from whence came the Queen of Sheba, all the long perilous way up the Nile, across burning sands and on up the steep hill country of Judah to sit at the feet of Solomon. Then, as at last she turned back toward home, it was with an ache in her heart and a confession her lips: "The half was never told me."

Such was Solomon! But as the years slipped away, sad and serious were the mistakes he made, entering into political marriages with the daughters of pagan kings. Gradually his spirituality declined as his Oriental luxury and opulence increased, and his harem dinned like Babel with hundreds of strange tongues. Jerusalem became the home of heathendom, also, as Solomon's wives imported their pagan gods and erected shrines to them. As Solomon began to lose his vision of the true and living God, he began to degenerate into a common Eastern despot. He multiplied his slaves, ground onerous taxes from his subjects, and at last followed his outlandish wives into the abominable rites of Ashtoreth and worshiped the abomination of the Zidonians, and even engaged in the savage worship of Milcom and Moloch. It is against this background of wisdom and wealth, women and worship that the books of Solomon should be read.

Proverbs

Not all the proverbs were written by Solomon and not all were collected by him. The wise (22:17), the men of Hezekiah (25:1), Agur (30:1), and King Lemuel and his mother (31:1) all shared in the production of this book. Likely, "the men of Hezekiah" included Isaiah and Micah. Perhaps some later editing was done by Ezra. The book of Proverbs is intended to do for our *daily* life what the book of Psalms is intended to do for our *devotional* life. They are filled with practical wisdom for all ages but, in a special way perhaps, should be taught to our young people.

Although the book of Proverbs does not lend itself to formal analysis, it richly repays study, abounding as it does with characters which stand in bold relief drawn by a skillful sage. Dr. Scroggie delineates many of them for us in graphic form. There is "the prating fool, winking with the eye; the practical joker, as dangerous as a madman casting firebrands about; the talebearer; the man who 'harps upon a matter,' separating chief friends; the whisperer whose words are like dainty morsels going down into the innermost parts of the belly; the backbiting tongue, drawing gloomy looks all around as surely as the north wind brings rain; the false boaster, compared to wind and clouds without rain; the haste to be rich; the liberal man that scattereth and yet increaseth, while others are withholding only to come to want; the speculator holding back his corn amid the curses of the people; the man of wandering life, like a restless bird; the unsocial man that separateth himself, foregoing wisdom for the sake of his own private desire; the cheerfulness that is a continual feast."[1]

The book of Proverbs contrasts "wisdom" and "folly." There are six different Hebrew words translated "wisdom" and three different Hebrew words for "fool" in this book. Solomon's own son, Rehoboam, turned out to be a fool, so he could not have paid much attention to the wisdom penned by his learned father. In these days of lowered moral standards every young person should be made familiar with the inevitable end of immoral living so clearly pictured in Proverbs. Happy are those teenagers whose parents have drilled them in the Scriptures and taught them those absolute moral standards demanded of all men by God.

Then, in Proverbs, we have Solomon's cure for disobedient children, a cure much neglected today (Proverbs 13:24; 19:18; 22:15; 23:13; 29:15). Some years ago a columnist in one of Chicago's largest daily newspapers printed a letter he had received from a distraught mother of a rebellious teenage son. In essence she said, "My son is running around with the wrong crowd and breaking my heart. He will not listen to me and defies me to my face. What can I do about it?" Jack Mably's answer was terse and to the point: "Shrink him down to seventeen months and begin all over again." In other words, for this lad, the mother's awakening had come too late. "Spare the rod and spoil the child" is the homespun English version of a truth that is deeply embedded in the book of Proverbs.

One fascinating way to study the book of Proverbs is to see its pearls of wisdom strung into the lives of Bible characters. Think, for example, how Proverbs 16:18, "Pride goeth before a fall and an haughty spirit before destruction," is illustrated in the lives of Asahel, Benhadad, Nebuchadnezzar, Herod Agrippa, and in the histories of Edom and Babylon. See how the first part of Proverbs 10:7, "The memory of the just is blessed," is illustrated in the lives of Elisha, Jehoiada, the Virgin Mary, and Dorcas, and how the second part of the proverb, "but the name of the wicked shall rot" is reflected in the lives of Cain, Balaam, Ahaz, Athaliah, Jezebel, Herod the Great, and Judas Iscariot. Almost all of the proverbs can thus be related to life—not only to the lives of Bible characters but to our own lives and the lives of those around us today.

Ecclesiastes

Solomon knew all about "the good life" for he tasted all that life could offer. All that wealth could demand, all that wisdom and love of learning could invent or devise, all that fame could bring—Solomon had it all and in full measure. In addition he had a proud ancestry, a godly father, a rich national heritage, and a personal knowledge of God and His Word. Solomon tasted that which life "under the sun" could offer and wrote Ecclesiastes to show that "all is vanity and vexation of spirit." The abiding value of Ecclesiastes is right here, for it proves that only God can satisfy the deepest hungers of the human heart. While much of the book is undoubtedly pessimistic, the last chapter is positive in its note of assurance. Beyond the sun is a living God who can and will fill the hearts of those who will let Him.

In his concluding remarks, Solomon addresses himself to young people for he would have them, above all, profit from his mistakes. Lord Beaconsfield, once prime minister of Britain in the heyday of the British Empire, came to the same conclusion about life as did Solomon, his illustrious and long-departed fellow Hebrew. "Youth," he said, "is a mistake, manhood a struggle, and old age a regret." Solomon could have told him that! Power, popularity, prosperity, prestige, and pleasure all in abundant measure and all combined cannot quench the burning thirst in man's soul which can be satisfied in God alone.

Outline of Ecclesiastes

This book is really a debate in which Solomon takes as his theme "life under the sun" and discourses on his subject from every angle. Its philosophies, observations, and arguments are typically those of the materialist, the "man of the world," and it is from this viewpoint that the book must be studied and understood.

I. THE PREACHER'S SUBJECT (1:1-11)
  A. He States His Text (1:1-2)
  B. He States His Topic (1:3-11)
    There seems to be:
    1. No Purpose in Anything (1:3-8)
    2. No Point to Anything (1:9-11)
II. THE PREACHER'S SERMON (1:12–10:20)
  A. Some of the Things He Had Sought (1:12–2:26)
    Observe:
    1. His Persistent Search (1:12–2:10)
    2. His Pessimistic Summary (2:11-26)
      a. The Barrenness of Life (2:11-16)
      b. The Bitterness of Life (2:17-19)
      c. The Boredom of Life (2:20-26)
  B. Some of the Things He Had Seen (3:1–6:12)

He had seen the vanity of:
1. Time Without Eternity (3:1-11)
2. A New Leaf Without a New Life (3:12-17)
3. Mortality Without Immortality (3:18-22)
4. Might Without Right (4:1-3)
5. Plenty Without Peace (4:4-8)
6. Prosperity Without Posterity (4:9-12)
7. Sovereignty Without Sagacity (4:13-16)
8. Religion Without Reality (5:1-6)
9. Wealth Without Health (5:7-20)
10. Treasure Without Pleasure (6:1-6)
11. Appetite Without Appeasement (6:7-10)
12. Life Without Length (6:11-12)
C. Some of the Things He Had Studied (7–10)
He had studied:
1. Some of Life's Frustrations (7)
He is cynical about:
a. The Better Things of Life (7:1-14)
b. The Bitter Things of Life (7:15-29)
2. Some of Life's Fallacies (8)
a. The Fiction of Being Great (8:1-9)
b. The Folly of Being Godless (8:10-13)
c. The Fantasy of Being Good (8:14)
d. The Frivolity of Being Glad (8:15)
e. The Fault with Being Gifted (8:16-17)
3. Some of Life's Failures (9)
Everything is overshadowed by:
a. Man's Brief Mortality (9:1-10)
b. Man's Bitter Moments (9:11-12)
c. Man's Bad Memory (9:13-18)
4. Some of Life's Facts (10)
According to his observations we can expect:
a. The Triumph of Folly (10:1-7)
(1) Over Everything Reasonable (10:1-3)
(2) Over Everything Right (10:4-7)
b. The Triumph of "Fate" (10:8-20)
(1) Over the Laboring Man (10:8-11)
(2) Over the Learned Man (10:12-17)
(3) Over the Lazy Man (10:18)
(4) Over the Laughing Man (10:19-20)
III. THE PREACHER'S SUMMARY (11–12)
A. He Repeats His Complaints about Life (11)
He does so by issuing three challenges:

       1. Look Well to Life's Future Prospects(11:1-6)
          Form those prospects if you can!
       2. Look Well to Life's Fleeting Present(11:7-8)
          Fill that present if you can!
       3. Look Well to Life's Frivolous Past(11:9-10)
          Forget that past if you can!
    B. He Relates His Conclusions about Life (12)
      These conclusions concern:
      1. Man and His Maker (12:1)
      2. Man and His Mortality (12:2-14)

The Fly in the Ointment

This outline of Ecclesiastes is reproduced here at length because this book is somewhat of an enigma to many, having indeed been called "the sphinx of Hebrew literature with its unsolved riddles of history and life." Like Job, Solomon did *not* have all the answers to life, and he was writing, under inspiration, from the viewpoint of a worldly man. The most valuable lesson to be learned from this book is that death is inescapable, and that its shadow falls on everything we do. The worldly man must be haunted by the specter of death, that is "the fly in the ointment" (10:1) of all that he accomplishes.

Now that Christ has come and conquered death we can take a new look at Ecclesiastes, for we now have the key that unlocks the riddles of history and life. One of the chief values of Ecclesiastes is its forceful exposure of materialistic and non-Christian philosophies of life. Without Christ all roads lead to the grave, with Him all roads lead to Glory.

Song of Solomon

To turn from Ecclesiastes to the Song of Solomon is like stepping out of the wilderness into the Promised Land. It is like the bright shining of the sun after rain.

If one book of the Bible may be said to be more sacred than another, then the Song of Solomon is that book, the very Holy of Holies of Scripture. The man with an impure mind will never understand this book. Under the figure of a bride and a bridegroom is expressed the love of Christ for His own, and the love which each believer has for his Lord. There is no sin, therefore, no shame.

There are several important interpretations for this book. The two main positions usually taken differ in their identification of the bridegroom of the Song.

According to one interpretation the bridegroom is Solomon, and the bride, a certain Shulamite woman. The Shulamite is seen awaiting the arrival of Solomon and, surrounded by ladies of the court, pouring out her rapture and longing. The king appears and takes her to his banqueting house, where the two lovers commune together. Then the Shulamite again confides in the court ladies, telling what tender regard she has for her beloved. With an overflowing heart she sings of the way in which her loved king found her, wooed her, how all nature awoke to new loveliness, how she lost him, found him again, and would not let him go. After this, Solomon is seen approaching Jerusalem with his bodyguard, wearing a splendid crown. He addresses the Shulamite with words of love, and to these she responds briefly but with rapturous delight. Then a cloud passes over the scene. Under the figure of a dream the bride describes a temporary separation of heart from her groom, her misery, her longing and search for him, and her appeal to her court companions to help her. In response to their questions the Shulamite tells why she loves her beloved so. Solomon returns and once more the two are united amid words of praise and assurances of love. The bride invites her husband to return with her to the scenes of her maiden life, and they are next seen enjoying the simplicity of country life, exchanging remembrances and confidences. Others are thought of, and the bride's joy reaches out to her kindred. The song ends with the bride singing and bidding her beloved to hasten to her side. In this view of the song, Solomon is taken to be a type of Christ and the Shulamite a type of the Church.

Another view of the song sees three main speakers and several subsidiary speakers. Solomon is seen as representing the world; the Shulamite, the Church; and the Shulamite's shepherd-fiancé, Christ. Solomon uses all the dazzle and splendor of his court to woo the girl away from her true love, seeking to get her to become one of his wives instead. In like manner the world is ever seeking to attract away from Christ those who are "espoused" to Him. Solomon is unable to accomplish his goal, however, for the Shulamite resists all his overtures and remains true to her beloved shepherd to whom, at last, she is reunited.

The abiding value of the Song of Solomon is clear whichever view is taken. As human life finds its highest fulfillment in the love of man and woman, so spiritual life finds its highest fulfillment in the love of Christ and His Church.

---

1. W. Graham Scroggie, *Analytical Old Testament*, "Know Your Bible," Vol. 1 (London: Pickering S. Inglis, 1940), pp. 140-141.

19

The Prophets:
Men Sent from God

The appearance of a prophet was always a mark of apostasy and rebellion in Israel. The prophets raised their voices in loud protest against the prevailing idolatry, corruption, and blindness of their times, calling the nation back to God. It is a mistake to think that a prophet's primary function was to foretell the future. The prophet did that of course, but he was first of all a man with a message from God for his own generation, a "forthteller" rather than a "foreteller." Often the prophets were statesmen with both insight and foresight, clearly seeing the end of the dangerous religious and political experiments of their contemporaries.

The prophets often failed to understand all of their own utterances, for the burdens they delivered sometimes had a double fulfillment: an initial and partial fulfillment close to the time the words were uttered, and a later, more complete fulfillment, at a remote date. They usually spoke from the standpoint of their own people, the Gentiles being mentioned only to the extent that the other nations would come into conflict with, or blessing through, Israel. Their themes were many and varied but, apart from the initial, immediate, and partial fulfillment of their predictions, their prophecies focused on two future events, the first and second comings of Christ. The prophets themselves probably could not distinguish between these two comings, and often, too, a message would be given only to be enlarged upon at a later date either by the same prophet or by another.

Three of the prophets directed their messages to Gentile nations: Obadiah, Jonah, and Nahum; the first to Edom and the other two to Nineveh. It often happened that the prophet was unpopular with the people to whom he delivered the message of God, and sometimes he was bitterly persecuted for his preaching, his message being considered subversive to the national interest and the prophet himself, a traitor. The prophets were the moral conscience of their age.

Bible Prophecy is Unique

The Bible is the only book which challenges unbelief by foretelling the future, staking its authority on the ultimate, certain, and complete fulfillment of its detailed predictions. It has been said that there were some 109 Old Testament predictions literally fulfilled at Christ's first coming, and that, of the 845 quotations from the Old Testament in the New Testament, 333 refer to Christ. There are some 25 prophecies concerning the betrayal, trial, death, burial, and resurrection of Jesus uttered by various prophets over a period of some five hundred years. These were literally fulfilled although the chances against such fulfillment have been shown to be one chance in 33,554,438. If the law of Compound Probabilities is applied similarly to all 109 predictions fulfilled at Christ's first coming, the chances that they could accidentally be fulfilled in the history of one person is one in billions.

The following chart shows that the writing prophets belong to three main periods of Hebrew history, either before, during, or after the Babylonian captivity. Since they group themselves mainly around Isaiah and Jeremiah, these two prophets will be discussed out of their chronological order so that some overall picture of the times can be given. Also it should be mentioned that Obadiah will be placed at the end of the pre-exilic prophets, although some authorities would place him at the beginning. There were, of course, other prophets besides the writing prophets, notably Elijah and Elisha. Others include Enoch, Nathan, Micaiah, and Huldah, a prophetess. Moses, Samuel, and David also must be counted as prophets. From the days of Samuel it would seem that schools were set up for the training of prophets, but the Holy Spirit by no means restricted Himself to these schools when calling a man to this office.

The Writing Prophets

CENTURY	PREEXILIC	EXILIC	POSTEXILIC
B.C.			
9th	Joel Jonah Amos Hosea		
8th	ISAIAH Micah Nahum Zephaniah Habakkuk		
7th	JEREMIAH Obadiah	EZEKIEL DANIEL	
6th			Haggai Zechariah
5th			Malachi

Background of the Prophets

The political and religious conditions of their times are constantly reflected in the writings of the prophets, so these need to be studied as part of the background of their books. The empires of Egypt, Assyria, Babylon, and Persia overshadow the whole prophetic era, while Greece and Rome color the visions of Daniel, too. Lesser kingdoms such as Moab, Edom, Syria, Philistia, Ammon, Phoenicia, Elam, and Ethiopia are also pictured on the prophetic page. The power struggles of these nations form the historical background against which the prophets poured out their warnings, their wooings, and their woes. Something should be known of all these nations, especially Assyria and Babylon, the empires which terminated the monarchies of Israel and Judah. Something should also be known of Persia, the nation which brought about the restoration of the Jews to their homeland.

The Prophetic Era

JUDAH	PROPHETS	ISRAEL	WORLD POWERS	PROPHETS
Rehoboam		Jeroboam I		
Abijam				
Asa				
		Nadab		
		Baasha		
		Elah		
		Zimri		
		Omri		
Jehoshaphat	Elijah »	Ahab	Syria	
	Elisha »	Ahaziah		
Jehoram		Jehoram		
Ahaziah		Jehu		
Athaliah		Jehoahaz		
Jehoash	« Joel	Jehoash		
Amaziah	Amos »	Jeroboam II	Assyria	Jonah (Nineveh)
Uzziah		Zachariah		
		Shalllum		
Jotham	Hosea »	Menahem		
		Pekahiah		
Ahaz		Pekah		
Hezekiah	« ISAIAH	Hoshea		
	« Micah	ASSYRIAN CAPTIVITY 722 B.C.		
Manasseh			Thebes destroyed	
				Nahum (Assyria)
Amon	« Zephaniah			
Josiah	« Habakkuk		Assyria overthrown 612 B C.	
Jehoahaz	« JEREMIAH		1st Babylonian invasion	Obadiah (Edom)
Jehoiakim				
Jehoiachin			2nd invasion	
Zedekiah			3rd invasion	
BABYLONIAN CAPTIVITY 586 B C	« EZEKIEL		Persia	DANIEL (Babylon)
			Cyrus	
Zerubbabel	« Haggai		Darius I	
	« Zechariah		Xerxes	
Ezra				
Nehemiah			Darius II	
	« Malachi			

Assyria

From the reign of Sennacherib on, Nineveh was the capital city of the Assyrian Empire and, as we are told in the book of Jonah, it was a great city. The Assyrians were fiendishly cruel, their kings often being depicted as gloating over the tortures inflicted on conquered peoples. They pressed their wars with the utmost ferocity, uprooting whole populations as a policy of state and deporting them to remote parts of their empire. The leading men of conquered towns were given over to torment and horribly mutilated before being put to death. It is no wonder that fear of Assyria fell on all her neighbors.

Babylon

The Assyrians were succeeded on the world scene by the Babylonians. God gave to Nebuchadnezzar a sweeping mandate over the other nations of the earth, including Judah. Nation after nation fell as the invincible Babylonians swept westward. Egypt was defeated in the famous battle of Carchemish on the Euphrates in 605 B.C., and with that nothing could halt the conquerors. Jerusalem fell and the Jews were deported as warned by Jeremiah and his contemporaries. Tyre was sacked, and Egypt handed over to Nebuchadnezzar by God in payment for this service. Many lesser kingdoms felt the weight of the Babylonian arm, and for about seventy years this empire reigned supreme, the Jews tasting complete captivity to their Gentile captors.

Persia

The Babylonian empire was ended by the Medes and Persians, with Persia emerging soon afterward as the supreme Gentile power. Cyrus the Great (whose name had been mentioned by Isaiah long before he was born) was a humane ruler. He issued a decree ending the Babylonian captivity of the Jews. Daniel, carried away to Babylon during the first deportation by Nebuchadnezzar, lived through the entire captivity period and on into the Persian era. He lived to see Judah restored to partial sovereignty and, in vision, saw Persia fall and Greece come into focus only to fall in turn before the Romans. His piercing eye saw still farther into the future than that, for he saw to "the time of the end." Such were the prophets, and they are unique in the history of the world. Their words still ring with authority as they bring a message for us even today. We shall now look at them one by one.

20

Joel: The Prophet of the Plague

A plague of locusts gave Joel (830-819 B.C.)[1] the illustration he needed to appeal to the conscience of his country. His book is not dated, and opinions vary widely as to when Joel lived and ministered, although it would seem that he was a prophet to Judah rather than to Israel.

Some contend that Joel prophesied about the same time as Ezekiel, one hundred years or more after Isaiah, and his prophetic utterances are said to relate to the end of the kingdom of Judah. Others claim that his prophecy was given after the exile because no mention is made of Assyria, Syria, or Babylon among the enemies of his people. Probably, however, Joel was the earliest of the writing prophets, coming with his message before any of these nations were a threat to Judah. The enemies he does mention—the Phoenicians, Philistines, Egyptians, and Edomites—belong to the days of Jehoash (2 Chronicles 21:16-17). Scofield says, "In his youth he may have known Elijah, and he certainly was a contemporary of Elisha." What a flood of light that statement casts on the days of Joel!

Analysis of Joel

Joel's prophecy may be divided into four parts:

Joel's Message

Locusts are the scourge of many lands, and those who have seen them swarm tell us that their countless legions blot out the sun, cover the ground, and fill the sky whichever way one looks. On the ground they march in regular lines like armies of soldiers, with their leaders in front. Nothing can stop them. They are "the incarnation of hunger," and the devastation they leave in their train is utter and complete.

It would seem that Judah had been invaded by just such a locust swarm, and Joel, seeing them, is caught up by the Spirit and given a message for his people of an invasion to come far worse than a mere locust plague. He sees the enemy coming in like a flood, and the Spirit of God raising up a standard against him. In view of this impending calamity, Joel urges the nation to repent.

Running through Joel's prophecy is a note none can miss. It is "the day of the Lord," one of the most important periods in Bible prophecy. Many of the prophets mention it, for it is that period which closes the present era of man's misrule of earth, ushering in the Lord Jesus as King of kings. The Day of the Lord is regarded as a day of terrible judgment, issuing at last in full and permanent blessing.

One of the best-known prophecies of Joel is in 2:28-32 concerning the outpouring of the Holy Spirit. This prediction began to be fulfilled on the day of Pentecost (Acts 2:16-21).

---

1. Note: The dating of many of the prophets' ministries cannot be given with absolute certainty and are therefore often given only approximately.

21
Jonah:
The Unwilling Prophet

The Lord Jesus believed that Jonah (784-772 B.C.) was a literal person and that Jonah's experience in the belly of the great fish is authentic history, for Jesus referred to the incident as an illustration of His own death, burial, and resurrection (Matthew 12:40). As Jonah was a sign to the Ninevites, so was the Son of Man to His generation (Luke 11:30). The Lord referred to Jonah in the same context as the Queen of Sheba and Solomon, thus placing him on the same level of validity.

Jonah lived in the northern kingdom of Israel and prophesied of the prosperity Israel enjoyed in the days of Jeroboam II (2 Kings 14:25). He must have lived, therefore, about this time or perhaps a little earlier. His name means "dove," and certainly his ministry to Nineveh was Spirit-anointed, resulting in one of the greatest religious revivals in history. His home was at Gath-hepher, not far from Nazareth, the well-known Galilean town where the Lord Jesus in later years spent the greater part of His life. Jonah is the only prophet to whom the Lord directly likened Himself.

Analysis of Jonah

Jonah's prophecy follows the chapter divisions of the Bible.

Jonah's History

Jonah was a Hebrew prophet commissioned to preach to a Gentile audience in Nineveh, one of the most important cities of Assyria. Probably Jonah knew well enough that Assyria would one day be used of God to punish the sins of his own people, so nothing would have pleased him more, as an ardent patriot, than the overthrow of Nineveh. The news, "Yet forty days and Nineveh shall be overthrown," must have sounded like music to his ears. Far from wanting to see Nineveh repent and escape the wrath of God, he longed to see the sentence executed (4:2). It seems that Jonah deliberately fled to Tarshish so that the forty-day sandglass of divine patience would run out and wrath would overflow.

Jonah's experiences in the fish's belly were so terrible that he called that awful prison house in which his disobedience landed him "the belly of hell." Like the Lord Jesus on the cross, Jonah's thoughts in his hours of anguish turned to the psalms. He quoted from many of them in his passionate outburst of prayer (Psalm 42:7; 31:22; 69:1; 3:8).

Jonah discovered that his efforts to thwart the divine will were futile, and all his agonizing experiences in vain. Delivered from the sea monster, he found himself again facing the mandate of God, for the "forty days" would begin from the hour his feet trod the streets of Nineveh, not before.

His eight-word message rang like the knell of doom through Nineveh, bringing immediate fruit as the city repented in sackcloth and ashes, much to Jonah's disgust. In grace, God reasoned with His petulant prophet, seeking to show him the sinfulness of his resentment. That the Lord's remonstrance was successful is seen in the fact that Jonah wrote the book which bears his name, keeping back nothing of his own sorry part in the narrative. The book of Jonah is a great Old Testament revelation of the grace of God, which reaches to even "lost sinners of the Gentiles."

22

Isaiah:
The Evangelical Prophet

I saiah (739-692 B.C.) was preceded, of course, by both Amos and Hosea, but we are considering him first because of the major role he played in the times of which both the others speak.

Isaiah lived through a stormy era. He was born during the days of King Uzziah, whose great power and prosperity were marred at last by his becoming a leper for usurping the priests' office. Isaiah was called to be a prophet "in the year that king Uzziah died." That year he saw a throne vacated on earth and an eternal throne in Heaven. He lived to see the brief glory of the reign of Jeroboam II of Israel give way to chaos as Assyria increasingly interfered in Israel's affairs upon the death of that king. He lived through those dark days when, away to the north, Samaria was besieged and sacked, and the ten tribes carried away captive by the Assyrians. He watched and warned as Judah, too, began to feel the ominous influence of Assyria. Amos, Hosea, and Micah were also lifting up their voices during this period, confirming the doom of the unrepentant people.

Despite the passionate entreaties of Isaiah, Ahaz, the grandson of Uzziah, deliberately followed suicidal political moves by seeking Assyrian aid against a threatened attack on Judah by Israel and Syria. Isaiah's warnings against an Assyrian alliance are found in chapters 7–9. Once under the Assyrian influence, Ahaz was trapped, and his infatuation for the Assyrians led him to great lengths of apostasy.

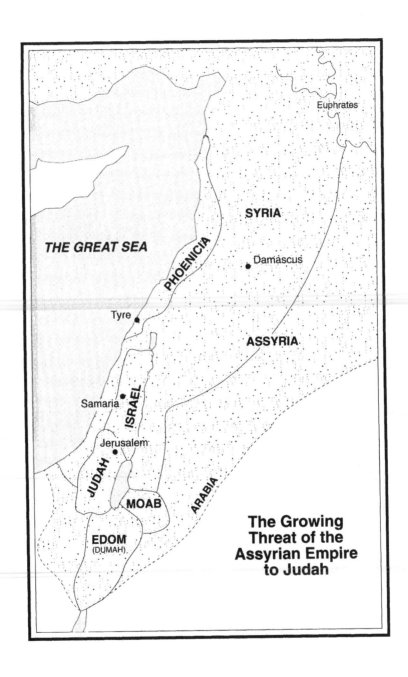

The Growing Threat of the Assyrian Empire to Judah

When Ahaz died he was succeeded on the throne of Judah by his son Hezekiah, who turned out to be one of the godliest of Judah's kings. Strongly influenced by Isaiah, he introduced sweeping reforms, abolishing idolatry and restoring the pure worship of Jehovah. He threw off the burden of tribute to Assyria and put his trust in the Lord to safeguard Jerusalem. His faith was soon tested, for the Assyrian armies hammered at the gates of Jerusalem, and cunning propagandists sought to subvert the allegiance of the defenders. Isaiah was a bulwark of strength to Hezekiah in those days (Isaiah 36–37). Encouraged by the prophet, Hezekiah held out against the threats and military might of the Assyrians and saw Jerusalem supernaturally delivered from the besieging armies by a direct act of God.

Long before the Babylonians became a world power, Isaiah foretold their rise and their conquest of Jerusalem. When Hezekiah was miraculously delivered from a fatal sickness, the Babylonians sent an embassy to court the goodwill of Hezekiah. Flattered, he foolishly showed the envoys all his treasures. Isaiah clearly foresaw that the cupidity of the Babylonians would be excited by the sight of such treasure and did not hesitate to roundly reprimand his king for such an exhibition of pride and folly.

Isaiah lived on into the reign of Manasseh, the son born to Hezekiah during the fifteen-year extension of his life. Manasseh reigned longest of all the kings and was one of the very worst to sit on the throne of David. Tradition has it that he murdered Isaiah by having him "sawn asunder."

Analysis of Isaiah

The prophecy of Isaiah falls into three main divisions, two prophetical and one historical.

I. ISAIAH'S PREDICTIVE STATEMENTS (1–35)
    A. His Prophetic Concern (1–4)
        1. The Wrong Standards of the Nation (1)
        2. The Wretched State of the Nation (2–4)
    B. His Prophetic Convictions (5)
        1. Judah's Complete Failure (5:1-7)
        2. Judah's Common Faults (5:8-23)
        3. Judah's Coming Foes (5:24-30)
    C. His Prophetic Call (6)
    D. His Prophetic Concepts (7–12)
        1. Judah's Monarchy (7–8)
        2. Israel's Misery (9:1–10:4)

It is an interesting coincidence that there are as many chapters in Isaiah as there are books in the Bible. Furthermore, these divide into thirty-nine and twenty-seven as do the books of the Bible into the Old and New Testaments. To further the comparison, the tone of the first thirty-nine chapters of Isaiah has an Old Testament ring, while the remaining chapters thrill with the evangel of the New Testament. These last twenty-seven chapters of Isaiah divide into three sections, each containing nine chapters. The center division deals with the Messiah of whom Isaiah was preeminently the prophet. Of the nine chapters in the "Messiah" section (49–57) the center chapter is the fifty-third, which gives us one of the clearest views of Calvary to be found anywhere in the Bible. Thus, at the very heart of Isaiah's evangelical message is the Cross. It seems appropriate that Isaiah's name means "salvation of Jehovah."

The Scope of His Vision

Isaiah's vision reached far beyond the borders of Judah and embraced Assyria, Babylon, Philistia, Moab, Damascus, Egypt, Edom, Arabia, Tyre—indeed, the wide world. Many of his predictions have passed into history, but some of them remain unfulfilled as yet. In chapter 10 he gives a graphic picture of the mission, motives, mistakes, and onward march of Assyria. In chapters 7 and 8 he denounces with passion the panic, the pride, and the policy of the foolish Ahaz. Isaiah was a terror to Ahaz and a tower to Hezekiah.

One moment his book is black with the thunder and the darkness of the storm. The next, the rainbow shines through, and he sweeps his readers on to the Golden Age that still lies ahead for the world. He speaks with equal conviction on the Messiah as a Savior, and the Messiah as a Sovereign, bringing both the Cross and the crown into focus in turn. Christ is as much the Lamb of God to Isaiah as He is the Lion of the tribe of Judah.

Isaiah is often quoted in the New Testament; indeed his book is one from which the Lord Jesus quoted frequently. It was from Isaiah 53 that Philip the Evangelist was able to lead the traveling Ethiopian chancellor to a saving knowledge of Jesus (Acts 8:32-33). As long as the message of the gospel is preached on earth, as long as there remains a soul to be saved, the great book of Isaiah will be needed. Jew and Gentile alike are caught up in its themes and led with directness and conviction to a consideration of the Person and work of God's beloved Son.

23

Amos:
The Country Cousin

A mos (764-755 B.C.), a native of Judah, was called to preach in and
against Israel. He was a herdsman, a backwoods "cowboy" from
the barren hill country some six miles southeast of Bethlehem,
overlooking the Dead Sea. He was called to preach at a time when both
kingdoms were experiencing a period of great power and prosperity.
Jeroboam II was on the throne of Israel, and with Syria roundly
defeated and Assyria in an era of temporary eclipse, wealth and
worldliness went hand in hand. Uzziah was on the throne of David in
Jerusalem, and Judah, like Israel, was experiencing imperialist expansion.

The outward prosperity of both kingdoms was deceptive, for
within a few years the Assyrians would be besieging Samaria, and
Judah would be living in daily terror. In Israel, especially, lawlessness
was but thinly veiled, and while the nation gave lip service to Jehovah,
immorality and superstition were at the heart of popular religion.

Outline of Amos

The opening of the book shows that Amos saw far beyond the
boundaries of his native land. His message embraced past, present,
and future, and was climaxed by a series of five visions.

I. THE VIGILANCE OF THE PROPHET (1–2)
Woes against:
A. Damascus (1:3-5)
B. Gaza (1:6-8)
C. Tyre (1:9-10)
D. Edom (1:11-12)
E. Ammon (1:13-15)
F. Moab (2:1-3)
G. Judah (2:4-5)
H. Israel (2:6-16)
II. THE VOICE OF THE PROPHET (3–6)
A. As to the Present—Privileges Despised (3)
B. As to the Past—Perversity Described (4)
C. As to the Prospect—Punishment Declared (5–6)
III. THE VISIONS OF THE PROPHET (7–9)
A. The Locust (7:1-3)
B. The Fire (7:4-6)
C. The Plumb-line (7:7-17)
D. The Over-ripe Fruit (8:1-14)
E. The False Altar (9:1-15)

At first, no doubt, Amos would have been welcomed as he poured out his prophecies against the surrounding nations. Even his country manners would have been forgiven. His idiomatic expression "for three transgressions and for four" means that the cup of iniquity was full and more than full. Even when Amos began to denounce Judah, the "Northerners" at Bethel listened probably with glee. But when he turned his attention to Samaria and denounced Israel's sins, it was a different matter.

Before long his preaching aroused the ire of Amaziah, the priest of Bethel (7:10-13), who complained to Jeroboam that Amos was a danger to national security. He also took it upon himself to order Amos out of the country. Amos told this man to his face that, regardless of his humble background and lack of formal education, he could clearly foresee the day when Amaziah's wife would be "an harlot in the city," a victim of the invader's lusts, his daughters put to the sword, his property divided by another, and Amaziah himself dying a captive in a heathen land. It took courage and conviction to be a prophet of the Lord.

The judgments God would bring upon the nation were of a twofold character. There was to be physical disaster. The nation would know famine, drought, blight, locusts and an earthquake. These would happen first. If they did not produce the desired result in national repentance then they would be followed by political disaster. The nation would be given over to the horrors of foreign invasion, it would know the terrors of war and the tragedy of utter defeat.

Although the burden of Amos was one of judgment, yet through his prophecy there runs a note of hope and an oft-repeated exhortation to "seek the Lord." In the three sermons (3–6) and the five visions (7–9) there is an increasing intensity to be noticed. Sins which Amos mentions are greed, injustice, drunkenness, immorality, profanity, and oppression. He shows that the nation, at the very summit of national prosperity, nevertheless was on the brink of disaster.

Amos has a message very much applicable to ourselves. God is patient and speaks again and again to the conscience of a nation. He allows things to go wrong; He brings the nation low. If He is still ignored then He raises up a foreign power to execute His will.

24

Hosea: Prophet of the Broken Heart and Broken Home

Hosea (755-714 B.C.) has been called "the Jeremiah of the northern kingdom," for like Jeremiah he was called to weep and suffer. He deals with the condition of Israel just before the fall of Samaria. His terrible statement in 13:16 is but a reflection on the typical savagery of the Assyrians: "Samaria shall become desolate; for she hath rebelled against her God: for they shall fall by the sword: their infants shall be dashed in pieces, and their women with child shall be ripped up." Hosea's contemporaries were Amos, Isaiah, and Micah. And he prophesied in the days of Uzziah, Jotham, Ahaz, and Hezekiah of Judah, and of Jeroboam II of Israel.

Amos and Hosea are a study in contrasts. Amos thundered out the righteousness of God; Hosea wept out the mercy of God. The first took the heathen nations into his prophecy, the second limited his utterances to Israel, with an occasional reference to Judah. The style of Amos is clear and lucid, his illustrations being drawn from the countryside. Hosea's style is simple but just as clear as he pours out his heart in short, sharp sentences, his broken home giving him ample illustration to convey the truths that were heavy on his heart.

Analysis of Hosea

I. THE TRAGEDY IN HOSEA'S HOMELIFE (1–3)

The Background

Hosea was commanded to marry a woman named Gomer who soon proved unfaithful to him. The children she bore were a source of sorrow. The first child Hosea owned as his own; the second, a little girl, he called *Lo-ruhamah* ("not beloved" or, as Baxter suggests, "she-that-never-knew-a-father's-love"). This child he disowned. The third child he likewise disowned, calling it *Lo-ammi* ("not my people" or "no child of mine"). Each step of the tragedy in his homelife is related to the tragedy in his homeland, for Gomer represented Israel, and her children, the people of the nation. Hosea's patience and pleading with the wife who broke his heart was a parable of God's love and longing for Israel. Even when Gomer forsook him to play the harlot, Hosea's love followed her, and at last he found her dishonored and deserted and, it would seem, in slavery. He purchased her (chapter 3) but refused to restore her fully until a time of chastening had passed. The whole sad story of domestic tragedy and heartache taught Hosea that Israel's sins were as adultery and harlotry in the sight of God.

The Burden

Hosea set himself the sad task of translating all this into a passionate wooing of and warning to Israel. The sins of the nation were many: swearing, lying, killing, stealing, adultery, drunkenness, idolatry, backsliding, pride, treachery, insincerity, forgetfulness, ingratitude, covetousness, craft, love of sin, oppression, highway robbery, and anarchy. All of these are reflected in Hosea's pages. The pagan priests aided and abetted murder (6:9), and the government was unstable. One faction urged compromise with Assyria, and another insisted on an alliance with Egypt (7:11).

Hosea's pleadings went unheeded, for Israel had "sown the wind" and would "reap the whirlwind" (8:7). Throughout the book can be heard the rumble of the gathering storm. But God is love, too, and that theme is ever present. Hosea tells us that sin hurts God; it not only breaks

His laws but it breaks His heart. Thus we find that there is a promise of ultimate salvation lightening the ever-darkening sky. "I will heal their backsliding, I will love them freely: for mine anger is turned away" (14:4). Hosea illustrates the "love that many waters cannot quench."

25
Micah:
A Tale of Two Cities

M icah (736-700 B.C.) was a younger contemporary of Isaiah and, although his chief ministry was to Jerusalem, he was also com- missioned to speak for God to Samaria. His ministry was during the reigns of Jotham, Ahaz, and Hezekiah of Judah, so he lived to see the evils he pronounced on Samaria in the North actually come to pass. No doubt his messages helped bring about the great spiritual awakening in the South during the days of Hezekiah (see Jeremiah 26:18). It must have been a great consolation to Isaiah to have his witness supported by such an able contemporary as Micah. Every spiritual man rejoices to see younger men taking up the burden of the things of God. Isaiah, we know, was a scholar who probably ministered to the upper classes in Jerusalem, for he had important contacts with King Hezekiah. Micah, on the other hand, was a man of the fields and probably had more to say to the rank and file of the nation.

Micah's home was in Moresheth-Gath near the Philistine border. He looked out over rich, fertile fields and could see the towns and fortresses that dotted the plain. Also he lived in an exciting hour. Samaria was about to fall and the dreaded Assyrian war machine roll on to the borders of Judah. Judah's sins were as scarlet as those of Israel so how could she expect to escape? Not far from his home Micah may well have seen the embassies hurrying from Jerusalem to Egypt and returning with empty promises of Egyptian aid. It was all so pointless, there was only one place from which help could come.

Analysis of Micah

The prophecy divides into three parts. Micah commands attention by use of the word "hear" (1:2; 3:1; 6:1).

I. THE PROPHECY OF RETRIBUTION (1–3)
    A. The Calamity of It (1)
    B. The Cause of It (2–3)
        1. The Sins of the People (2:1-13)
        2. The Sins of the Princes (3:1-4)
        3. The Sins of the Prophets (3:5-10)
        4. The Sins of the Priests (3:11-12)
II. THE PROMISE OF RESTORATION (4–5)
    A. The Restoration Depicted (4:1-8)
    B. The Restoration Delayed (4:9–5:6)
        1. The Times of Judah's Misery (4:9-13)
        2. The Times of Judah's Messiah (5:1-6)
    C. The Restoration Described (5:7-15)
III. THE PLEA FOR REPENTANCE (6–7)
    A. The Standards of the Nation (6:1-8)
    B. The Sins of the Nation (6:9-12)
    C. The Sorrows of the Nation (7:1-6)
    D. The Savior of the Nation (7:7-20)

Micah's Message

No class was exempt from the corruption of his day, so no class was exempt from Micah's message. There were many false hireling *prophets* who plied their trade for gain, giving themselves over to spiritism and consulting demons to gain a knowledge of the future. Micah fearlessly denounced these men. He spoke out also with great boldness against the *people*, bluntly naming their sins. Royalty did not escape his lash as, turning on the *princes,* he accused them of violence, oppression and corruption. They were merciless in their treatment of the poor, and cruel in their greed for gold. Finally Micah denounced the *priests,* accusing them of unblushing graft.

Despite all the corruption in the moral, religious, and national life of the people, the prevailing attitude was one of complacency. God was in the midst of His people, therefore they could come to no harm. Micah plainly told them otherwise. Like so many of the Old Testament prophets, he prophesied not only in the context of his day but also in the context of the Day of the Lord. He saw far into the future, speaking of "the last days" (4:1) and vividly describing the great restoration which is future even to us. Both comings of the Messiah are foretold, and Micah closes his prophecy with a passionate plea for repentance.

Micah liked to play on words, employing as puns the names of Gath, Aphrah, Saphir, Zaanan, and Beth-ezel, various towns he mentions. Indeed he concludes his prophecy with a pun on his own name, Micah, which means "Who is like Jehovah?" He concludes with the challenge, "Who is a God like unto thee?" The more we get to know of this great and living God, the more we shall appreciate the parting thrust of Micah.

26
Nahum: The Prophet of Nineveh's Doom

T here was not a cloud in the Assyrian sky when Nahum wrote (648-620 B.C.). Mighty Nineveh, capital of Assyria and mistress of the world was at the peak of its prosperity and power. The dates of Nahum's prophecy can be fixed with fair certainty. His book was written after 663 B.C., for that was the year when No-Ammon (Thebes, the famous Egyptian city) fell. This city had fallen to Assyrian arms, and Nahum used its fall as a parable of the impending fall of Nineveh (3:8). It was written before 612 B.C., for that was when Nineveh itself fell, and this fall was the subject of Nahum's prophecy.

The city of Nineveh seemed impregnable. Standing on the left bank of the Tigris, its walls towered one hundred feet into the air and were further strengthened by more than twelve hundred mighty towers. The walls were wide enough for three chariots to drive abreast on them, and they enclosed 1,800 acres. The city could maintain its own food supply in case of a siege, and the sides not protected by the Tigris were surrounded by a moat. Nothing seemed more unlikely than the fate Nahum announced against Nineveh.

Analysis of Nahum

I. NINEVEH'S DOOM DECLARED (1)
A. The Lord's Patience (1:1-3a)

The history of the Assyrian empire had been long and bloody. The Assyrians were notoriously warlike, blood-thirsty, and cruel, and had long been a scourge to surrounding nations. Israel had been uprooted by them, and Judah threatened, invaded, and cowed. The brief repentance of the Ninevites under the preaching of Jonah more than a century before had long been forgotten. Nothing but judgment remained. Having abused the mercy of God, Nineveh must now taste His wrath.

Nahum foretold for Nineveh utter desolation, and this was something new. Normally empires fell, but cities survived. Babylon, for example, the seat of the Babylonian empire, passed in turn to the Persians and the Greeks, but not so Nineveh. God reserved for it "an utter end" (1:8). At the time Alexander the Great was pushing his conquests eastward, he marched over its site not knowing that the capital of a world empire was buried beneath his feet. The city of Nineveh passed so completely into oblivion that for centuries the place where it had once stood was not known.

Nahum's language is very fierce and his vision is focused strictly and sharply on one greatly longed-for event—the fall of Nineveh. For a hundred years and more the Hebrews had longed for the downfall of Assyria. As Sir George Adam Smith puts it, "Nahum's book is one great At Last!" Nahum has eyes for nothing else. To him, God is a God of vengeance. His arsenal is vast. He has storms and hurricanes and thunderbolts and earthquakes and volcanoes to command. When finally He rises up in judgment His foes must go down before Him like standing corn before a scythe. Nor all the vaunted strength of Nineveh, nor all its military might shall stand before the outpoured wrath of God.

Nahum foretold, in chapter 1, the destruction of Nineveh and the subsequent peace of Judah, and he based his warnings on the revealed character of God. In chapter 2 Nahum gave a graphic portrayal of the siege and sack of the city. In chapter 3 he set out the reasons why such a complete overthrow was inevitable and righteous.

The swollen waters of the Tigris inundated a part of the city, making possible the invasion of this otherwise impregnable fortress by the Medes and Babylonians. Nahum foretold this in 2:6. The city was then given over to fire as described in 3:13-15. The fate of Nineveh had hung over the city for centuries and was long delayed, but over its ruins might well be written the words, "The mills of God grind slowly, but they grind exceeding small." When God finally settles accounts, He settles them in full.

27

Jeremiah and Lamentations: The Weeping Prophet

A s Isaiah lived through the turbulent Assyrian period, so Jeremiah (627-575 B.C.) lived through the equally heartbreaking Babylonian period. In Isaiah's day, Israel was carried into captivity, and in Jeremiah's day a like fate overtook Judah. Jeremiah stood in the same relationship to godly King Josiah of Judah as Isaiah had to godly Hezekiah. As Amos, Hosea, and Micah had clustered around Isaiah, so Zephaniah, Habakkuk, and possibly Obadiah clustered around Jeremiah.

Jeremiah saw five kings on the throne of David in Jerusalem: Josiah, Jehoahaz, Jehoiakim, Jehoiachin, and Zedekiah. Probably he lived almost a century after Isaiah. Isaiah had lived to see Judah delivered from the Assyrians, but Jeremiah wept out his prophecies on deaf ears and lived to see his beloved people given over to famine and the sword. His loftiest counsels were ignored, his writings torn to shreds by a tyrant king, his name blackened, his life hunted, and his worst predictions horribly fulfilled before his tear-filled eyes. He was indeed a weeping prophet, "a man of sorrows and acquainted with grief." The bitterest feelings of his broken heart he recorded in the book of Lamentations. He was forbidden by God to marry. And, even when his preaching produced results, as in the days of King Josiah, he could clearly see that the reforms were superficial and could not last.

Idolatry and corruption had seeped too deeply into the lives of the people. The sepulcher of Judah might be whitened by a godly and well-meaning king, but inwardly it was filled with corruption and dead men's bones.

Jeremiah's Style

Jeremiah has been criticized because so many of his utterances are in no kind of order. It has been well said concerning this that "it is the historical portions, which concern Jehoiakim and Zedekiah, that are chiefly so affected. And who was Jehoiakim that his history should be of any importance? Was it not he who 'cut up the word of Jehovah' with a penknife, and cast it into the fire? Why should not his history be 'cut up'? Zedekiah rejected the same word of Jehovah. Why should his history be respected? Secular authors take the liberty of arranging their own literary matter as they choose; why should this liberty be denied to the sacred writers?"

Historical Background

Jeremiah was born during the days of Manasseh, the wicked son of Hezekiah. He was called to prophesy at the tender age of fourteen, and his feelings of helplessness and incompetence are recorded in the opening chapter. He continued to pour out his heart for over forty years. It was in the thirteenth year of godly King Josiah that Jeremiah began to preach. The short-lived reforms of Josiah came to an abrupt end with his death, and his son Jehoahaz reigned only three months, when he was deposed by the Egyptian Pharaoh Necho. His father, Josiah, had lost his life in a vain attempt to stem an Egyptian army marching across Judah on the way to Carchemish.

From this point on, Judah was a mere pawn in the power play between Egypt and Babylon. Pharaoh Necho put the brother of Jehoahaz on the throne in Jerusalem, carrying the rightful king to Egypt as a hostage. Jehoiakim reigned for eleven years and, coming out boldly for idolatry, was a bitter foe of Jeremiah. But by now the Babylonians felt themselves strong enough to curb the ambitions of Egypt, and in 605 B.C. the first Babylonian invasion of Judah took place. Still Jeremiah went unheeded, and Jehoiakim was deposed and threatened with deportation to Babylon. Jehoiachin, his son, was placed on the throne of David as a mere puppet of Babylon. A second and severer invasion of Judah took place in March, 597 B.C., to end this evil king's short reign, and every able-bodied man, including Jehoiachin, was carried into captivity.

The last king of Judah was then set on the throne by Nebuchadnezzar who, generously enough, chose Zedekiah, a prince of the royal Davidic line and another son of Josiah. Zedekiah was a weakling who, although inclined to be friendly to Jeremiah, was little better than a tool in the hands of the princes. In the face of solemn warning from Jeremiah, this king broke his oath to the Babylonian monarch and rebelled. Assured of success by false prophets, he listened to accusations of treachery against Jeremiah and allowed him to be persecuted.

Soon the Babylonians were back. This time, after a bitter siege, Jerusalem fell. The book of Lamentations speaks of the horrors of this time. Jerusalem was razed to the ground, and the temple burned. Zedekiah fled, only to be captured and treated after the barbarous fashion of the times, while Jeremiah, taken prisoner by Nebuchadnezzar, was kindly treated. Allowed to remain in Jerusalem after the final deportation, his woes were not yet over, for more intrigues took place, and Jeremiah was forcibly carried to Egypt by a fleeing remnant of Jews. In Egypt he continued to weep out his warnings but, as ever, he went unheeded. Ancient tradition has it that Jeremiah was finally stoned to death.

Analysis of Jeremiah and Lamentations

The broken nature of his prophecies makes the book of Jeremiah difficult for formal analysis. This outline suggests one way of grouping his material—by subject matter. Another way is to group it chronologically, but either way the chapter sequence is broken.

    I. THE PROPHET'S MANDATE (1)
       A. The Time of the Mandate (1:1-3)
       B. The Terms of the Mandate (1:4-19)
    II. THE PROPHET'S MESSAGES (2–51)
       A. To the Nation of Judah (2–45)
          1. During Days of Incomplete Revival (2–12)
            a. Prior to the Finding of the Law (2–6)
            b. Pertinent to the Finding of the Law (7–9)
            c. Pursuant to the Finding of the Law (10–12)
          2. During Days of Increasing Rejection (13–45)
            a. By Signs
               (1) The Sign of the Linen Girdle (13:1-27)
               (2) The Sign of the Drought (14:1–15:21)
               (3) The Sign of the Unmarried Prophet (16:1–17:18)
               (4) The Sign of the Potter's House (18:1–19:13)

(5) The Sign of the Figs (24:1-10)
(6) The Sign of the Yokes (27:1–28:17)
(7) The Sign of the Field of Hanameel (32:6-44)
(8) The Sign of the Rechabites (35:1-19)
(9) The Sign of the Hidden Stones in Egypt (43:8-13)
b. By Sufferings
(1) Jeremiah in the Stocks (19:14–20:18)
(2) Dangers—the Murder of Urijah (26:20-24)
(3) Jeremiah in Prison (32:1-5)
(4) Jeremiah's Prophecy Destroyed by Jehoiakim
(36:1-32)
(5) Jeremiah Imprisoned by Zedekiah (37:1–39:18)
(6) Jeremiah Forcibly Carried to Egypt (43:1-7)
c. By Sermons
(1) Messages concerning the Sabbath (17:19-27)
(2) Message to Zedekiah regarding Babylon
(21:1–22:30)
(3) Restoration Promised (23:1-40)
(4) Prophecy of the Seventy-year Captivity
(25:1-38)
(5) Message to Jehoiakim (26:1-19)
(6) Message to the Jews of the First Captivity
(29:1-32)
(7) Message regarding the Time of Jacob's
Trouble (30:1-24)
(8) Message on the Last Days (31:1-40)
(9) Message on the Millennium (33:1-26)
(10) Message to Zedekiah concerning His Captivity
(34:1-22)
(11) Message to the Poor Remnant of the Land
(40:1–42:22)
(12) Messages in Egypt (43:8–44:30)
(13) Message to Baruch in the Days of Jehoiakim
(45:1-5)
B. To the Neighbors of Judah (46–51)
1. Concerning the Conquests of Babylon (46–49)
2. Concerning the Collapse of Babylon (50–51)
III. THE PROPHET'S MISERY (52 and Lamentations)
A. He Records the Facts of History (52)
B. He Records the Feelings of His Heart (Lamentations)
1. Jerusalem's Wretchedness (1,5)
2. Jehovah's Wrath (2,4)
3. Jeremiah's Woe (3)

Summary of Jeremiah

Jeremiah 2–6 gives us a summary of his preaching during the days of Josiah. Josiah's vigorous attacks on idolatry, carried even to the abandoned cities of Manasseh, Ephraim, Naphtali, and Simeon (2 Chronicles 34:1-7), form the background. The first five years of Jeremiah's ministry are recorded here. Josiah then began to repair and cleanse the temple, and a copy of the law was found, the reading of which greatly troubled the good king (2 Chronicles 34:18-32). Jeremiah 7–9 covers this period. Following the finding of the law more drastic reforms than ever were carried out, climaxing in the commemoration of the Great Passover (2 Chronicles 35:1-19). Jeremiah's notes of his ministry during this period are given in chapters 10–12.

From this point on, his prophecies were many and varied and were given in various ways—by signs, by personal sufferings, and by sermons. Not everyone disbelieved Jeremiah. It was doubtless Jeremiah's great prophecy of the seventy years (25), for example, that inspired Daniel's great intercession toward the end of the Babylonian captivity (Daniel 9).

Jeremiah saw far beyond his own immediate times, foretelling the coming Great Tribulation ("the time of Jacob's trouble" in chapter 30) as well as the millennial reign of Christ (33). With graphic detail he described the great conquests of the Babylonians, his messages embracing Egypt, Philistia, Moab, Ammon, Edom, Syria, Kedar, and Elam. He also clearly foresaw the ultimate collapse of the Babylonian world empire.

His Lamentations, written in the form of an acrostic dirge, consist of five poems. The first, second, and fourth are of twenty-two verses each, corresponding to the letters of the Hebrew alphabet. The third, or center, poem is built on the same principle except that each letter of the alphabet is repeated three times. The acrostic is dropped for the fifth poem. The dirge has to do with the fall of Jerusalem and the terrible sufferings connected with its overthrow. "O Jerusalem, Jerusalem," wept Jeremiah, as did the Lord Jesus Himself in later years. No wonder some thought Jesus was Jeremiah returned from the dead (Matthew 16:14; 23:37-38).

28
Zephaniah: The Royal Prophet

Z ephaniah (634-625 B.C.) gives his ancestry more fully than any of the other prophets. Mention is made of "Hizkiah" in his opening sentence, and there is every reason to believe that this name is the same as Hezekiah. Zephaniah would therefore be the great-great-grandson of that illustrious and godly king of Judah. He would also be related to good king Josiah in whose reign he ministered. This would make Zephaniah a contemporary of Jeremiah and, probably, a leading figure in the great religious revival in Josiah's day.

The kings of Judah vacillated between good and evil, between the worship of the living God and the worship of idols. Each revival and reformation was followed by a lapse back into idolatry; only with each return to paganism, Judah sank lower than before. Little lasting effect resulted from the various reforms, for it always seemed to be the old story of "too little and too late." Josiah's valiant attempts to bring the nation back to God represented the last flicker of the nation's candle before it was finally extinguished. In Babylon, the cradle of idolatry, the nation would have to learn the hard and bitter way that idolatry is a mockery and a lie.

Zephaniah's prophecies were pronouncements of wrath to come, and over and over again he spoke of "the great day of God." He looked squarely at the coming Babylonian invasion with all its horrors and then, borne on the wings of divine inspiration, looked far beyond that terrible event to even worse sufferings for the Jews at the end of the age. Like Jeremiah, Zephaniah's clear prophetic vision took in other nations besides Judah. So far as his main subject is concerned, he stands shoulder to shoulder with Joel, mentioning "the day of the Lord" some twenty times within the compass of his short book.

Analysis of Zephaniah

    I. THE DETERMINATION OF THE LORD (1:1-6)
      A. To Judge Fully (1:2-4)
      B. To Judge Fairly (1:5-6)
    II. THE DAY OF THE LORD (1:7–3:8)
      A. The People Mentioned (1:7-13)
        1. The Mighty: Too Independent to Listen (1:7-8)
        2. The Mob: Too Iniquitous to Listen (1:9)
        3. The Merchants: Too Involved to Listen (1:10-11)
        4. The Majority: Too Indifferent to Listen (1:12-13)
      B. The Period Mentioned (1:14-18)
        1. Its Nearness (1:14)
        2. Its Nature (1:15-18)
      C. The Places Mentioned (2:1–3:8)
    III. THE DELIVERANCE OF THE LORD (3:9-20)
      A. Israel's Regathering (3:9-10)
      B. Israel's Repentance (3:11-13)
      C. Israel's Rejoicing (3:14-15)
      D. Israel's Redeemer (3:16-20)

It is interesting to see how God asserts His sovereignty both in terms of judgment (1:2-4) and in terms of mercy (3:18-20). The emphasis in both these portions is on the divine assertion, "I will."

Joel, Hosea, Amos, Micah, Isaiah, and other prophets besides Zephaniah make mention of the "day of the Lord." It is toward this great focal point of Hebrew prophecy that world events are surely moving so rapidly today. The same theme is picked up in the New Testament in 2 Thessalonians 2:2. The nature of the "day of the Lord" should not be confused with the nature of the "day of Christ." The first has to do with Israel and the nations, the second with the Church. The Day of the Lord has to do with that coming time when the wrath of God will be poured out upon the earth and to the time of blessing thereafter. It is one of the chief themes of the book of Revelation.

Zephaniah has none of the tender wooing of Jeremiah; instead he hammers hard at the nation's conscience. However he does end on a happier note, looking beyond the time of wrath to the blessings that follow. His message was very pertinent to his own day and generation, and it is very pertinent to ours as well.

29

Habakkuk: The Prophet with a Problem

Habakkuk (619-610 B.C.) has been called "the doubting Thomas of the Old Testament." He seems more concerned with solving a problem than with delivering a message. We can learn a valuable lesson from Habakkuk, for this man, when faced with a seemingly unsolvable problem, took it to God, instead of abandoning his faith as some would do. He was a contemporary of Jeremiah and clearly saw the handwriting on the wall for Judah. The rising power of the Chaldeans (the Babylonians) filled his vision, and herein lay his problem. That the Judeans were wicked was an obvious fact, but still they were the people of God. Habakkuk could see that God must punish sin, and that Judah could not possibly escape the chastening hand of God. But when he looked at the Babylonians, the people God would use to chastise Judah, he could see that they were worse than the Jews. How could God punish a nation by a less righteous nation? War is God's scourge, and with it He whips the rebellious nations. Habakkuk's problem is perennial and is as pertinent today as it was then. How Habakkuk took his doubts and difficulties to God and how he found his answer is the theme of the book.

Analysis of Habakkuk

Habakkuk had a burden, a vision, and a prayer. In his short book we observe faith sighing, faith seeing, and faith singing.

I. THE PROPHET IS TROUBLED (1)
  A. By the Crimes of Judah (1:1-4)
  B. By the Coming of Judgment (1:5-17)
    1. The Invincibility of the Chaldeans (1:5-11)
    2. The Iniquity of the Chaldeans (1:12-17)
II. THE PROPHET IS TAUGHT (2)
  God is righteous. This applies:
  A. Individually (2:1-4)
  B. Internationally (2:5-20)
    1. The Rapaciousness of the Chaldeans (2:5-8)
    2. The Relentlessness of the Chaldeans (2:9-11)
    3. The Ruthlessness of the Chaldeans (2:12-14)
    4. The Repulsiveness of the Chaldeans (2:15-18)
    5. The Religion of the Chaldeans (2:19-20)
III. THE PROPHET IS TRIUMPHANT (3)
  A. Faith Surrenders (3:1)
  B. Faith Sees (3:2-16)
  C. Faith Soars (3:17-19)

The key verse of Habakkuk is 2:4b: "The just shall live by faith." This great statement is repeated three times in the New Testament (Romans 1:17; Galatians 3:11; Hebrews 10:38). Habakkuk, like so many of us, wanted to understand everything, but God showed him this could never be. Instead he must trust—trust God in the dark—for God is not going to give all the answers in this life.

When Habakkuk learned this simple lesson he soon discovered that God *could* be trusted. The world has the saying, "Seeing is believing," but faith replies, "Believing is seeing." God showed Habakkuk that if the Babylonians were going to be used to punish Judah, He in turn was going to visit the sins of the Babylonians upon their own heads in due time. But more, not only would the Babylonians be overthrown but ultimately God's loving purposes for His people would be fully realized. The book which opens with a sob closes with a song.

There has probably never been a darker hour in this world's history than the one in which we live. When our hearts begin to fail us with fear, looking on those things that are coming upon the earth, it is time to turn back to this little-known book of Habakkuk and again read his message. He tells us that "God is still on the throne" and that all appearances notwithstanding, His wise and loving purposes cannot be thwarted.

> Deep in unfathomable mines
>   Of never-failing skill,
> He treasures up His bright designs
>   And works His sovereign will.

30
Obadiah: The Prophet of Edom's Doom

The prophecy of Obadiah is a classic warning against anti-Semitism. The nation that curses and persecutes the Jew will inevitably reap what it sows. The nation that harbors and protects the Jew will surely enjoy the blessing of God (Genesis 12:2-3).

There is wide disagreement as to the date of Obadiah. Some would place him as the earliest of the prophets, whereas others place him in the days of Jeremiah. Although there are a number of people in the Old Testament with the name of Obadiah, none of them can be positively identified as the prophet of that name. The dating of Obadiah hinges on the interpretation of verses 11-14. It is thought by some that the reference here is to events in the days of Jehoram (2 Chronicles 21:16-17), whereas others see in the reference events in the days of Ahaz (2 Chronicles 28:17). Others link the passage with Jeremiah 49:14-16 and make these two prophets contemporaries. It is not necessary to assume that either prophet quoted the other, although there is a close similarity between these two passages. Jude and 2 Peter give us an example of God inspiring two men with a like message.

Outline of Obadiah

This short prophecy is in two parts, one part dealing with Edom and the other with Israel. This is instructive when we remember that

Jacob and Esau, from whom these two nations sprang, were twins. There was little love lost between the twin brothers from the very first, and with the passing of time the gap between their descendants widened into bitter national hostility.

    I. THE DOOM OF EDOM PREDICTED (1-16)
       A. The Doom Declared (1-2)
          1. The Ambassador's Mission (1)
          2. The Ambassador's Message (2)
       B. The Doom Described (3-9)
          1. Edom's Territory Subdued (3-4)
          2. Edom's Treasure Stolen (5-6)
          3. Edom's Treaties Subverted (7)
          4. Edom's Troops Slaughtered (8-9)
       C. The Doom Deserved (10-14)
          Edom had:
          1. Encouraged Judah's Foes (10-11)
          2. Enjoyed Judah's Fall (12-13)
          3. Enslaved Judah's Fugitives (14)
       D. The Doom Dawns (15-16)
          1. The Fixed "Day of the Lord" (15a)
          2. The Fearful "Day of the Lord" (15b-16)
    II. THE DELIVERANCE OF ISRAEL PREDICTED (17-21)
       A. The Character of It (17a)
       B. The Completeness of It (17b-20)
       C. The Climax of It (21)

The Fierce Hatred of the Edomites

When the children of Israel were on their way to Canaan after their exodus from Egypt, the Edomites refused them passage through their territory. In later years the Edomites were thrashed again and again by kings of Judah but were never completely subdued. When at last Nebuchadnezzar sacked Jerusalem, the joy of the Edomites knew no bounds, and they did all they could to befriend and assist the Babylonians. As the wall of Jerusalem was assaulted, the Edomites screamed with delight, "Down with it, down with it, even to the ground" (Psalm 137:7). Their exultation was brief, however, for within four years Edom itself was invaded by Nebuchadnezzar and completely overthrown. This was clearly foreseen by Obadiah (assuming he was a contemporary of Jeremiah) and stated in a most emphatic way. Long centuries afterward we find Edomite hostility to the things and people of God still in evidence, for Herod the Great, who massacred the babes of

Bethlehem in his efforts to slay the infant Christ, was an Idumean and a descendant of the Edomites.

The False Security of the Edomites

The Edomites dwelt in Mount Seir, a mountainous region reaching from south of the Dead Sea to the Gulf of Akabah. (The territory is now included in the Hashemite Kingdom of Jordan.) Bozra was its ancient capital. In Obadiah's day the capital was Sela (Petra), the rock city which, although desolate now, still remains one of the wonders of the world. The Edomites had good grounds for thinking their city impregnable. They failed, however, to reckon on God.

The Day of the Lord

Edomite territory comes back into focus in the last days though as far as the Edomites or Idumeans are concerned as a race or nationality, the last remnants were wiped out in A.D. 70 helping to defend Jerusalem against the Romans. No one today can trace his ancestry back to the Edomites. Thus it will be the residents in the old Edomite territory whom Christ will judge (Isaiah 63:1-6). It appears that in a coming day the nation occupying the Edomite territory will assist the armies of Antichrist against the Jews as once the Edomites assisted Nebuchadnezzar. The ultimate triumph, however, is for Israel.

31

Ezekiel:
The Exile Prophet

E zekiel (593-559 B.C.) probably belonged to the upper class of the people and, like Jeremiah, was a priest as well as a prophet. He was carried away to Babylonia in 597 B.C. by Nebuchadnezzar together with the cream of Judean nobility. In Babylonia his home was at Tel-abib (3:15), to the north of Babylon and on the river Chebar (1:1). He dwelt in his own house (8:1) and was married, his wife dying in the year that the final siege of Jerusalem began.

Thirteen of the visions and prophecies of Ezekiel are dated. His prophetic ministry began in the fifth year after his arrival in the land of his exile (1:2). For the first six years of his ministry he preached to the exiles, and all this time Jerusalem was still standing. Later he had the difficult task of keeping before the generation born in captivity the national sins which had led to that exile. His visions were far-reaching and some of them still await fulfillment. Ezekiel felt called to justify God's dealings in judgment with his people. The expression "they shall know that I am God" occurs some seventy times and runs like a refrain through the book. He continually claimed divine inspiration for his prophecies. Scofield suggests that the main prophetic strains of this book are indicated by the sevenfold repetition of the expression "the hand of the Lord was upon me" and that the subdivisions are indicated by the formula "and the word of the LORD came unto me."

Ezekiel dramatized the message of God, continually doing things calculated to arrest attention and fire the imagination. His ministry seems to have been particularly calculated to make an impression upon the minds of children. It is worth remembering that the children of Ezekiel's day were, generally speaking, those who in later years returned to Jerusalem at the end of the seventy-year captivity. Ezekiel was a younger contemporary of Jeremiah, and while that great man of God was concluding his prophecies in Jerusalem, Ezekiel was commencing his ministry among the exiles.

Analysis of Ezekiel

The book of Ezekiel is in three well-defined divisions. The prophet first addresses his own exiled people before the final siege of Jerusalem. At the time of the fall of Jerusalem he turns his attention to the Gentile nations and addresses seven of these. Then again he turns his attention to his own people and, with Judah fallen and her people in exile, comforts the captives with glowing accounts of the glory yet future.

    I. THE FALL OF JUDAH (1–24)
      (Prophecies before the siege of Jerusalem)
      A. Judgment Decided (1–3)
      B. Judgment Demonstrated (4–5)
      C. Judgment Declared (6–7)
      D. Judgment Demanded (8–11)
      E. Judgment Decreed (12–19)
      F. Judgment Deserved (20–24)
    II. THE FOES OF JUDAH (25–32)
      (Prophecies during the siege of Jerusalem)
      A. Ammon (25:1-7)
      B. Moab (25:8-11)
      C. Edom (25:12-14)
      D. Philistia (25:15-17)
      E. Tyre (26:1–28:19)
      F. Sidon (28:20-26)
      G. Egypt (29–32)
   III. THE FUTURE OF JUDAH (33–48)
      (Prophecies after the siege of Jerusalem)
      A. The Nation's Troubles Removed (33–36)
      B. The Nation's Tribes Regathered (37–39)
      C. The Nation's Temple Rebuilt (40–47)
      D. The Nation's Title Restored (48)

Ezekiel's prophetic utterances were in the forms of visions, signs, and direct prophecy. He also made use of parables, poems, and proverbs to convey the message of God.

Ezekiel's Call

Ezekiel's call was accompanied by a majestic vision of the glory of God. He saw the mysterious cherubim, the throne, and the burning likeness of One like unto a man. The prophet was addressed by God as "son of man" (2:1), and this important title was used by God of Ezekiel one hundred times. The corresponding title "the Son of man" is found in the Gospels eighty-eight times where all but two of the occurrences were as Christ spoke of Himself. On the other two occasions the expression was used by others referring to Christ. The title "son of man" denotes a natural human being, a descendant of Adam. The title "the Son of man" applies only to Christ and marks Him as "the second man, the last Adam," the One who came to take the place the original Adam forfeited.

The vision and title were intended to make Ezekiel feel his own utter insignificance. He was informed that judgment upon Israel had been decided on. His was the thankless task of delivering the message of doom, but he was not to be afraid, for strength would be given to him to meet every situation. To him also was given the solemn charge to be a "watchman" to the nation (3:16-21).

Ezekiel's Signs

Before the fall of Jerusalem Ezekiel constantly set forth the message of God by acting out the prophecy. Indeed God had told his servant that he would be dumb (3:26-27) except when God chose to relieve him of the affliction for the delivery of specific utterances. There are ten such messages given in the sign language of the dumb in the first twenty-four chapters. A tile, filthy food, a razor, a pot, and a fire were things he used to convey the divine message. He was to lie for a while on his left side, then for a while on his right side; he was to prepare baggage for moving; he was to smite his hands together; he was not to mourn when his wife died. All these actions were intended to draw the attention of his rebellious and unheeding fellow exiles.

Back in Jerusalem, those left behind after the first deportation were congratulating themselves. Ignoring Jeremiah's warnings, they looked upon themselves as Heaven's favorites. They imagined Jerusalem to be impregnable, and in this were encouraged by false prophets.

Likewise in Babylonia, the exiles fondly imagined their captivity would be brief, and in their midst, also, false prophets buoyed up false hopes.

The prophet Jeremiah wrote a letter to the exiles in Babylon in an effort to disillusion them concerning their vain expectations. Not only was Jeremiah ignored but Ezekiel also was resisted when he raised his voice in the same vein. To a people unwilling to listen to His voice, God became, as it were, largely dumb, and instructed His prophet to resort to sign language so that at least some curiosity and inquiry might be aroused.

Judgment Declared and Demanded

In chapters 6–7 we find some of the more conventional-type prophecies of judgment. In no uncertain terms Ezekiel spelled out the imminent doom about to fall upon the mountains of Israel. In chapters 8–11 he showed why judgment could not be averted. He was given visions of the unspeakable abominations being practiced in Jerusalem in the very temple of God, and saw the Shekinah cloud slowly, reluctantly, but surely departing from Jerusalem. Once more it could be written *Ichabod*, "the glory is departed." He conveyed to his fellow exiles what he had seen in vision and was ignored.

Judgment Decreed and Deserved

Once more the prophet resorted to signs and sermons. Faithfully he reiterated the fact that judgment had been decreed and was inevitable. He went on to show why, and spoke of the spiritual whoredoms of Jerusalem which exceeded even the wickedness of Sodom and Samaria. His last warning before Jerusalem was besieged was brought home in a way which spelled tragedy for him. His wife ("the desire of thine eyes") died, and Ezekiel was forbidden to mourn. This at last evoked a response from the exiles: "Wilt thou not tell us what these things are to us that thou doest so?" (24:19). The meaning was as solemn as it was sad. His own personal sorrow was swallowed up in a far greater sorrow, for the day his wife died the armies of Nebuchadnezzar invested Jerusalem. Compare 2 Kings 25:1 with Ezekiel 24:1, 15-18.

The Gentile Nations

Turning to the Gentile nations, Ezekiel pronounced briefly the doom that was to fall upon the Ammonites, Moabites, and Edomites, all hereditary foes of Israel. In each case the reason is given—taking pleasure in the misfortunes of Jerusalem. Longer utterances are given against Tyre, Sidon, and Egypt. Tyre's scorn for Israel had its roots in commercial rivalry, Sidon's was founded on religious rivalry, and Egypt's in political rivalry. In each of these cases the prophet saw beyond the immediate crisis to the far distant future.

Visions of Judah's Future

Returning to his ministry to the exiles, Ezekiel was again reminded of his duty as a watchman (33:1-9). In 33:21 we are told how Ezekiel was visited by one who reported, "The city is smitten." This led Ezekiel once more to spell out the reasons for judgment, but he looked forward, too, to the regathering of Israel and to the discomfiture of Israel's foes.

In chapter 37 is given the remarkable vision of the valley of dry bones, a far-reaching prophecy of the political rebirth of Israel. There are many reasons for thinking that we are seeing this prophecy at least partially fulfilled today. This vision was followed by the last "sign." Ezekiel was to take two sticks, one for the house of Judah and one for the house of Joseph (Israel), and join them. They became one stick in his hand, thus signifying the fact that the nation would no longer be divided but would once more become one people.

The vision of Israel's political rebirth is followed by two chapters (38 and 39) speaking of the invasion of Israel in the last days by Gog of the land of Magog. A vast Northern confederacy is seen as allied to certain nations of the Middle East and to certain African peoples. Israel is seen as surrounded by countless, well-armed, implacable, ambitious, and determined foes who invade the land. Certain Western powers ("Tarshish") make a formal protest against this invasion but make no move to intervene. The invaders are overthrown by direct intervention of God. Many people see in this a prophecy of the coming invasion of Israel by Russia and her satellites, virtually resulting in the complete annihilation of the invaders.

The collapse of this invasion having been described, Ezekiel devotes eight chapters to a description of the millennial temple. Much of the *description* seems to be symbolic, although the *fact* of a coming temple seems to be literal. The tribes are regathered by name and the new Jerusalem is renamed Jehovah Shammah "the Lord is there." On this majestic note Ezekiel ends his book. Thus the book which begins with the heavenly glory concludes with that glory at home on earth.

32

Daniel: The Prophet Greatly Beloved

D aniel (605-536 B.C.) was both a saint and a seer, and his book is both practical and prophetical. The courage, conviction, and committal of Daniel and his friends, as recorded in the first half of the book, teach valuable lessons. Those who would "know their God and do exploits" in days of testing and trial should spend much time in the good company of these choice young men.

Since much of Daniel's prophecy has now been fulfilled in history, and that in minute detail, the book is especially valuable. It not only confounds the critics but it confirms the faith of the believer. It is little wonder, therefore, that the book of Daniel has been a storm center of criticism. The battle has been waged around four chief issues: the miracles, the predictions, the language, and the history. Today, archaeology and philological studies by men like Dr. Robert Dick Wilson have done much to refute the claims of the critics.

Daniel was an actual historical person famed even in Ezekiel's day for his piety. Ezekiel mentioned Daniel by name three times and regarded him as such an outstanding person as to link his name with those of Noah and Job. The Lord Jesus mentioned Daniel by name, looked upon him as a historical person, and regarded his prophecies as inspired. He identified Himself with the Son of man of Daniel's vision (cf. 7:13 with Matthew 16:13; 26:64), and in Matthew 24:15 (Mark 13:14)

He referred to Daniel 8:13; 9:27; 11:31; 12:11. In Matthew 24:30; 26:64; Mark 14:62; Luke 22:69 the Lord referred to Daniel 7:13, and in Matthew 24:15-17 He referred to Daniel 12:1. For the believer this settles the issue.

Daniel was deported from Judah in 605 B.C., began his ministry three years later and lived through the entire period of the seventy-year captivity. He was probably of royal descent, good-looking, intelligent, courageous, and devout. He was a contemporary of Jeremiah, Habakkuk, Ezekiel, and possibly Obadiah.

Outline of Daniel

The book of Daniel is in two parts, one part largely historical and the other largely prophetical. In the original it is written chiefly in two languages, Aramaic and Hebrew.

I. DANIEL AND HIS PERSONAL FRIENDS (1–6)
   Key Thought: Personal Victory
   A. Times of Testing (1–3)
      1. The Challenge of a Believer's Walk (1)
         The matter of the king's meat
      2. The Challenge of a Believer's Witness (2)
         The dilemma of the king's dream
      3. The Challenge of a Believer's Worship (3)
         The implications of the king's image
   B. Times of Truimph (4–6)
      1. The Triumph of Truth (4–5)
         a. Resulting in the Conversion of Nebuchadnezzar (4)
         b. Resulting in the Condemnation of Belshazzar (5)
      2. The Triumph of Trust (6)
         The den of lions
II. DANIEL AND HIS PEOPLE'S FUTURE (7–12)
   Key Thought: Prophetic Vision
   A. The Character of the Future (7–8)
      1. The Nature of the Facts (7)
         Four beasts: Babylon, Persia, Greece, and Rome
      2. The Narrowing of the Focus (8)
         Two beasts: Persia and Greece
   B. The Control of the Future (9–10)
      1. Daniel's Vision (9)
         a. He Believes an Old Prophecy (9:1-23)
            The seventy years
         b. He Receives a New Prophecy (9:24-27)
            The seventy "weeks"
      2. Daniel's Visitor (10)

       a. The Herald Angel
       b. The Hindering Angels
       c. The Helping Angel
    C. The Course of the Future (11)
       1. The Coming of the Typical Antichrist (11:1-35)
       2. The Ccoming of the True Antichrist (11:36-45)
    D. The Climax of the Future (12)
       1. The Turmoil Is Seen (12:1-4)
       2. The Tribulation Is Sure (12:5-7)
       3. The Truth Is Sealed (12:8-10)
       4. The Times Are Set (12:11-13)

Daniel carefully dates his various prophecies and writings. It is helpful to see their relationship to the kings of Babylon and Persia under whom he lived and attained such prominence.

The Dating of Daniel's Prophecies

HISTORICAL		PROPHETICAL	
Chapters	Kings	Chapters	Kings
1-4	Nebuchadnezzar		
5	Belshazzar	7-8	Belshazzar
6	Darius	9	Darius
		10-12	Cyrus

The Historical Section

While still a youth and an exile in Babylon being trained as a courtier, Daniel showed remarkable conviction and courage. Not fearing the wrath of the king, Daniel and his friends determined to obey God rather than man. The issue they made over the king's meat might have seemed fanatical to some, but to these faithful Hebrews their whole loyalty to God was at stake. They made up their minds to trust God and enthrone Him in all things, great and small. They would walk according to God's revealed will, cost what it might, and regardless of whether or not some thought the issues unimportant.

The challenge to their walk was followed by a challenge to their witness. The wise men of Babylon were unable to tell the king the meaning of a strange dream he had, and were delivered over to death. The daring of Daniel's faith is seen in his offering to do what others were impotent to do. Daniel was given divine enlightenment to recount to the king the outline of the dream which he claimed to have forgotten and then to give the king the meaning of that dream, bearing bold witness to the true God while doing so. Nebuchadnezzar was so impressed that he promoted Daniel to the rank of prime minister and gave his companions important posts in his kingdom. The chart below gives a brief outline of the king's vision and its main points of interpretation.

The Rise and Fall of Gentile World Empires

World Empires	NEBUCHADNEZZAR'S DREAM Daniel 2:31-45	DANIEL'S DREAMS	
		Daniel 7:1-28	Daniel 8:1-27
Babylonian	Head of gold	Lion	
Medo-Persian	Breast and arms of silver	Bear	Ram
Grecian	Belly and thighs of brass	Leopard	He goat
Roman	Legs of iron	The beast with ten horns	
Antichrist's	Ten toes of iron and clay		
Christ's	The stone cut out without hands		

Next followed a challenge to worship. Having erected a great golden image, Nebuchadnezzar demanded that all should bow and worship it or face death in a fiery furnace. Probably Daniel's duties had taken him away from the capital at this time, for it is unthinkable that he would have bowed. Indeed had he been at home very likely the king would never have erected the image in the first place. In any case, Daniel's three friends refused to worship the image and remained standing when all the others in a vast assembly bowed low in homage before the idol. The infuriated king consigned these faithful believers to the roaring flames only to be deeply moved when God vindicated their faith in the deliverance of His own.

Daniel was able to witness to Nebuchadnezzar, Belshazzar, and Darius. The humbling of Nebuchadnezzar, foretold by Daniel, led to the conversion of this king who immediately issued a most remarkable document in which he bore witness to his faith in the living God. Unlike Nebuchadnezzar, Belshazzar refused to be humbled when he came to power. Though terribly frightened when his blasphemous feast was interrupted by God, whose hand wrote its message of doom on the palace wall, this dissolute king refused to repent. Daniel, now probably in his late eighties, preached this king a notable sermon before proceeding to give an interpretation of the mystical symbols which had appeared upon the palace wall. The expression "In that night was Belshazzar the king of the Chaldeans slain. And Darius the Median took the kingdom" is significant. It marked the passing of world empire from the Hamitic and Semitic races into the hands of the Japhetic peoples as foretold by Noah (Genesis 9:27). Darius, representative of the Medo-Persian powers, proved to be a warm friend to Daniel. Trapped into condemning Daniel to the den of lions, Darius acted swiftly to testify to his faith in the Lord when he witnessed Daniel's miraculous deliverance. The historical part of Daniel ends with the conversion and testimony of the Median conqueror.

The Prophecies of Daniel

The vision given to Nebuchadnezzar (chapter 2) and the vision given to Daniel (chapter 7) are thought to cover the same ground only from different perspectives—the coming and character of Gentile world dominion. With the fall of Jerusalem the "times of the Gentiles" began, and political control over Jerusalem passed from Jewish to Gentile hands, where it has remained practically unchallenged ever since. The proof of Gentile dominion over the earth is the captivity of Jerusalem (Luke 21:24). Although the government of the modern, reborn State of Israel is located in Jerusalem, and the Old City is now in the hands of the Jews, the Dome of the Rock, a Muslim mosque, still stands on the ancient site of Solomon's temple. Although the "times of the Gentiles" appear to be drawing rapidly to a close today, they have not yet done so.

The Image and the Beasts

Nebuchadnezzar's dream (chapter 2) and Daniel's own vision (chapter 7) show the rise and fall of the Gentile world empires. Not all world empires are seen in this survey, only those important from the standpoint of prophecy. Babylon is represented as a unit (a head of gold), Medo-Persia as a duality (breast and arms), Greece as a fourfold unity (four horns), and Rome, or the last world empire yet to come, as a tenfold entity (ten toes in the image and ten horns on the final beast). Finally the Gentile world empire becomes a multiplicity of ruins, and the kingdom of God (the "stone cut without hands") fills the scene.

The empires move generally in a westerly direction following the course of the sun, and Gentile misrule of the earth closes at last with a gory sunset—the Great Tribulation. The downward trend is evident in Nebuchadnezzar's dream. The focus descends from the head to the feet, from gold to silver, silver to copper, copper to iron, and from iron to clay. It descends also from the head (the seat of the intellect) to the breast (the seat of the vital organs), from the breast to the belly (the seat of the digestion), and from the belly to the feet which walk in the dust. The notable difference between Nebuchadnezzar's view of Gentile power and Daniel's is significant. The one was a heathen ruler, the other a holy man of God. One saw world empire as a mighty human figure worthy of universal worship, the other saw so many wild beasts. The whole thing seemed brilliant to Nebuchadnezzar (Daniel 2:31), but to Daniel it appeared brutal and bestial.

The Visions of Daniel 7 and 8

Chapter 7	Chapter 8	INTERPRETATION
MEDO-PERSIA		
Bear	Ram	Medo-Persia
Two sides Raised on one side	Two horns One horn higher than the other	A dual empire Persia the predominant one of the two powers
	The higher horn raised up after the other	Persia raised up after Media
Three ribs between teeth	Pushed west, north, and south	Conquests
GREECE		
Leopard	He-goat Came from the west	Greece Its conquests eastward
Dominion given to it	Over the face of the earth	Extent of conquest
Four wings of a bird	Touched not the ground	Rapid conquest
	A notable horn	Alexander the Great
	Four notable horns	Alexander's generals
	A "little horn"	Antiochus Epiphanes

The Focus Narrowed

In chapter 8, Daniel was given a further vision, only in this one the focus was narrowed from Babylon, Persia, Greece, and Rome to the central two, Persia and Greece. Babylon's days were almost done when this vision was received (in the days of Belshazzar), and Rome's days were in the far future. In this chapter the focus is on *Persia,* the last of the Eastern, Asiatic world powers, and on *Greece,* the first of the Western, European powers. These two empires also lay nearer to Daniel's times. This vision of Daniel 8 is augmented in Daniel 11, and the period there covered spans the gap between Malachi and Matthew.

The chief characteristics of the visions in chapters 7 and 8 are tabulated on page 154.

The Seventy Weeks

The vision of Daniel 9 is remarkable, for it predicts the actual time of the Lord's crucifixion centuries before it happened. In the first year of Darius, while pondering Jeremiah's prophecy of the seventy-year exile, Daniel came to the conclusion that the captivity was due to end. He took the matter to the Lord in earnest intercessory prayer and was granted a further vision of the future of Israel.

He was told that seventy "weeks" would fulfill his people's history. (In Daniel 9:24-26, the word translated "weeks" may be legitimately taken as "sevens" and there can be little doubt that it refers to sevens of years.) The period was to begin with the commandment to restore and rebuild Jerusalem. We know from Nehemiah 2:1-8 that the commandment to restore and rebuild Jerusalem was given in March (Nisan) of the twentieth year of Artaxerxes, who ascended to the throne of Persia in 464 or 465 B.C. Thus the beginning of the prophetic period would be 445 B.C. Some commentators actually fix the date at March 14, 445 B.C., and claim the support of astronomy for so doing. After sixty-nine of these "weeks," the Messiah would be "cut off" (69 x 7 = 483 years) bringing us to A.D. 39. Since the Biblical year is 360 days and not 365 days, the difference (5 x 483 = 2,415 days = 6.6 years) must be deducted, bringing us to A.D. 32.

The Lord's ministry began in "the fifteenth year of Tiberius Caesar" (Luke 3:1). This Caesar began to reign on August 19, A.D. 14, so that the Lord commenced His public ministry early in A.D. 29. The first Passover of the Lord's ministry was in the month of Nisan of that year. Three Passovers later, in A.D. 32, He was crucified. Sir Robert Anderson contends that this prophecy of Daniel was fulfilled to the very day.

The seventieth "week" is yet future, the whole Christian era being interposed. Thus there remains a period of seven years during which

God will resume direct dealings with Israel and during which Gentile misrule of the earth will come to a head. The last half of the coming "week" is known as "the Great Tribulation" and will be a time of terrible persecution, especially of the Jews. The period will end with the battle of Armageddon and the personal return of the Lord in power and glory to set up His kingdom on earth.

The Greek Empire

The history of the Greek Empire is given further analysis in Daniel 11, truly one of the most remarkable prophecies in the entire Bible for detail. In perfect sequence the prophet chronicled in advance the coming of Alexander the Great, the division of his empire into four parts; the quarrels between Syria and Egypt, Israel's miseries as the pawn between these two rival powers (called the "king of the north and the king of the south"), the dark days of the tyrant Antiochus Epiphanes who most certainly prefigures the Antichrist, and the struggle of the Maccabees. He even saw prophetically the intervention of Rome in the affairs of Palestine. Then, leaping the ages, he spoke of the last days and of the coming of the actual Antichrist of whom Antiochus was but a type. In the closing chapter of the book, Daniel dwelt on the Great Tribulation period. Truly this book is one of the most fascinating in the entire Bible.

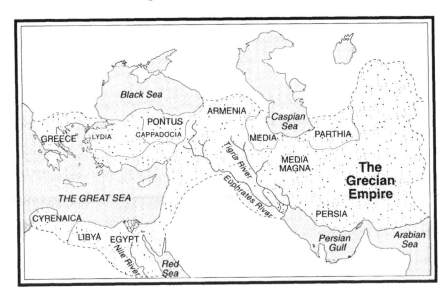

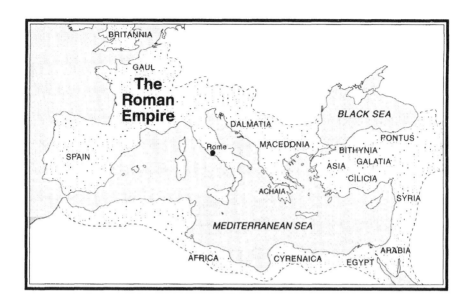

33
Haggai:
First Things First

The prophets Haggai, Zechariah, and Malachi are known as "postexilic" prophets because they prophesied to the returned remnant after the Babylonian exile was over. Haggai and Zechariah were contemporaries, and Malachi prophesied about a century later.

The prophecies of Haggai (520-504 B.C.) are all dated and were given over a period of four months against the background of Ezra 5 and 6. Zechariah's prophecy began midway between Haggai's second and third messages.

There can be no doubt that the returned remnant had become greatly discouraged. For one thing the prophets had painted glowing pictures of the Promised Land. But it was a far cry from the refinements of the Babylonian culture, to which they had grown accustomed, to the rigors of pioneer life in the homeland. There was nothing romantic about having to hoe the flinty soil, quarry stones and stay up nights on watch against a bitter and persistent foe. For some years before the voice of Haggai was raised in the land things had been allowed to drift. Poor harvests, declining income and repeated discouragements had taken their toll.

The chief theme of Haggai was the rebuilding of the temple, work on which had ceased. Fourteen years had passed since the remnants had returned, and not only was the temple unfinished but its foundation had become overgrown with weeds. At the same time the people were building and ornamenting their own houses. Haggai insisted that first things be put first.

Analysis of Haggai

    I. A CALL TO BUILD (1)
    (1st day, 6th month)
    A. The Background of the Message (1:1-2)
    B. The Burden of the Message (1:3-11)
    C. The Blessing of the Message (1:12-15)
    II. A CALL TO BEHOLD (2:1-9)
    (21st day, 7th month)
    A. The Present—Dealing with the Temple (2:1-3)
    B. The Past—Dealing with the Covenant (2:4-5)
    C. The Promise—Dealing with the Messiah (2:6-9)
    III. A CALL TO BEHAVE (2:10-19)
    (24th day, 9th month)
    A. The Blessing Wanted (2:10-14)
    B. The Blessing Withheld (2:15-17)
    C. The Blessing Waiting (2:18-19)
    IV. A CALL TO BELIEVE (2:20-23)
    (24th day, 9th month)
    A. God Will Manifest His Power (2:20-22)
    B. God Will Manifest His Prince (2:23)

Haggai appeared at a critical time in the history of his people. The incomplete temple was not only a bad testimony to the surrounding nations but a source of spiritual peril to Israel. With the throne of David gone it was imperative that the nation realize its true center in the temple. Within the compass of his brief book Haggai mentions three temples: Solomon's (2:3a), Zerubbabel's (3b-5), and the Messiah's (2:6-9).

A wrong attitude toward prophecy on the part of the people was partly responsible for the national lethargy. "The time is not come, the time that the Lord's house should be built," was their excuse (1:2). This fatalistic attitude toward the work of God has its counterpart in the Church today. Prophecy is never intended as an excuse for inaction but always as a spur to holy, consecrated living.

The prompt obedience on the part of prince, priest, prophet, and people must have been a tremendous encouragement to Haggai. Not all the prophets by any means had the joy of seeing the people respond thus to their messages, but Haggai did. Within three weeks of his first message, Zerubbabel was stirred up by God to give fresh leadership to the work.

The completion of the temple was not looked upon with undiluted joy by all. Some of the senior citizens lamented the fact that it was far inferior to Solomon's, so Haggai's second message was to remind the people that the Messiah Himself would grace the courts of Zerubbabel's temple, something which could not be said about Solomon's.

Haggai's third message was addressed to the priests and called for a renewal of consecration. The blessing of God, long wanted and long withheld, was waiting for them. "From this day and upward" is the key expression in this section, signifying, according to some, that this date terminated the "desolations" to come upon Jerusalem as predicted by Jeremiah. "From this day will I bless you." God is ever more willing to bless than we are to receive His blessing.

Haggai's final message was apocalyptic in character. Looking down the long ages, he finished his book by pointing to the coming Golden Age. This part of his prophecy remains unfulfilled and we are called upon to believe it just as much today as Israel was then.

34
Zechariah:
Looking Ahead

Zechariah (520-489 B.C.) was a priest as well as a prophet. His grandfather, Iddo, was one of the priests who returned from the Babylonian exile with Zerubbabel and Joshua (Nehemiah 12:4). Zechariah was probably a very young man when he began to prophesy. The difference in style between chapters 9-14 and the earlier part of his book is usually explained on the ground that these later chapters were probably written when the prophet was a much older man. Also, the circumstances would probably be much different.

The original circumstances which called for the ministries of Haggai and Zechariah were the same. Zechariah began to prophesy two months later than his contemporary, and while Haggai concentrated on the need for finishing the temple, Zechariah had a wider vision. He saw Israel in a world context and looked far ahead to the end times with great clarity.

Analysis of Zechariah

> I. REVELATIONS CONCERNING ISRAEL'S FUTURE (1–6)
>   A. The Voice of Zechariah (1:1-6)
>   B. The Visions of Zechariah (1:7–6:15)
>   1. God Sees (1:7-21)

Zechariah's task was not only to support Haggai in his urgent call to the nation to complete the temple but also to put the restoration in its proper perspective. There was every reason for the returned remnant to be discouraged. The glowing predictions of Isaiah and Jeremiah had not materialized, and Zechariah had to show that God's promises were not forgotten, though they might indeed be postponed.

Zechariah's visions savor of the apocalypse. First, God sees; the vision of the four horsemen tells us that. He has not failed to observe the attitude of the Gentiles toward His people, neither will He allow it to continue indefinitely. The vision of the four carpenters guarantees redress.

The vision of the man with the measuring rod promises great future prosperity for Jerusalem. The vision of Joshua, the high priest, defended against Satan by Jehovah Himself, gives comforting assurance that divine favor has returned to His people. The vision of the candlestick speaks of spiritual revival.

The vision of the flying roll is essentially one of conviction, for evil must be expelled if God is to bless. The vision of the ephah (the largest of the dry measures used by the Jews), together with the woman (often used as a symbol of religious error in the Scripture), is next seen. The ephah is returned to Babylon from whence, in the beginning, all religious error stemmed. In the vision of the four chariots is symbolized the coming of divine judgment upon the nations.

The Branch is one of the great Old Testament titles of the Lord Jesus. There are twenty-three words translated "branch" in the Old Testament, but one, occurring twelve times, is used specifically of the Messiah on four great occasions: Jeremiah 23:5-6, 33:15; Zechariah 3:8, 6:12; and Isaiah 4:2. It will be seen from the context of these references that the Messiah is referred to as King, Servant, Man, and Jehovah; and it is from these four viewpoints exactly that the four Gospels are written.

Zechariah's visions are followed by a discussion of the relationship of fasts to the returned remnant, and the glad conclusion is that the time will come when all fasting will give way to feasting. Zechariah's closing chapters, probably written some thirty years after the earlier portions of his book, deal with the coming, rejection, and ultimate triumph of the Messiah. The greatest national folly of Israel was the rejection and crucifixion of Christ, and it is this folly that Zechariah clearly foresaw and described in chapters 9-14. It is a folly which would be unbelievable were it not for the fact that, although it is now past history, millions today are perpetuating it by rejecting Christ and, as it were, crucifying afresh the Son of God. But God will not suffer human folly to thwart His own good purposes concerning His Son, and the day will come when Jesus shall reign as Zechariah also foretold. The nations will one day "worship the king" (14:17), and "holiness unto the Lord" will yet pervade the earth (14: 20).

35

Malachi:
The Gathering Gloom

alachi's voice is heard in the gathering gloom. It is the last
prophetic call (436-416 B.C.) before a long silence of four hundred years descended upon mankind. His name means "my
messenger" and he has been called "the unknown prophet with the
angel's name." He prophesied possibly a whole century later than
Haggai and Zechariah. At any rate it was long enough after these
prophets for a sharp decline to have set in both religiously and
morally. Sacrilege and profanity characterized the religious attitude;
witchcraft, adultery, perjury, fraud, and oppression were prevailing
moral sins; disregard of family responsibility highlighted social conditions; and "robbing God" reflected the gross materialism of the age.
The attitude of the people was one of sneering self-defense. The
formalism and skepticism of Malachi's day are seen in full bloom in the
Pharisaism and Sadduceeism of the time of Christ.

Analysis of Malachi

I. THE LORD'S COMPLAINTS (1–2)
   A. The Nation's Spiritual Sins (1:1–2:9)
      1. Denying God's Love (1:1-5)
      2. Despising God's Name (1:6)

      3. Defiling God's Altar (1:7-14)
      4. Disregarding God's Law (2:1-9)
   B. The Nation's Special Sins (2:10-17)
      1. Their Detestable Worship (2:10-13)
      2. Their Deserted Wives (2:14-16)
      3. Their Distorted Words (2:17)
II. THE LORD'S COMING (3–4)
   A. To Deal in Judgment with Sinners (3:1-15)
   With their:
      1. Ungodly Actions (3:1-5)
      2. Ungodly Attitude (3:6-12)
      3. Ungodly Arguments (3:13-15)
   B. To Deal in Justice with Saints (3:16–4:6)
   The righteous are to be:
      1. Remembered (3:16-18)
      2. Rewarded (4:1-4)
      3. Revisited (4:5)
      4. Revived (4:6)

Malachi not only cataloged the sins of the nation (sins which were never fully arrested but which took deep root and produced the conditions which climaxed in the murder of the Lord Jesus). He also spoke emphatically of the Lord's coming. He pointed back to Moses, the great representative of the law, and to Elijah, the great representative of the prophets. Then he foretold the coming again of Elijah, a coming which had, at least, an initial fulfillment in the ministry of John the Baptist. The last word of Malachi, the last word of the Old Testament, and the last word before a long silence fell, was the solemn, sobering word "curse." With that fearful word ringing in his ears, the Jew came to an end of his Bible.

The New Testament begins where the Old Testament ends. Without the New Testament, the Old Testament tells of a beginning without an ending, relates hundreds of promises and predictions without any lasting fulfillments, and begins with blessings and ends with a curse. Gratefully we now acknowledge that the silence of God has been broken. God has spoken to us in these last days in His Son.

36

The Silent Years

Between Malachi and Matthew are about four hundred "silent years" during which God remained silent so far as fresh revelation was concerned. The broad outline of these years is given in Daniel 11, but much that meets us when we first turn from the Old Testament to the New Testament is new indeed. We read of sects and parties unknown in Old Testament times: Scribes, Pharisees, Sadducees, and Herodians. Who were these? We find Hebrew a dead language and Aramaic and Greek the languages of intercourse, culture, and commerce. We find Palestinian cities bearing Greek names, and Persia long replaced by Rome as the power dominating the Land of Promise. We read of "the twelve tribes which are scattered abroad" (James 1:1), otherwise known as the Dispersion. We discover that a Greek version of the Scriptures is in common use among the Jews, and that idolatry, the great snare of Israel in the Old Testament, is completely rooted out of the nation. We read of an Idumean reigning as king in Jerusalem and of an official Jewish council known as the Sanhedrin holding some form of religious and political power in the land. We even find that the temple in Jerusalem is not identical with the one we left in the Old Testament, and that far and wide among the Jews synagogues have come into existence as places of worship. Naturally we are curious about these things. Indeed, if we are to properly understand the New Testament, we need some information about them.

History

The Old Testament closes with Palestine still under Persian rule. A remnant of the Jewish people are in the land, but the majority are dispersed more as colonists than captives throughout the Persian Empire. In 333 B.C. Alexander the Great brought Syria under his control, and Palestine was merged into the growing empire of Greece. Upon the death of Alexander, the land became a pawn in the power struggles of Syria and Egypt, being ruled by whichever power happened to be the strongest at the time. The persecutions of the Syrian king Antiochus Epiphanes provoked the revolt of the Maccabees who led the Jews in a struggle for independence 167-141 B.C. This was followed by the rule of the Hasmonaeans, descendants of the Maccabees, until 63 B.C., when Pompey the Great conquered Palestine and brought the country under the iron rule of Rome. Christ was born in Bethlehem in the days of Caesar Augustus. This Caesar appointed Herod the Great as king after the Battle of Actium in 31 B.C., when Augustus overthrew the alliance of Anthony and Cleopatra of Egypt. Herod the Great ruled Judea, Samaria, Galilee, Persia, and Idumea, and was the king responsible for the massacre of the babes of Bethlehem shortly after the birth of Christ. Herod the Great also rebuilt the temple in Jerusalem which had not been ornate enough to suit his tastes. The entire reconstruction took about eighty-five years and was not fully completed until the time of Agrippa II.

Sects and Parties

We frequently read of the *scribes* in the Gospels. These men were held in high esteem by the Jewish people as the interpreters and teachers of the Scriptures. As a class they first came into prominence after the return of the captives from Babylon, Ezra himself being described as both a priest and a scribe. They were bitterly opposed to Christ and were frequently denounced by Him for making the Scriptures of no effect by their traditions. The *Pharisees* were an influential Jewish sect which arose in the time of the Maccabees. They were originally a group of people who separated themselves from the ambitious political party in the nation. They were zealous guardians of the law and were conservative in belief, accepting both the supernatural and the concept of an afterlife. The *Sadducees* on the other hand were rationalists, the liberals of their day, who denied the existence of spirits as well as the resurrection and the immortality of the soul. Numerically they were a much smaller group than the

Pharisees and belonged for the most part to the wealthy, influential, priestly parties, the aristocracy of the Jewish nation. They also came into prominence during the days of the Maccabees. Both Pharisees and Sadducees opposed Christ, and those who did so were condemned by Him. The *Herodians* were in no sense a religious cult but were a political party who took their name from Herod and their authority from the Roman government. The Herodians looked upon Christ as a revolutionary and opposed Him on those grounds. The *Zealots* were an extremist group who were fanatical defenders of the theocracy and engaged in acts of violence against the Romans. One of Christ's disciples might have been a Zealot (Matthew 10:4; Luke 6:15).

The Sanhedrin

In New Testament times the Sanhedrin was the supreme civil and religious body within the Jewish nation. The president of the Sanhedrin was the high priest, and twenty-three members composed a quorum. The body eventually known as the Sanhedrin likely came into existence during the Greek period of Palestinian history, was dissolved during the Maccabean revolt, and was restored after the victorious conclusion of that struggle. The Sanhedrin had the right, granted by the Romans, to pass sentence of death but not the right to execute it. Christ and later Peter, John, and Stephen were tried by the Sanhedrin.

The Synagogue

During the Babylonian captivity the Jews, with no temple in which to worship, began to meet in smaller assemblies for worship and religious instruction, and in this way the knowledge of the law was kept alive among the Jews. The institution of synagogues in all the lands of the Dispersion helped draw the attention of the Gentiles to the great truths entrusted by God to Israel.

The Dispersion

The scattering of the Jews from their homeland was originally a divine punishment for sin. In New Testament times dispersed Jews were to be found in all parts of the Roman Empire and were often wealthy, influential, and outstanding citizens. Living as they did among pagans, the Jews of the Dispersion were able to win many proselytes to Judaism and, on the whole, while maintaining strict separation from idolatry, were more liberally minded than the Jews of the homeland. The common language of the ancient world was Greek, so it is not surprising that the Jews of the Dispersion felt their need for a Greek translation of the Scriptures. This translation was made at Alexandria in Egypt between 285 and 130 B.C and is known as the Septuagint.

Prepare the Way of the Lord

During the "silent years" God had not been inactive. Indeed these four hundred years were years of intensive preparation of the world for the coming of His Son. The *Jews* of the Dispersion had done much to spread abroad the basic ideas on which the gospel was to be so firmly founded. The Jewish Sabbath, synagogue, and Scriptures became well known. Jewish separation, while it antagonized some, attracted others. The Jewish Messianic hope was kept alive so that when the apostles began to spread the news that the Christ had come, many were ready to believe. The *Greeks* had left a lasting mark upon the ancient world. Greek logic and learning and, above all, Greek language had made a cultural climate which, when the time came, greatly expedited the missionary outreach of Paul. The *Romans* had hammered the world into one vast empire and flung their arterial highways across the whole empire. Indeed a "Roman peace" had descended on the world, enforced by a central government with a genius for organization and the armed might to make it effective. Added to all this was the bankruptcy of pagan religions, which only served to accentuate the spiritual needs of mankind.

So "when the fulness of the time was come, God sent forth his Son, made of a woman, made under the law, to redeem them that were under the law, that we might receive the adoption of sons" (Galatians 4:4-5).

37

The Four Gospels

Some people seem to think the four Gospels are not trustworthy. There are those who will believe without question what Josephus wrote about the Jews, what Plutarch wrote about the Romans, and what Seutonius wrote about the Caesars, but they will not believe what Matthew, Mark, Luke, and John wrote about Jesus Christ. There are those who will accept the writing of secular authors at their face value but who treat with scorn and skepticism the works of sacred writers. Such an attitude is not only unfair, it is fatal. For if the New Testament documents be true, then those who neglect or reject their message are making one of the biggest mistakes possible to man.

One of the greatest American lawyers of the past was Simon Greenleaf, who wrote one of the most important works on the law of evidence ever to appear in the English language. His book, A *Treatise on the Law of Evidence,* was unsurpassed on the subject for nearly one hundred years. It ran through sixteen editions. When he was a mature lawyer at the age of sixty-three, just seven years before his death, Simon Greenleaf published a volume in which he examined the testimony of the four evangelists to Jesus Christ. He used the same laws of evidence employed in courts of justice in the civilized world. He said: "Our profession leads us to explore the mazes of falsehood, to detect its artifices, to pierce its thickest veils, to follow and expose its sophistries, to compare the statements of different witnesses with severity, to discover truth and separate it from error." In this book, which ran to 543 pages, Simon Greenleaf came to the conclusion that the Gospels are absolutely trustworthy and that the four evangelists could not possibly have lied about Jesus Christ, for their testimony rings true. Paul put it this way: "This statement is completely reliable and should be universally accepted—Christ Jesus entered the world to save sinners" (I Timothy 1:15, Phillips translation).

The four Gospels give us four views of Christ. They were written by different men, they were written for different audiences, they were written at different times, and they were written from different perspectives. Matthew, Mark, and Luke are known as *synoptic* Gospels because they present Christ from a similar viewpoint, while John is known as the *autoptic* Gospel because it has a different emphasis from the other three.

There are some important differences between the first three gospels and the fourth. In the first three most of the action takes place in Galilee, in John it is mostly in Judea. Had we only the first three gospels we might easily come to the conclusion that Christ's public ministry lasted only a year. John, with his repeated chronological notes (he mentions three Passovers) shows that the ministry extended over a little more than three years. The first three gospels concentrate on Christ's works, John concentrates on His words. Even where the first three devote space to what Jesus said they repeat messages quite different from those found in John. The synoptic writers concentrate mostly on Christ's parables; John gives no parables but, instead, records a number of lengthy discourses. But taken together, the four gospels make up a harmonious whole.

Matthew

Matthew was a Jew and wrote primarily for the Jewish people. He answered the kind of questions a Jewish person would ask about Jesus of Nazareth. Jews, for example, would want to know whether Jesus could trace His ancestry back to David to prove that He was the rightful king of Israel. They would want to know what relationship Jesus had to the law and the prophets. Did He uphold the law? Did He fulfill the Old Testament prophecies concerning the Messiah? To answer these questions Matthew traced the ancestry of Jesus back to David through the legal line of Joseph, His foster father. Matthew constantly quoted Old Testament scriptures to prove the Messiahship of the Lord, and he was at pains to show that Christ had come to found a kingdom.

Mark

Mark's Gospel, written primarily for the Romans, sets forth Christ as the Servant of Jehovah. It is short and to the point and written in the coarse Greek language of the slave market. Mark took pains to explain Jewish customs which would not be understood by his Roman readers. His emphasis was on the doings of Jesus rather than on His sayings, for he wished to impress the businesslike Romans that Jesus was essentially a Man of action. The words *immediately* and *straightway* are key words in Mark. Things which one would expect to be of interest to a servant are prominent in Mark's Gospel: clothing, food, utensils, service, trade, boating, fishing, and animals. It is a down-to-earth Gospel.

Luke

Luke was a Greek, a physician by profession, a close companion of the Apostle Paul, and a scholar. His Gospel, written especially for Greeks, presents the Lord Jesus as the perfect Man and does so with simplicity and dignity. Luke tells us that he carefully examined all the facts before he began to write. He traced the ancestry of the Lord Jesus back to Adam, the first man, showing us that Jesus is "the last Adam" and "the second Man." His Gospel arrests the individual for it is full of human interest; it deals with sympathy and forgiveness; it brings women and children before us more than any other Gospel. Luke showed us Jesus as the Savior of sinners. His key verse is: "For the Son of man is come to seek and to save that which is lost" (Luke 19:10). Typical of the beautiful simplicity of Luke's style is the fact that this verse does not have one word in it containing more than one syllable.

John

John, known as "the disciple whom Jesus loved," wrote much later than the synoptic writers and mainly for believers, to emphasize the deity of Jesus. He gave us the reactions of belief and unbelief to the ministry of Jesus. His material supplements what the others wrote. Half of John's Gospel is made up of the actual words of Jesus, and the discourses recorded are different from those in the other Gospels. John also selected certain miracles of Jesus which he set forth as "signs" of Christ's deity.

Here then are the four Gospels. Without doubt they are the most important documents in the world. They do not give us "a life of Christ" but partake more of the nature of memoirs. They are very brief and are as remarkable for the things they omit as for the things they contain. The emphasis of each one is heavily weighted toward the death of Christ. Matthew gives eight chapters, or two-sevenths of his Gospel, to the Passion Week; Mark gives six chapters, or three-eighths of his Gospel; Luke gives five and a half chapters, or one quarter of his Gospel; while John gives ten chapters, or about one half of his Gospel, to the Passion Week. The reason for this is obvious: important as the life of Christ is, through His death on the cross at Calvary He wrought redemption for lost sinners. Jesus did not die as a martyr for a noble cause. He died as a Redeemer for sinful men. His death was not an accident but an accomplishment (Luke 9:31).

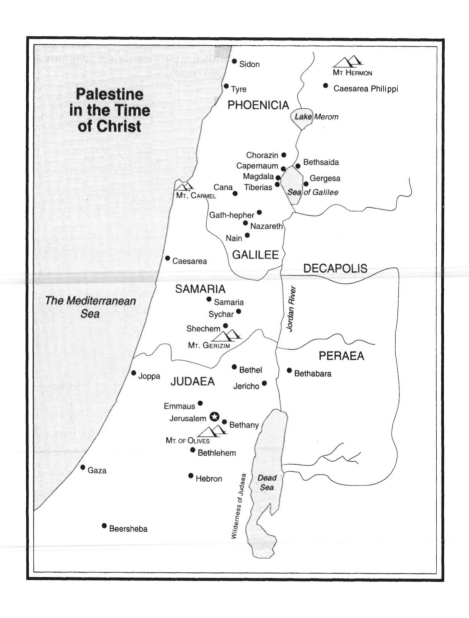

Palestine
in the Time
of Christ

38
Matthew: Behold Thy King

B efore being called by Christ to be one of His disciples, Matthew had been a publican (a tax gatherer) for the government of Rome and a member of a caste utterly despised by all patriotic Jews. Upon his call, Matthew had thrown a great feast to which he had invited all his former colleagues, and to which he also invited Jesus and His disciples. This was a great way to begin a life dedicated to the Christ of God. Being a Jew himself, Matthew fully understood the Jewish Messianic hope, and His Gospel is designed to convince his own nation that the long-awaited Messiah is none other than Jesus of Nazareth.

There are about thirty sections in Matthew which are peculiar to his Gospel, and most of these sections have some bearing on Matthew's main theme—the King and His kingdom. Words and expressions peculiar to Matthew have the same purpose, such as "the kingdom of heaven" (an expression occurring thirty-two times and not once in any of the other Gospels), "Father in heaven" (fifteen times in Matthew and only twice in Mark), "son of David" (ten times in Matthew), "that it might be fulfilled which was spoken" (nine times in Matthew and in none of the other Gospels), and "that which was spoken" or "it was spoken" (fourteen times in Matthew and nowhere else). Matthew's Gospel is saturated with Old Testament quotations, containing some sixty references to that portion of the Bible. Matthew never lost sight of his audience: Jews trained to believe that when the Messiah came He would conquer all Israel's foes and make Jerusalem the capital of a Jewish world empire. Such people believed in the Christ but did not believe *Jesus* was the Christ.

Matthew's material is not always in chronological sequence. He tends to group his material in order to produce a cumulative effect for the point he is making that Jesus is the Messiah of the Jews. For example, beginning in chapter five, we have the Sermon on the Mount—what Jesus *taught*. This is followed by a series of miracles in chapters eight to nine, by no means in the order of occurrence, but which show what Jesus *wrought*. These miracles are followed in turn by a series of reactions to Jesus illustrating what people *thought*. It seems clear that Matthew's material is arranged so that it can be easily remembered and certainly the contents of his gospel are more easily remembered than the contents of the other synoptics.

Outline of Matthew

The outline of Matthew shows clearly that Jesus is the long-awaited Son of David, King of Israel, and God's promised Messiah.

    I. THE KING IS REVEALED (1–9)
       A. His Person (1:1–4:11)
          1. His Ancestry (1:1-17)
          2. His Advent (1:18–2:23)
          3. His Ambassador (3:1-17)
          4. His Adversary(4:1-11)
       B. His Purpose (4:12–7:29)
          1. His Method Revealed (4:12-25)
          2. His Mandate Revealed (5–7)
       C. His Power (8–9)
    II. THE KING IS RESISTED (10:1–16:12)
       A. The Resistance Foretold (10)
       B. The Resistance Felt (11)
       C. The Resistance Focused (12:1–14:12)
          1. The Malice of the Pharisees (12)
          2. The Mysteries of the Kingdom (13)
          3. The Murder of John (14:1-12)
       D. The Resistance Fades (14:13-36)
       E. The Resistance Fanned (15:1–16:12)
    III. THE KING IS REJECTED (16:13–27:66)
       A. The Shadow of That Rejection (16:13–25:46)
          1. The Private Discussions (16:13–20:34)
          2. The Public Disputes (21–23)
          3. The Prophetic Discourse (24–25)

Introducing the King

The genealogy of Christ as given by Matthew is not the same as that given by Luke. Matthew gave the *regal* line ending in Joseph, the foster-father of Jesus, and showed Christ as the Son of David and the Son of Solomon. Luke gave the *legal* line through Nathan, an elder brother of Solomon (2 Samuel 5:14), ending in Mary, the Lord's mother. The prophet Isaiah, speaking of the death of Jesus long years before, challenged the people with the words, "Who shall declare his generation?" (Isaiah 53:8). Matthew proved conclusively that Jesus had every right to the throne of David, for He was indeed "the king of the Jews." At His birth Gentile wise men paid Him this tribute, and at His death the Gentile Pilate, in the superscription over the cross, acknowledged the same thing.

Jesus was introduced to the nation by John the Baptist, His cousin according to the flesh, and the appointed forerunner spoken of in Malachi. Jesus was baptized by John in the River Jordan and was immediately led into the wilderness by the Spirit to be tempted of the devil. The resounding victory the King won over man's ancient foe was but the opening campaign in that bitter struggle which climaxed at Calvary. Returning from this victory, the King selected certain of His disciples and manifested His power over demons and disease.

Matthew had a tendency to group his material so as to produce a cumulative effect. There are five major sections to his Gospel (4:12–7:29; 8:1–11:1; 11:2–13:53; 13:54–19:2; 19:3–26:2), all ending with the phrase "and it came to pass when Jesus had finished ..." Each section ends with a discourse reflecting the Jewish manner of teaching in ancient days. The Sermon on the Mount is one of the most revolutionary passages in the Bible. In sweeping statements the King revealed

His concept of the kingdom as spiritual, other-worldly, and yet intensely practical. He boldly lifted the law of Moses to a higher plane and, brushing aside all cumbersome traditions and evasive interpretations, faced men with laws of behavior that, humanly speaking, are impossible to obey. Yet He practiced the life He preached, living it out day by day, moment by moment, for thirty-three and a half magnificent years.

The King Resisted

It was not long before the impact of Christ's message produced adverse results. This was not the kind of king the people wanted, nor the kind of kingdom they expected. Resistance began to stiffen despite the marvelous proofs and credentials Jesus gave in His mighty miracles. The leaders, moved with jealousy, began to attack both the Person and the work of Christ and were made even fiercer in their opposition by the Lord's withering denunciations of their hypocrisy. Again and again the Lord warned the disciples that His enemies would triumph temporarily and that they would succeed in having Him crucified. Calmly He announced to them not only His death but His certain resurrection. He spoke of these events more frequently after His unveiling on the Mount of Transfiguration.

In private discourses, public disputes, and prophetic declarations the Lord showed a clear grasp of future events both near and far. The Olivet Discourse for example (chapters 24–25) is one of the most concise yet comprehensive prophetic utterances in the Bible. At last Judas defected to the enemy camp and betrayed the Lord to His foes. A mock trial ensued before both the Jews and the Gentiles, and God's King was crowned with thorns and nailed upon a Roman cross. Three days later He rose in triumph from the tomb, and none of the enemy's lies have been able to halt the spread of the spiritual empire of the risen Christ of God around the globe.

Happy are they who, faced with such a risen, living, reigning, returning King, bow the knee to Him and crown Him Lord of their lives.

39
Mark: Behold My Servant

J ohn Mark was the son of the Mary who lived in Jerusalem and whose home was one of the meeting places of the early church (Acts 12:12). John was his Jewish name, and Mark, his Roman name. When Paul and Barnabas set out on their first missionary journey, John Mark went along to minister to them in the capacity of a servant (Acts 13:5). No sooner did the missionaries reach the mainland of Asia Minor, however, than Mark abandoned the enterprise and thus sowed the seeds of a later serious quarrel between Paul and Barnabas. Afterward Mark made good in the Lord's work and was even commended by Paul who had felt so strongly about Mark's desertion. It would seem that Mark came strongly under the influence of Peter, and there are substantial reasons for thinking that Mark's Gospel is, in essence, the result of Peter's influence upon Mark.

It has often been pointed out that the ground covered by Mark is really an expansion of Peter's sermon as it is reported in Acts 10:34-43. It begins with the ministry of John the Baptist and ends with the ascension of the Lord Jesus. In other words, Peter was Mark's chief source for his material although not his only source.

It is interesting that Mark, who at first so dismally failed as a servant, should present the Lord Jesus to us as the Servant of Jehovah, God's perfect Servant. The key verse of Mark is 10:45: "For even the Son of man came not to be ministered unto, but to minister, and to give his life a ransom for many."

One of the world's great missionary societies has, as its logo, a picture of an ox. On one side of the ox is a plow; on the other side is an altar. Underneath the pictures are the words: "Ready for either!" That is exactly how Mark presents to us the Lord Jesus. In the opening chapters is the plow; the Son of Man gives His life in service. In the closing chapters is the altar; the Son of Man gives His life in sacrifice.

Analysis of Mark

The key verse of Mark gives us the clue to the Gospel's analysis.

I. THE SERVANT GIVES HIS LIFE IN SERVICE (1–10)
   A. The Servant's Work (1–3)
      1. The Work Begun (1)
      2. The Work Belittled (2:1–3:6)
      3. The Work Blessed (3:7-19)
      4. The Work Blasphemed (3:20-25)
   B. The Servant's Words (4–5)
      1. Exact in Purpose (4:1-34)
      2. Executive in Power (4:35–5:43)
   C. The Servant's Ways (6:1–8:26)
      1. The Attitude of Others to God's Servant (6:1-29)
      2. The Attitude of God's Servant to Others (6:30–8:26)
   D. The Servant's Worth (8:27–9:13)
   E. The Servant's Will (9:14-29)
   F. The Servant's Wisdom (9:30–10:52)
      1. Perfect Wisdom (9:30-50)
      2. Penetrating Wisdom (10:1-31)
      3. Practical Wisdom (10:32-52)
II. THE SERVANT GIVES HIS LIFE IN SACRIFICE (11–16)
   A. He Precipitates the Crisis of Calvary (11–12)
      1. His Provoking Acts (11:1-26)
      2. His Provoking Arguments (11:27–12:44)
   B. He Portrays the Consequences of Calvary (13:1–14:31)
      1. In Public (13)
      2. In Private (14:1-31)
   C. He Permits the Cross of Calvary (14:32–15:47)
      1. The Will of God (14:32-41)
      2. The Wickedness of Man (14:42–15:15)
      3. The Way of Sacrifice (15:16-47)
   D. He Proves the Crime of Calvary (16)
      1. The Conquest of the Grave (16:1-14)
      2. The Conquest of the Globe (16:15-20)

Mark's Gospel begins with God's Servant busy. His credentials are presented by John the Baptist; His companions are being taken from physical toil to be prepared for spiritual toil; and His capabilities are proven in the healing of countless sick. Satan's wilderness assault is passed over in a single verse, for the whole of Mark's Gospel shows us the Servant of Jehovah destroying the works of the devil.

The critics of God's Servant were soon seeking to undermine His work, for they were angered at His evident authority, His love for the lost, and His undisguised scorn for their petty religious scruples and taboos. Mark shows us the Servant as mighty in word and deed. He speaks with the voice that stills the storm, that delivers the demoniac, that heals the sick, and that raises the dead. Mark presents us with a Christ who is tenderly concerned with people—with their happiness, their hunger, their hardships, their health, and even their hypocrisy. Mark tells us how Jesus succored the stranger, delivered the dumb, fed the famished, rebuked the radicals, and taught those who would hearken to His words. He tells how Peter confessed the Servant's matchless worth, and how God opened heaven to honor Him, too.

The narrative hurries on with the Servant ever busy, pouring out His life in service that must end in sacrifice. The crisis was precipitated when Jesus rode into Jerusalem on the colt and summarily cleansed the temple. Fiercely His foes sought to trap Him in His talk, but they failed and were roundly castigated by Christ for their hypocrisy. As the last week wore on to its tragic climax, the Lord sketched an outline of the ages from the time of His rejection to the time of His return. In private, He told His disciples what to expect in the immediate future and then led them to dark Gethsemane where, after His agony, He was betrayed by Judas and delivered over to the will of His foes. Mark describes with a graphic, concise, realistic, and forceful style the sad events surrounding the trial and crucifixion of Jehovah's perfect Servant. He tells how He was buried by wealthy men and how He rose again, His work on earth being finished. The closing verses of Mark have been much discussed and often disputed, but they seem to be in keeping with Mark's theme. They tell us of the commissioning of the disciples and of the way they went forth in the Spirit and power of the risen Lord Himself to tell the good news of the gospel.

Mark's Gospel concludes with a world vision and a task entrusted to those who love the Lord. The servants of Jehovah's Servant "went forth and preached everywhere, the Lord working with them and confirming the word with signs following." To this task all those who love Him must dedicate themselves until He comes again.

40
Luke: Behold the Man

As Mark came under the influence of Peter so Luke came under the influence of Paul. By profession Luke was a physician, and his medical knowledge is reflected in many expressions used both in his Gospel and in the book of Acts, which also came from his pen. It has been suggested that Luke might well have undertaken his medical studies at the university of Tarsus. Attached to that university was a school of philosophy and literature and it is not at all unlikely that Luke and Paul were contemporary students. Perhaps it was there that they began their life-long friendship. There is a striking similarity between the thought and language of Paul and Luke. Luke emphasizes such Pauline words and concepts as *faith, grace, repentance, mercy* and *forgiveness.*

As Mark had written for the Romans so Luke wrote for the Greeks. The Greeks were noted for their intellectual power, and Luke's Gospel was written in a polished literary style and in a more classical style than the others. So strong was the Greek ideal of perfect manhood that they had made all their gods in the image of men, deifying in the process their vices as well as their virtues. Luke presented Christ as the perfect Man—One who, being both Man and God, could fully realize the deepest aspirations of the Greeks.

Luke's Gospel is characterized by its comprehensiveness, beginning as it does with the annunciations of John and Jesus and continuing to the ascension of Jesus.

Analysis of Luke

I. INTRODUCTION (1:1-4)
II. EVENTS RELATING TO THE SAVIOR'S COMING (1:5–4:13)
  A. His Birth at Bethlehem (1:5–2:39)
    1. The Announcements of Gabriel (1:5-38)
    2. The Anthems of Elisabeth and Mary (1:39-56)
    3. The Arrival of John (1:57-80)
    4. The Advent of Jesus (2:1-39)
  B. His Boyhood at Nazareth (2:40-52)
  C. His Baptism in Jordan (3:1-22)
  D. His Background in History (3:23-38)
  E. His Battle with Satan (4:1-13)
III. EVENTS RELATING TO THE SAVIOR'S CAREER (4:14–21:38)
  A. The Work in Galilee (4:14–9:50)
  His Anointing in Focus
    1. The Work Is Commenced (4:14–5:17)
    2. The Work Is Criticized (5:18–6:11)
    3. The Work Is Climaxed (6:12–9:50)
      a. The Dependent Savior (6:12-16)
      b. The Dynamic Savior (6:17–9:17)
      c. The Divine Savior (9:18-45)
      d. The Discerning Savior (9:46-50)
  B. The Way to Golgotha (9:51–21:38)
  His Adversaries in Focus
    1. The Scholastic Approach (9:51–10:42)
    2. The Slanderous Approach (11:1-28)
    3. The Sophisticated Approach (11:29-52)
    4. The Systematic Approach (11:53–13:9)
    5. The Sermonic Approach (13:10-30)
    6. The Scare Approach (13:31-35)
    7. The Subtle Approach (14:1-35)
    8. The Sarcastic Approach (15:1-32)
    9. The Scoffing Approach (16:1–17:10)
    10. The Selfish Approach (17:11-19)
    11. The Snobbish Approach (17:20–19:27)
    12. The Straightforward Approach (19:28–20:19)
    13. The Seductive Approach (20:20–21:38)
IV. EVENTS RELATING TO THE SAVIOR'S CROSS (22–24)
  A. The Table (22:1-38)
  B. The Tears (22:39-53)
  C. The Trials (22:54–23:31)

D. The Tree (23:32-49)
E. The Tomb (23:50-56)
F. The Triumph (24:1-53)

Luke gave us the fullest account of the Christmas story and did so with delicacy, feeling, and much human interest. We never tire of reading of the visits of the herald angel, the sweet confidences which passed between Mary and her cousin Elisabeth, the birth of John the Baptist, the humble birth of God's beloved Son, the worship of the shepherds, and the glad messages of Simeon and Anna. We love to read Luke's account of the boyhood of Jesus as a twelve-year-old. We trace with interest Luke's impressions of the ministry of John the Baptist and his account of Christ's baptism and temptation. We appreciate Luke's thorough and painstaking compilation of the Lord's genealogy right back to Adam.

The greater part of Luke's Gospel, of course, shows us the Savior at work, for Luke presents us with Christ the Savior as much as he presents us with Christ the Man. We do not read far into Luke's gripping account of Christ's ministry before we meet the Lord's enemies who coldly criticize Him on religious grounds. These enemies of Christ are very prominent in Luke. But Luke sweeps us on, showing us the dynamic Christ: dynamic in His words and in His works, in His ways and in His walk, in His wisdom and in His will. Distance cannot prevent the going forth of His power as the centurion whose servant was sick discovered; neither can death, as the widow of Nain found out. Neither the tempest nor the terrorist can thwart His will, for the dynamic Savior is also divine.

But Christ had His enemies—many of them—and Luke dramatically shifts the emphasis to them and shows how the perfect Man handled all His foes. The *scholastic approach* was tried by a certain lawyer who "stood up, and tempted him, saying, Master, what shall I do to inherit eternal life?" (10:25). Certainly this man was convicted when the Lord told the parable of the Good Samaritan and then drove the point home. The *slanderous approach* drew forth a terrible warning of the unpardonable sin from the lips of God's Son. The *sophisticated approach* was tried by a certain Pharisee who, having invited Jesus to dinner, sneered at Him secretly for not washing His hands. The *systematic approach* was tried next, for we read, "The scribes and the Pharisees began to urge him vehemently, and to provoke him to speak of many things: laying wait for him, and seeking to catch something out of his mouth, that they might accuse him" (11:53-54). Of course they failed. The *sermonic approach* was tried by the ruler of the synagogue, who was indignant because Jesus healed a crippled woman on the

Sabbath day. "There are six days in which men ought to work," carped this man. "In them therefore come and be healed and not on the Sabbath day." Jesus bluntly and publicly told this man he was a hypocrite. The *scare approach* was tried next as some warned Jesus that Herod would kill Him. Jesus' answer was to call Herod a fox. The *subtle approach* was tried by one of the chief Pharisees who, having invited Jesus home with him to break bread on the Sabbath, waited to pounce should Jesus heal a man afflicted with dropsy. The *sarcastic approach* was used by the Pharisees and scribes on yet another occasion as they sneered, "This man receiveth sinners, and eateth with them" (15:2). This sarcastic thrust only drew forth the three pearly parables of the lost sheep, the lost silver, and the lost son. The *scoffing approach* was also evident, for we read that "the Pharisees . . . derided him" (16:14) for His teaching on covetousness. The *selfish approach* was manifested in the ingratitude of the nine lepers, something which deeply hurt the Lord. The *snobbish approach is* apparent in the Pharisees' demanding of Him "when the kingdom of God should come" (17:20). The *straightforward approach* of Christ's enemies becomes increasingly prominent after the triumphal entry into Jerusalem. "The chief priests and the scribes . . . sought to destroy him," we read. The *seductive approach* was the last recorded as they threw at Him questions which were "loaded" both politically and religiously and then hired Judas for his act of treachery.

Luke's account of the crucifixion and resurrection of the Savior is as graphic as the rest of his Gospel. But he goes beyond the others, taking us to Bethany and showing us the risen Lord ascending to Heaven. It is at this point that Luke lays down his pen only to take it again later to pick up the thread once more and trace the history of the early Church in the book of Acts.

41
John: Behold Your God

J ohn's purpose was to present Jesus as God, and this is evident in his first and in almost his last references to Christ (1:1; 20:28, 31). John omits both the temptation in the wilderness and the agony in the garden, for neither of these would have been in keeping with his theme. He gives us no genealogy of Jesus but takes us straight up to the throne and back to the beginning. The only incidents John records in common with the other evangelists are the work of John the Baptist, the Last Supper, the anointing at Bethany, the Passion, the resurrection, and two miracles—the feeding of the five thousand and the walking on the Sea of Galilee. The synoptic Gospels place great emphasis on Christ's ministry in Galilee, but John concentrates on Jerusalem and Judea, hence the Lord's visits to the feasts are given special prominence (2:13–3:21; 5:1; 6:4; 7:10; 10:22; 11:55). It is from John's Gospel that we can decide the length of the Lord's public ministry, approximately three and a half years.

Dr. Graham Scroggie points out that Luke's Gospel and John's dovetail the one into the other in a most remarkable way. It is just as if two halves of a broken jug were to be brought together so that every indentation of the one corresponds to every protuberance of the other. In fact John seems to carefully avoid relating incidents related by Luke.[1]

Analysis of John

John's key words are *life, light, love, believe,* and *witness.* These are prominent not only in his prologue and epilogue but also throughout the Gospel.

I. PROLOGUE (1:1-18)
   A. The Divine Life in Its Essence (1:1-5)
   B. The Divine Light in Its Evidence (1:6-13)
   C. The Divine Love in Its Experience (1:14-18)
II. THE SIGNS OF THE SON OF GOD (1:19–12:50)
   His Deity Is in Focus
   A. His Deity Is Declared (1:19–4:54)
     1. TheTestimony of John (1:19-51)
     2. The Triumphs of Jesus (2:1–4:54)
       a. Over Life's Sudden Disappointments (2:1-12)
         The wine at the wedding
       b. Over Life's Secular Debasements (2:13-25)
         The traffic in the temple
       c. Over Life's Spiritual Deceptions (3:1-21)
         The night with Nicodemus
       d. Over Life's Saddening Discouragements (3:22-36)
         The Jews who went to John
       e. Over Life's Sordid Defilements (4:1-42)
         The woman at the well
       f . Over Life's Sorrowful Disablements (4:43-54)
         The faith of a father
   B. His Deity Is Disputed (5:1–10:42)
     1. The Impact of His Life (5:1–6:71)
       a. In Urban Jerusalem (5:1-47)
       b. In Rural Galilee(6:1-71)
     2. The Implications of His Life (7:1–10:42)
       a. As He Expounds the Word of God (7:1-53)
       b. As He Exposes the Wickedness of Men (8:1–9:41)
       c. As He Expresses the Way of Life (10:1-42)
   C. His Deity Is Disowned (11:1–12:50)
     1. Some Examples of His Rejection (11:1–12:36)
     2. Some Explanations for His Rejection(12:37-50)
III. THE SECRETS OF THE SON OF GOD (13–17)
   His Disciples Are in Focus
   A. The Talk in the Upper Room (13–14)
   B. The Walk on the Gethsemane Road (15–17)
IV. THE SORROWS OF THE SON OF GOD (18–20)
   His Death Is in Focus
   A. He Is Falsely Condemned (18:1–19:15)

Isaiah described the coming Messiah as the "child born" and as the "Son given" (Isaiah 9:6), thus expressing the humanity and deity of Christ. Matthew and Luke, in their genealogies, gave a glimpse of the Child born. John told of the Son given, for we read "God so loved the world that he gave his only begotten Son" (John 3:16). This notable verse also highlights one of John's purposes in writing—to present us with reactions to Christ, belief on the one hand and unbelief on the other.

Having introduced the Eternal Word made flesh, John got right down to his theme, showing how John the Baptist faithfully witnessed to Jesus both as Lord and as Lamb. He showed how the disciples of the Baptist "heard him speak, and . . . followed Jesus" (1:37). He told how they recognized Him as Messiah, and how Nathanael confessed Him as "Son of God" and "King of Israel."

John's selection of miracles was deliberate. He called them signs, for they signified the deity of Christ. The first miracle was at a wedding, and the last, at a funeral; Christ made Himself equal to life's gladdest and saddest hours. In Jerusalem for His first Passover as Israel's revealed Messiah, the Lord cleansed the temple (2:13-17), an act He repeated later toward the end of His public ministry. This event was no doubt uppermost in the mind of the religious Pharisee, Nicodemus, when he paid Christ his famous night visit and learned of his need of being born again. In contrast to Christ's interview with Nicodemus was His talk with the woman at the well in Samaritan country. Rich and poor, moral and immoral, all need to come to Christ and find in Him the answer to life's deepest needs.

John showed how the Jews took issue with Jesus over the Sabbath question. Indeed, it was Christ's attitude toward the Sabbath as much as anything else which gave His enemies something on which to hang their criticisms. Again and again John showed the people taking sides, some believing, and some disbelieving. The words of Jesus in the Gospel of John, as well as His works, were misunderstood by Christ's foes. The discourses in John are much different than those recorded in the synoptics. In John the well-known parables are all missing and, instead, we have deep, mystical utterances on well-chosen but often difficult and abstract themes. Sometimes the Lord's miracles gave rise to discourses such as that on the bread of life, which resulted from the feeding of the five thousand. Again and again in John, Jesus is shown to be the I AM, the great Jehovah Himself. But all Christ's signs and sayings were in vain, for opposition to Him strengthened, coming to a head shortly after the amazing resurrection of Lazarus.

Much of John's Gospel is devoted to the Passion week and the Lord's intimate talks with the disciples. These discourses, while warm, were often beyond the disciples' power to comprehend, so that the Lord had to promise them the gift of the Holy Spirit, Who would in due course not only bring His sayings back to mind but make them clear as well. Just before He left the upper room for Gethsemane, the Lord poured out His heart in prayer for believers of all ages, and John was careful to record this magnificent prayer.

John seemed to have access to places closed to the other disciples. It was he who gained entrance for Peter into the palace of the high priest. With the same restraint as the other evangelists, John recorded the mock trials and the crucifixion, telling only what was necessary and leaving out all the emotion-packed details human imagination would hasten to add. True to his theme also, John showed how the resurrection of Christ affected people and closed his magnificent Gospel with the statement that the world itself could not contain the books which could have been written about the life and death of Christ, the Son of God. Enough has been written, however, to face people with the challenge of believing.

---

1. See W. Graham Scroggie, *A Guide to the Gospels,* pp. 437-446.

42

Acts:
The Early Church in Action

The writer of Acts was Luke. The book has the same introductory address as his Gospel and resumes the history where that document leaves off. Actually the book describes not the "acts of the apostles," for only a few of them are given any degree of prominence, but the acts of the risen and ascended Lord through the Holy Spirit. Luke used a number of sources for his information, and some of his facts are firsthand. The "we" sections of the book (16:10-17; 20:5-15; 21:1-18; 27:1–28:16) indicate that he was often in the company of the Apostle Paul.

The book of Acts traces the history of the Church from its origin on the day of Pentecost to its spread throughout the western part of the Roman Empire; from being a small Jewish minority to a populous group predominantly Gentile. The key to the book is 1:8: "But ye shall receive power, after that the Holy Ghost is come upon you: and ye shall be witnesses unto me both in Jerusalem, and in all Judea, and in Samaria, and unto the uttermost part of the earth."

Analysis of Acts

The book of Acts is in three parts, each with a different emphasis. The first describes God's man, Simon Peter; the second deals with

God's martyr, Stephen; and the third displays God's missionary, Saul. Around these three men the three movements of the book are centered.

 I. THE FOUNDATION EMPHASIS OF THE CHURCH (1 – 5)
  Dominated by Simon Peter
  A. Its Preparation (1)
  B. Its Power (2)
  C. Its Persecution (3)
  D. Its Progress (4 – 5)
 II. THE FORWARD EMPHASIS OF THE CHURCH (6 – 12)
  Dominated by Stephen
  A. New Voices (6 – 8)
   1. Stephen the Martyr (6 – 7)
   2. Philip the Missionary (8)
  B. New Victories (9 – 11)
   1. Saul of Tarsus is Saved (9)
   2. Simon Peter is Sent (10 – 11)
  C. New Violence (12)
 III. THE FOREIGN EMPHASIS OF THE CHURCH (13 – 28)
  Dominated by Saul (called Paul)
  A. Paul the Pioneer (13:1 – 21:26)
   1. Exploration—the First Missionary Journey (13:1 – 15:35)
   2. Expansion—the Second MissionaryJourney (15:35 – 18:23)
   3. Exhortation—the Third Missionary Journey (18:23 – 21:26)
  B. Paul the Prisoner (21:27 – 28:31)
   1. His Treatment as a Prisoner (21:27 – 23:35)
   2. His Triumphs as a Prisoner (24 – 26)
   3. His Travels as a Prisoner (27 – 28)

Beginnings

For forty days before His ascension the Lord prepared the disciples for their great task, giving them the blueprint for world evangelization and promising them the power. After his ascension the disciples chose Matthias to succeed Judas as an apostle and waited for the promised coming of the Holy Spirit.

In Acts 2 we are told of the coming of the Holy Spirit "when the day of Pentecost was fully come." The day of Pentecost had come many times in Hebrew history, for it was one of the national feasts. It did not *fully* come until that day when the Spirit descended in a new way to baptize the believers into the body of Christ, thus bringing into being the Church. Phenomenal signs accompanied this marvelous event, and soon thousands were converted to Christ and swept into the Church. It was not long before official Jewry, led by the Sadducees, began to persecute the Church. But nothing could stay its power, except sin, and the first manifestation of that was the dissimulation of Ananias and Sapphira. The Apostle Peter judged the hypocrisy and pretense of this covetous couple with such power that, accused of lying to the Holy Spirit, they each collapsed and died in turn.

Broadening Horizons

The persecution of the infant Church reached its climax in the martyrdom of Stephen, one of the "deacons" of the church, a gifted and eloquent man whose arguments for Christianity could not be refuted by its foes. Far from stemming the rising tide of belief in Christ, the martyrdom of Stephen seemed to give it impetus, for the believers were scattered far and wide from Jerusalem, taking the good seed of the gospel wherever they went. Philip, one of the deacons also, took the message to Samaria, where a church was founded which was soon in happy fellowship with the Jewish church in Jerusalem. Prejudice of ancient vintage could not stand before the dynamic of the gospel. Then Saul of Tarsus, arch-persecutor of the Church, was saved. Soon the Church would have in him a new apostle—Paul. With a few further notes regarding Peter's great ministry in opening the door of the Church to the Gentiles in the home of a Roman centurion, Cornelius, and with an account of Herod's persecution of the Church and his untimely death, Luke hastened on to tell of Antioch and the real beginnings of Gentile Christianity.

The Uttermost Parts of the Earth

The greatest missionary of all times was Paul. When Paul and Barnabas were commended to the work of world evangelism by the church at Antioch, at first Barnabas took the lead. Leaving Antioch, the missionaries went to Cyprus; then, Paul taking the lead, they went on into Galatia. Enduring hardship as good soldiers of Jesus Christ, the missionaries saw a number of churches established. Returning to Antioch, they found the church in a turmoil because Jewish teachers were insisting that all Gentile converts be circumcised and keep the law of Moses. Paul and Barnabas led a deputation to Jerusalem where the issue was settled in a great conference at which emancipation from Judaism was endorsed for all Gentile believers.

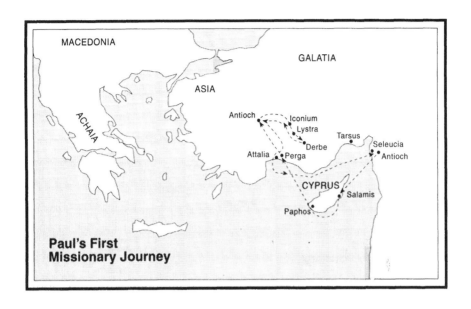

Paul's First Missionary Journey

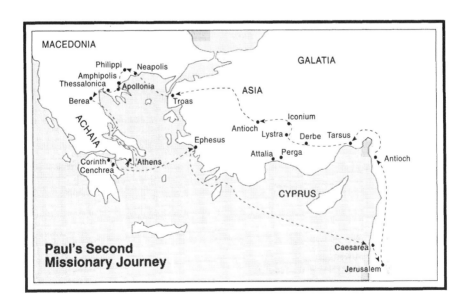

Paul's Second Missionary Journey

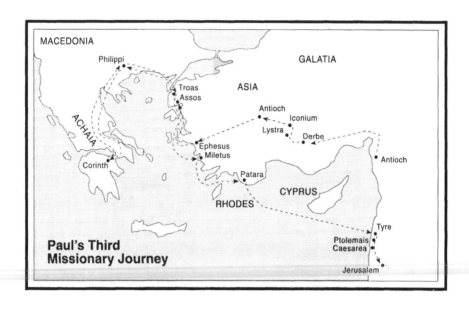

Paul's Third Missionary Journey

Roman Provinces and Paul's Journey to Rome

Paul's second missionary journey began on a sad note, for he and Barnabas quarreled over John Mark, a young man who had deserted them on their first missionary journey. Parting with Barnabas over this issue, Paul took Silas with him and revisited the churches which had been founded on his first missionary journey. Then, moving ever westward until he came to Troas, he received the "Macedonian call" and invaded Europe for Christ. Soon a trail of churches were founded in Macedonia and Greece: Philippi, Thessalonica, Berea, and Corinth. Hurrying back to Jerusalem, Paul paid a flying visit to Ephesus, which was to be the scene of some of his greatest triumphs in the gospel on his third journey.

Paul's third journey was largely occupied, except for his stay at Ephesus, with teaching, establishing, and exhorting the churches founded before. Ephesus, an important city in western Asia Minor, was where Paul spent considerable time on this last recorded missionary journey. A strong and thriving church was established and became a beacon to all the surrounding countryside.

Back in Jerusalem, Paul was attacked by Jewish enemies who resented his preaching and his success. He was arrested and began his long, tedious, and often perilous journey to Rome as a prisoner. Paul's captivity was fruitful, for it brought him before great men to whom he testified unashamedly and with power. Also during his captivity he wrote some of the greatest epistles of the New Testament. The book of Acts closes with Paul, still a prisoner in Rome under house arrest but, as Christ's ambassador in bonds, still conducting a vigorous onslaught on the strongholds of sin. Such is the book of Acts. A grasp of it is a key to understanding the epistles.

43

Romans:
Theology of the Gospel

Before beginning a survey of Romans we should first get a clear picture of the relationships of the various New Testament books. The following chart will help.

Categories of New Testament Books

NARRATION	EXPLANATION		CONSUMMATION
	Paul's Epistles	General Epistles	
	To Churches		
Matthew	Romans	Hebrews	
Mark	1 Corinthians	James	
Luke	2 Corinthians	1 Peter	
John	Galatians	2 Peter	
	Ephesians	1 John	
Acts	Philippians	2 John	Revelation
	Colossians	3 John	
	1 Thessalonians	Jude	
	2 Thessalonians		
	To Individuals		
	1 Timothy		
	2 Timothy		
	Titus		
	Philemon		

If for the purpose of memorization, we count Revelation with the epistles, we have nine church epistles (Romans to 2 Thessalonians) followed by four pastoral-personal epistles(1 Timothy to Philemon) followed by nine general epistles (Hebrews to Revelation). This pattern is easily memorized(9–4–9). Now taking the church and general epistles, each section containing nine books, we observe the following similarities and differences. Both sections begin with a thorough doctrinal treatise (Romans and Hebrews). Both sections close with an unveiling of the future (2 Thessalonians and Revelation). Both sections were written to special groups, the first to Gentile and the second to Hebrew Christians.

Concentrating now on the Pauline church epistles we see that the following pattern, based on 2 Timothy 3:16, is evident:

A. Doctrine and Instruction—Romans
  B. Reproof (for practical failure) 1 and 2 Corinthians
    C. Correction (for doctrinal error) Galatians

A. Doctrine and Instruction—Ephesians
  B. Reproof (for practical failure) Philippians
    C. Correction (for doctrinal error) Colossians

A. Doctrine and Instruction—1 and 2 Thessalonians

From this it will be seen that Paul wrote three epistles which are pivotal and which unfold doctrine and instruction. In Romans he expounded the mystery of Christ's *Cross;* in Ephesians, the mystery of Christ's *Church;* and in the Thessalonians, the mystery of Christ's *coming.* The Thessalonian epistles come last though written first, and there are no "church" epistles beyond these because no higher truth can be taught; the consummation is reached.

Paul had not been to Rome when he wrote his epistle to the church there, but he planned to go as soon as occasion presented itself (1:10, 13; 15:23-24, 28). He wrote from Corinth (16:1) while on his third missionary journey during the "three months" referred to in Acts 20:3, just before his final visit to Jerusalem. As we have seen, Paul's great ambition to preach in Rome was fulfilled in an unexpected way. He went there as a prisoner.

Some of the key words in Romans are: *law* (78 times), *all* (71 times), *righteousness* (66 times), *faith* (62 times), *sin* (60 times), *death* (42 times), *in Christ* (33 times), *flesh* (20 times), *impute* (19 times), and *God forbid* (10 times). Matthew, Mark, Luke, and John gave the facts about Christ's sojourn on earth, but Paul gave the meaning of it all. In

Romans we have the Gospel according to Paul. There are more Old Testament quotations in Romans than in all the other epistles put together—some seventy quotations from fourteen Old Testament books. In this way Paul demonstrated the fact that the Gospel message is the same throughout all ages.

Analysis of Romans

I. PROLOGUE (1:1-17)
II. THE PRINCIPLE OF CHRISTIANITY (1–8)
    A. The Question of Sin (1:18–3:20)
    B. The Question of Salvation (3:21–5:21)
    C. The Question of Sanctification (6–8)
III. THE PROBLEM OF CHRISTIANITY (9–11)
    A. God's Past Dealings with Israel (9)
    B. God's Present Dealings with Israel (10)
    C. God's Promised Dealings with Israel (11)
IV. THE PRACTICE OF CHRISTIANITY (12–16)
    A. The Laws of Christian Life (12:1–13:7)
       1. The Spiritual Life of the Christian (12:1-13)
       2. The Social Life of the Christian (12:14-21)
       3. The Secular Life of the Christian (13:1-7)
    B. The Laws of Christian Love (13:8–16:24)
       1. Love's Conscience (13:8-14)
       2. Love's Consideration (14:1–15:3)
       3. Love's Convictions(15:4-13)
       4. Love's Concern (15:14-33)
       5. Love's Contacts (16:1-16)
       6. Love's Conquests (16:17-20)
       7. Love's Companionships (16:21-24)
V. EPILOGUE (16:25-27)

Christian Belief

In the first three chapters of Romans Paul painted a black picture of human sin. Jew and Gentile alike are condemned before God and found without exception to be without excuse and without escape, facing the wrath of God. Then Paul turns to the question of salvation and shows that when God forgives He does so fully, freely, and forever. Paul sees man's case as hopeless apart from the sovereign grace of God. He traces human sin back to Adam and shows that "in Adam all die," and then shows that God has a second federal head for the human race, Christ in whom all are made alive. By natural birth we are children of Adam, but by being born again we become children of God, for Christ's sake being adopted out of Adam's family of ruined men into God's family of the redeemed. The key to salvation is faith in Christ, works being totally excluded as a means of procuring the favor of God.

With Paul, salvation meant security but not freedom to sin. In chapters 6 through 8 he showed that God saves from the power of sin as well as the penalty of sin and that through the indwelling of the Holy Spirit sin, self, and Satan can all be subdued in practical daily Christian living.

The Problem of the Jew

Paul had a special sympathy for and understanding of the Jewish dilemma, for he himself was a Jew. For years he had resisted Christianity, sensing its basic challenge to Judaism. In chapters 9 through 11 Paul dealt with the effect of the Christian gospel on the ancient promises of God to the nation of Israel. In a masterful way he showed that God had always been sovereign in His dealings with Israel and had traditionally dealt with a believing remnant rather than with the unbelieving masses of the nation. Paul showed that, for the present time, there is but one basis of salvation for Jew and Gentile alike—faith in Christ. "Whosoever shall call upon the name of the Lord shall be saved" (Romans 10:13). Then he proved that the time will yet come when God will resume His dealings with Israel as a nation and will fulfill all His glorious promises to His ancient people. The Christian gospel does not cancel the purposes of God with Israel as a nation, although it does indeed postpone them, not because God has changed His mind but because Israel refuses to believe.

Practical Christianity

The closing chapters of Romans are intensely practical and relate the principles of the earlier chapters to daily living. Beginning with the call to full consecration (Romans 12:1-3) Paul showed how Christianity relates to the various relationships of life. In the church, the believer is to humbly exercise his gift. He is to be generous, forgiving, kind, honest, considerate, and impartial. He is to obey the law of the land, give honor to dignities, and pay his taxes.

Love is the fulfilling of the law, so love is to dominate in all a Christian's conduct and conversation. He is to respect the convictions of others, consider the weak brother, hold fast to vital truth, have a keen interest in world evangelism, and uphold God's servants in prayer.

In conclusion Paul showed how wide were his interests and how much he prized his friends. He mentioned name after name of those he knew in Rome (although he had never been there), commending some, commenting on the service of others, and sending greetings to groups of Christians here and there all over Rome. He conveyed salutations from some of the saints at Corinth and at last closed his epistle with four amens. A good grasp of this vital epistle is essential to all those who would tell others of Christ and lead them into a full gospel experience.

44

1 and 2 Corinthians: Order in the Church

P aul founded the church at Corinth on his second missionary
journey. Some time after this, Apollos came to Corinth from
Ephesus and made a deep impression on the believers with his
eloquence. Then a party of Judaizers appeared and soon there were
factions in the church. There were other dangers as well. Paul had
already written to the Corinthians (1 Corinthians 5:9), warning them
against the dangers of immorality, for Corinth was one of the most
licentious cities of antiquity. But the saints at Corinth evidently were
more tolerant of vice than Paul, for they allowed an incestuous man to
continue in their fellowship without rebuke (1 Corinthians 5:1-2). In
addition to this, the Corinthians had written to Paul asking advice on
certain questions. All in all, Paul had a number of very vital matters
with which to deal in this young church, and in 1 Corinthians he
addressed himself to their quarrels and their questions with vision
and with vigor. First Corinthians is the longest of Paul's letters and is
an important treatise on order in the church.

Analysis of 1 Corinthians

I. INTRODUCTION (1:1-9)
II. DIVISIONS IN THE CHURCH (1:10–4:21)

The key to 1 Corinthians is found in 1:30 where we read: "But of him are ye in Christ Jesus, who of God is made unto us wisdom, and righteousness, and sanctification, and redemption." The four divisions of the epistle form a commentary on this verse.

Wisdom

In sharp sentences Paul showed the folly of sectarianism and especially that particularly odious form which pretends not to be sectarian at all while saying, "I of Christ" (1:12). Paul utterly repudiated such a spirit and refused to have his name linked with a religious party in the church. Then, knowing the Greek love of intellectualism, Paul denounced all worldly wisdom as being out of place in the believer's thinking. At the heart of divine wisdom is the Cross, which is a source of stumbling to the Jews, and foolishness to the Greeks. Returning to his theme of sectarianism, Paul showed that only carnal Christians have a party spirit and warned that in view of the Judgment Seat of Christ, Christians would be wise to cease glorying in men and begin living lives acceptable to God.

Righteousness

Having rebuked the folly of denominationalism and worldly wisdom, Paul next condemned the Corinthians for allowing a flagrant case of immorality to remain in their midst. He demanded action against the offending brother in the strongest terms. Then he admonished them all for using the civil courts to settle their disputes, saying that a Christian should suffer loss rather than take such action. He concluded by showing that the righteousness of Christ in the life is a very practical antidote against moral sin.

Sanctification

Having dealt with disorders in the church, Paul dealt with questions which had been raised by the Corinthians in a letter to him. He gave some practical counsel on sanctification in marriage, and considered the very touchy problem of eating meat offered to idols and then placed on sale in the markets. The principles he set forth are of abiding value. The place of women in the local church, disorders at the Lord's table, and the misuse of gifts were all dealt with in turn in terms of sanctification. Gifts, for example, are to be exercised in love. Paul devoted a whole section of his letter to a definition of Christian love.

Redemption

The redemption of the body at the resurrection was Paul's closing theme in this letter. Arguing powerfully from the resurrection of Christ, he quelled all doubts as to the future portion of the believer. In conclusion he gave some practical advice on church collections and spoke of a visit he hoped to make to them in the near future. He closed his epistle with commendations and greetings.

2 Corinthians

Paul's letter to the Corinthians described above produced a good effect on the whole. The immoral brother, for example, was expelled from the fellowship and showed deep repentance. However, a vocal minority in the church was stirring up trouble against Paul, challenging his apostleship and attacking him in a slanderous manner. They accused him of being fickle (1:17-18, 23), of being proud and boastful (3:1; 5:12), of being weak and of a displeasing personal appearance (10:10), of being dishonest (12:16-19), and even of being practically insane (5:13; 11:16-19; 2:16).Paul answered his detractors in warm, passionate language in 2 Corinthians. Of all his letters this one probably gives us our best glimpse of the personality of the great Apostle.

Comparison of 1 and 2 Corinthians

1 CORINTHIANS	2 CORINTHIANS
• Insight into the life, character and conditions of the church • Objective and practical • Deliberate • Warns against pagan influences	• Insight into the life, character and conditions of the apostle Paul • Subjective and personal • Impassioned • Warns against Judaistic influences

Analysis of 2 Corinthians

I. INTRODUCTION (1:1-2)
II. PAUL AND HIS COMMISSION (1:3–5:21)
    A. Paul Defends His Motives (1:3–2:17)
    B. Paul Defends His Message(3:1–5:21)
III. PAUL AND HIS CONVERTS (6–9)
    A. Their Faithful Partnership in the Gospel (6–7)
    B. Their Financial Partnership in the Gospel (8–9)
IV. PAUL AND HIS CRITICS (10–13)
    A. His Personal Appearance (10)
    B. His Proven Apostleship (11:1–12:13)
    C. His Passionate Appeal (12:14–13:10)
V. CONCLUSION (13:11-14)

Paul suffered many things for the cause of Christ. In this letter he appealed again and again to the things which he suffered as evidence of his sincerity. Paul explained to the Corinthians that a proposed visit of his had been unavoidably delayed, but this was no proof that he was fickle. Indeed, one reason why he had postponed his visit to Corinth was because he had no desire to hurt them and had no wish for a painful visit. He told them how glad he was that the excommunicated brother had repented and recommended that he be forgiven and restored to the fellowship. He explained that his previous letter had been a sort of a test to see if they would bow to his apostolic authority (2:9). Then, in glowing words, he described the glory of the apostolic ministry, telling them they themselves were the living proof of his commission (3:1-3).

Paul warmly thanked the Corinthians for their faithful partnership in the gospel and assured them that his heart was completely open toward them. He urged them to live in separation from the world and then again assured them, that, despite the sharp words he had to use, he nevertheless loved them deeply. Next he spoke of their financial support and used great plainness of speech on the whole subject of Christian stewardship of money.

The closing chapters tell us much about Paul's outlook. He felt he had something more worthwhile than mere good looks: spiritual strength, stateliness, and stature (chapter 10). "He that glorieth," he said, "let him glory in the Lord."

Then Paul warned against giving heed to "another Jesus," "another spirit," and "another gospel" (11:4). He exalted his apostleship, saying he came behind none of the apostles (11:5). He described briefly some of his great sufferings for the cause of Christ and went on to describe a heavenly vision he had received, a vision so magnificent that it had necessitated his being given "a thorn in the flesh." But even this "thorn" was a blessing in disguise, for it taught him fresh dependence upon God's grace.

He concluded with a warning that the next time he came to Corinth he would not be lenient with his critics but would put them to the test and deal with them in power. But his last remarks were full of endearment, grace, love, and fellowship.

45
Galatians: Magna Charta of Christian Liberty

P aul's epistle to the Galatians has been likened to "the sketch for the finished picture of Romans," and certainly the two letters have much in common. Both emphasize salvation, the believer's emancipation from the law, and the removal before God of any difference between Jew and Gentile. Paul's Galatian letter also has common ground with 2 Corinthians, for both letters emphasize the fact of his apostleship.

The area covered by Galatia varied from time to time. Originally it was a country in northwestern Asia Minor settled by the Gauls who gave the area its name. Later Galatia was taken over by the Romans who enlarged the territory southward and incorporated it into the empire as a province. It is a disputed point as to whether or not Paul addressed his Galatian epistle to churches located in the southern part of the province and founded on his first missionary journey, or whether he addressed churches located in the northern part of the province and founded on his second missionary journey.

The Galatians themselves were generous, inconsistent, impulsive, and quarrelsome, and these characteristics are reflected in Paul's letter to them. Of the fifteen "works of the flesh" listed by Paul (5:20-21), eight are sins of strife.

Outline of Galatians

I. INTRODUCTION (1:1-2)
II. AN EXPLANATION (1–2)
    A. The Declaration of the Gospel (1:3-5)
    B. The Distortion of the Gospel (1:6-10)
    C. The Dynamic of the Gospel (1:11-24)
        1. Paul's Reception of the Gospel (1:11-17)
        2. Paul's Reputation in the Gospel (1:18-24)
    D. The Defense of the Gospel (2:1-21)
        1. How Paul Challenged the Church at Jerusalem (2:1-10)
        2. How Paul Challenged the Church at Antioch (2:11-2l)
III. AN EXPOSITION (3–4)
    A. How Paul Interrogated the Galatians (3:1-5)
    B. How Paul Instructed the Galatians (3:6–4:31)
        1. Believers Are the Seed of Abraham (3:6-29)
        2. Believers Are the Sons of God (4:1-31)
IV. AN EXHORTATION (5:1–6:10)
    A. The Law of Liberty in Christ (5:1-15)
    B. The Law of Likeness to Christ (5:16-26)
    C. The Law of Love for Christ (6:1-6)
    D. The Law of Life in Christ (6:7-10)
V. CONCLUSION (6:11-18)

Paul's Narrative

Paul saluted the Galatians in a curt and formal way and in his very first sentence positively asserted his apostleship. He told them he was astonished at the suddenness of their defection from the simple gospel, and he hurled his anathemas at those who had seduced them from Christ. He assured the Galatians that the gospel he preached was given to him by direct revelation from God, and he related how the "pillars" of the Jerusalem church had given him the right hand of fellowship. He told how he had championed the cause of Christian liberty, even going so far as to publicly rebuke Peter when his behavior seemed to jeopardize it. He explained in graphic language and in biographical form that he could afford to be dogmatic about the gospel, for it was delivered to him by God. He had declared it and defended it and knew his gospel was genuine.

Doctrinal Argument

Going back to the Old Testament and citing Abraham as an example, Paul showed that the doctrine of salvation by faith was by no means new. Abraham had been justified this way long before the law was given. As a matter of fact the true function of the law was to convict of sin and to prepare the way for the gospel.

Next Paul contrasted the position of a "child" under the law with that of a "son" under grace and illustrated his points by contrasting the child of Hagar, the bondwoman, with the child of Sarah, the free. Paul was saddened because the Galatians seemed so anxious to put themselves under bondage to the law when they might have been truly free in Christ.

Practical Exhortation

Paul urged the Galatians to stand fast in their Christian liberty and to allow the Spirit of God to lead them into a life of true victory over the works of the flesh. The true burden a Christian should bear is that of love. He warned also that there was a law which applied even to believers in Christ—the law of sowing and reaping. His parting words were biographical again and gave further insight into his physical sufferings and showed afresh the greatness of the Apostle's heart.

Martin Luther loved this epistle. "The epistle to the Galatians is my epistle," he said. "I have betrothed myself to it. It is my wife." The Christian today can obtain like blessing in the letter to the Galatians.

46
Ephesians: Higher Ground

T he epistles of Paul to the Ephesians, Colossians, Philippians, and to Philemon are known as prison epistles because they were written during his first captivity at Rome. The book of Acts records Paul's arrival under armed escort at Rome and his two-year detention in his own hired house. Paul turned his imprisonment to good account, making important contacts in the very household of Caesar (Philippians 1:13; 4:22), and writing four of the greatest and most Christ-exalting books of the New Testament. It is helpful to see the relationship the prison epistles have to Paul's other letters:

Imprisonment and Paul's Epistles

Written Before Imprisonment	Written During Imprisonment	Written After Imprisonment
1 Thessalonians	Colossians	1 Timothy
2 Thessalonians	Ephesians	Titus
Galatians	Philippians	
1 Corinthians		
2 Corinthians		
Romans	Philemon	2 Timothy (Paul was back in prison when he wrote this)

Paul's epistle to the Ephesians was probably a circular letter intended for the Ephesian church and also for the other churches of Asia mentioned in Revelation 2–3. The church at Ephesus was located in one of the great cities of the Roman Empire. At the close of Paul's second missionary journey he spent a weekend at Ephesus with Aquilla and Priscilla, promising to return as he left. On his third missionary journey he came back to Ephesus, remaining for about three years and establishing one of the greatest of all his churches. Tradition has it that the Apostle John spent the last years of his life at Ephesus and that he died there.

Outline of Ephesians

    I. INTRODUCTION (1:1-2)
   II. CONSIDERING THE HEIGHTS (1:3-14)
     A. The Mercies of God the Father (1:3-6)
     B. The Mediation of God the Son (1:7-12)
     C. The Ministry of God the Holy Spirit (1:13-14)
  III. CLIMBING THE HEIGHTS (1:15-23)
  IV. COMPREHENDING THE HEIGHTS (2–3)
     A. Redemption (2:1-10)
     B. Relationship (2:11-14)
     C. Reconciliation (2:15-18)
     D. Reconstruction (2:19-22)
     E. Revelation (3:1-6)
     F. Responsibility (3:7-13)
     G. Resources (3:14-21)
   V. CLAIMING THE HEIGHTS (4:1–6:9)
     A. The Vitality of the Body of Christ (4:1-16)
       1. Its Greatness (4:1-6)
       2. Its Gifts (4:7-16)
     B. The Victory of the Believer in Christ (4:17–6:9)
       1. The Christian and Self (4:17-24)
       2. The Christian and Satan (4:25-27)
       3. The Christian and Sin (4:28–5:4)
       4. The Christian and Salvation (5:5-14)
       5. The Christian and Service (5:15-21)
       6. The Christian and Society (5:22–6:9)
  VI. CONQUERING THE HEIGHTS (6:10-20)
     A. The Adversaries (6:10-12)
     B. The Armor (6:13-17)
     C. The Attack (6:18-20)
 VII. CONCLUSION (6:21-24)

The theme of both Colossians and Ephesians is Christ and the Church. In Colossians Christ is set forth as the Head of the Body (the Church), and in Ephesians the Church is set forth as the Body of Christ, the Head. In Ephesians Paul was at pains to promote more unity between Jews and Gentiles in the Church, since there were not two churches, only one. This idea runs through the epistle.

There is "one body, and one Spirit . . . one hope . . . one Lord, one faith, one baptism, one God and Father . . ." (4:4-6). The Church is depicted as a building (2:20-22), a body (4:4-13), and a bride (5:23-33), but there is only one church. Paul sets before us the wealth, the walk, and the warfare of the Christian. The epistle contains two great prayers (1:15-23; 3:14-21).

The opening verses of Ephesians introduce us to the heights. The Apostle's very language illustrates the magnificence of his theme. We are "blessed," "chosen," "predestinated," "accepted," and "sealed." We have "redemption through his blood," we have "forgiveness of sins," and we have "obtained an inheritance." We are faced with "the mystery of his will" and with "the praise of his glory."

Next, Paul bursts into prayer. With him we climb the heights to where Christ sits "far above all principality, and power, and might, and dominion." Then we see before us a panoramic view of the heights we are to enjoy in our Christian experience. We are redeemed and the middle wall of partition between Jew and Gentile is broken down. Complete reconciliation has been effected and the divine Architect is now engaged in building with living stones "an habitation of God through the Spirit"—His glorious Church.

The "mystery," long hidden, had now been revealed. So Paul set forth the glorious secret that the Gentiles were "fellow heirs and of the same body."

Paul next discussed the greatness and the gifts of the Church. The apostles and prophets (4:11) are associated with the foundation of the church (2:20), and their unique function is no longer needed. Evangelists, pastors, and teachers are still needed to exercise their ministry to sinners and to saints.

But the Church is composed of individuals. So Paul devoted an important section to the believer, showing the way to victory and focusing attention on the need for being filled with the Spirit. Only a Spirit-filled Christian can properly deal with the various relationships of life in which his lot is cast.

Paul concluded the epistle by showing how to conquer the heights and come to grips with spiritual adversaries "in heavenly places." It is important to observe that both our blessings and our battles are in the heavenlies, and it is this aspect of truth which makes Ephesians in the

New Testament so parallel to Joshua in the Old Testament. God has provided us with the armor we need for the fray and has placed His Word as a sword within our hands that, in prayer, we may press the attack against all our spiritual foes.

47
Philippians: Continual Rejoicing

P aul's letter to the Philippians was sent to the first Christian church he planted in Europe. His first visit to this city was on his second missionary journey, and he was accompanied by Silas and Timothy and probably Luke (Acts 16). The city of Philippi, a Roman military colony in Macedonia, probably had very few Jews in its population. Persecution of the missionaries at Philippi had arisen from Gentile sources. Only twice in the book of Acts is Gentile hostility thus manifested, and on each occasion it was because the gospel had threatened vested financial interests. The Philippian believers had retained their first love for Paul and had helped him more than once with his financial needs. The Apostle's gratitude is shown repeatedly in the epistle.

The church at Philippi was quite free from the many errors which called forth most of Paul's other letters. Paul's reasons for writing were twofold. He wished to acknowledge the receipt of a financial gift delivered by Epaphroditus, and he wished to urge some of the members of the church to lay aside animosity and live in peace one with another. Written in prison by a man chained day and night to a soldier—a man with few friends in Rome, a man with numerous vocal enemies—this letter, nevertheless, resounds with a note of joy. The word *rejoice* and its synonyms occur sixteen times in four short chapters.

Outline of Philippians

    I. PAUL'S TRIUMPHANT EXPERIENCES (1)
    Prison could not keep Paul from:
    A. His Pen (1:1-8)
    B. His Prayers (1:9-11)
    C. His Purpose (1:12-18)
    D. His Prospects (1:19-26)
    E. His Pulpit (1:27-30)
    II. PAUL'S TREMENDOUS EXAMPLES (2)
      A. The Lord: Triumphant in Sacrifice (2:1-18)
        1. The Implications for Christ (2:5-11)
        2. The Implications for Christians (2:1-4, 12-18)
      B. Timothy: Triumphant in Service (2:19-24)
      C. Epaphroditus: Triumphant in Sickness (2:25-30)
    III. PAUL'S TYPICAL EXHORTATIONS (3–4)
      A. You Cannot Defraud a Man Who Knows the Power of
        Proper Theology (3:1-21).
      B. You Cannot Defile a Man Who Knows the Power of
        Positive Thinking (4:1-9).
      C. You Cannot Defeat a Man Who Knows the Power of
        Perpetual Thanksgiving (4:11-20).
    IV. CONCLUSION (4:21-23)

Satan might keep a man like Paul from traveling but he can never keep him from triumphing. The epistle to the Philippians illustrates the words "more than conquerors." There was one man in the Philippian church who knew that Paul's emphasis on joy was real. That man was the jailer who had learned that neither chastisement nor chains could blunt the edge of Paul's triumph in Christ. He could date his conversion from the night that Paul and Silas had sung the songs of Zion in the Philippian jail until the very foundations of the prison had rocked.

The epistle to the Philippians gives us the key to this triumphant joy which could laugh at tribulation. "For to me to live is Christ," says Paul, "and to die is gain" (1:21). This outlook on life transformed misery into melody, prisons into palaces, and Roman soldiers into souls to be won for Christ. The first chapter of Philippians throbs with this triumph. "My bonds!" exclaimed Paul again and again. "My bonds! My bonds! Thank God for these bonds! Through these bonds the entire praetorian guard has been told of a greater king than Nero. Through these bonds many have taken courage to be bold for Christ. Yes, these very bonds have taught me to prize my prospects of an abundant entrance into the Savior's presence."

Paul's triumphs can be shared by all because of the triumph of Christ. Paul bade the saints to arm themselves with the mind of Christ and manifest the true Christian spirit. For did not Christ Himself lay aside His glory and stoop to conquer? Did He think equality with God a thing to be grasped after? Did He not rather clothe Himself with humanity, humble Himself, and become obedient unto even the death of the cross? And from this great stoop had He not been exalted on high and given the Name supreme? And were not the implications clear for all Christians? Would not those who followed in His steps experience a transformation of conduct, character, and concept? Yes indeed!

Next Paul cited the examples of Timothy and Epaphroditus, who became more than conquerors in service and in sickness. He reminded the Philippians that Timothy's service was exemplified by a true, total, and tested commitment to Christ (2:19-24). He told, too, how the sickness of Epaphroditus had affected himself and the patient, and how it should affect the Philippians, too (2:25-30).

In the last two chapters Paul made some practical applications. We need a proper theology of Christ if we are to experience His triumph. "That I might win Christ," said Paul, bringing into focus the truth of reward. "That I may know him," he said, underlining the truth of sanctification. "That I might apprehend," he said, emphasizing the truth of service.

Paul showed how "positive thinking" has its place in the life of a child of God. After all, we can only think of one thing at a time. If the mind is occupied with things which are true, honest, just, pure, and lovely—things indeed which are of good report—then indeed virtue and praise will flow from the life.

Paul did not forget that the praising man is the prevailing man, for he closed the epistle on a note of thanksgiving, contentment, and praise. The man who has learned how to take the circumstances of life and interpret them in the light of Calvary can thank God come what may. "I have learned in whatsoever state I am therewith to be content . . . I can do all things through Christ which strengtheneth me" (4:11, 13). Those who have learned this secret will not *react* to adverse situations but will *act* in triumph. They will be "more than conquerors."

48

Colossians:
Christ Supreme

C olossians stands in the same relation to Ephesians as Galatians does to Romans. Like Galatians, Colossians is polemic, that is, written to combat error. The error against which Paul warned in Colossians later became known as Gnosticism. Besides the Gnostic teachings, Jewish ideas were being entertained in the church at Colossae. Paul's answer to this subtle mixture was the supremacy of Christ.

The Gnostic heresy, a philosophy based on the notion that matter is evil, concerned itself with the origin of the universe and the nature of evil. The Gnostics watered the gospel down to a mere philosophy. Their great goal was for knowledge. On this they put their emphasis rather than on faith.

The Gnostics assumed that, since God is good and evil exists, and since (according to their assumption) evil is inherent in matter, God could not have created evil matter. Between God and matter they placed a series of emanations, spirits, and angels.

The Gnostics' idea was that one of these spirits came from God, then another from this one, and so on until there was one far enough away from God to have the power to create evil matter and yet not contaminate God. The bottom aeon or spirit was called Demiurge. The god of the Gnostics was not the God of the Bible who, according to them, was only one of the emanations.[1]

Confronted with the Person of Christ, the Gnostics placed Him either at the bottom of the list of spirits or somewhere in the center. In other words, they interpreted Christ in the light of their pagan philosophy. Some denied the humanity of Jesus, others took an opposite view, maintaining that whereas Jesus was an ordinary man until His baptism, at that time the aeon Christ came upon Him and remained with Him until just prior to His death on the cross.

The Gnostics' view that matter was essentially evil caused them to take divergent views of ethical problems. Some argued that since the body was evil it should be subdued, and the result was asceticism. The Essenes, and to some extent the Stoics, followed this line. Others took the view that the only way to overcome sensuality was to indulge bodily cravings to the full, even to excess, exhaustion, and satiety. The Epicureans were examples of this.

Grafted onto this pagan philosophy was a form of Pharisaical Judaism. The narrowest view of Jewish ritualism, insisting on circumcision, dietary laws, observance of feasts and fasts, and the whole cumbersome apparatus of ceremonial religion, was wedded to the original Gnostic heresy and presented as truth to the Colossian Christians. This special form of knowledge was presented as a "mystery," a secret available only to the initiated to be received by revelation and not by scientific deduction. Much of this type of "teaching" has been revived by present-day cults. Paul, in Colossians, wrote an inspired "nonsense" across the whole thing.

Outline of Colossians

I. INTRODUCTION (1:1-14)
II. THE TRUTH ABOUT THE CHRIST (1:15-29)
    A. The Deity of Christ (1:15-19)
    B. The Death of Christ (1:20-22)
    C. The Demands of Christ (1:23-29)
III. THE TRUTH ABOUT THE CULTS (2:1-23)
    A. We Are to Experience the Truth (2:1-7)
    B. We Are to Expose the Lie (2:8-23)
        1. That Christianity Depends on Secular Reasoning (2:8-15)
        2. That Christianity Relies on Sundry Rituals (2:16-17)
        3. That Christianity Looks for Special Revelations (2:18-19)
        4. That Christianity Adheres to Stricter Regulations (2:20-23)
IV. THE TRUTH ABOUT THE CHRISTIAN (3:1-4:6)
    A. The Statement of What Is Expected (3:1-4)
    B. The Steps to What Is Expected (3:5-4:6)

The Magnificence of Jesus

There are few more magnificent passages in the New Testament than Colossians 1:15-18, in which Paul set forth the Deity of Christ. He showed that all the divine personality, power, and purposes are centered in Christ. "All fulness" is in Him. He is the Creator and Sustainer of the entire universe, yet He died to reconcile men to God and therefore has every right to expect that those who trust in Him will "continue in the faith" and not be "moved away." Paul made known the true mystery: "Christ in you, the hope of glory" (1:26-27). In the New Testament, of course, a "mystery" is something which can be understood only by the initiated (the saved). It is an open secret, a truth once hidden but now revealed, a truth which would have been unknown without special revelation. Thus Paul cut right across the Gnostics' pretensions of "mysteries" by showing that all true believers are initiated into the true mysteries.

The Claims of the Cult

There are always those who would add human reasoning to divine revelation. Paul warned the Colossians against intellectualism. "Beware," he said, "lest any man spoil you through philosophy and vain deceit." J. B. Phillips translated it thus: "Be careful that nobody spoils your faith through intellectualism or high-sounding nonsense." Next Paul attacked the teaching that ritualism could add to the simplicity of the Christian faith. He showed that the rituals of the law were "shadows" (2:17), but that since the reality had come the shadows were done away. The shadow of a meal cannot satisfy a starving man; the shadow of a key cannot liberate a prisoner. Neither can religious shadows bring peace with God. As for the Gnostic pretensions about angels, Paul showed that they were talking of things which they claimed to have experienced but in so doing they were completely missing Christ. Finally he demolished the idea that Christianity had anything to gain from rules and regulations, fastings, bodily punishments, and the like. Such things, he said, tended to produce pride rather than perfection.

The Christian Life

As usual, Paul turned his attention to practical issues. In the closing chapters of Colossians he discussed the outworking of proper belief in proper behavior. The Christian truly is "risen with Christ" and is to set his affections on things above, manifesting the life of Christ in every situation as he lives in an evil world. His personal life is to be characterized by purity and love. In his spiritual life the Word of God is to issue in songs that ring out from the heart. Everything he does is to be governed by the Name. In his domestic life, the Christian is to quietly take the place of wife or husband, child or parent, and radiate Christ. In his business relationships, the believer is to be considerate of the rights of others, be he employer or employee, master or slave. In all the secular aspects of life the Christian is to so live that others will wish to become Christians, too. His prayers are to be pointed, his time is to be properly invested, and his conversation is to be pungent.

Paul closed the letter by referring to a dozen believers dear to him and known to the Colossians. These believers—Tychicus, Onesimus, Aristarchus, Marcus, Justus, Epaphras, Luke, Demas, Nymphas, and Archippus—are well worth getting to know with the aid of a concordance and a Bible dictionary. May our names shine as gloriously in the Book of God as do the names of some of these.

There's another lesson to be learned from these names as well. Says Alexander Maclaren, "There is something very solemn and pathetic in these shadowy names which appear for a moment on the page of Scripture, and are swallowed up of black night, like stars that suddenly blaze out for a week or two, and then dwindle and at last disappear altogether. They too lived and loved and strove and suffered and enjoyed: and now—all is gone, gone; the hot fire burned down to such a little handful of white ashes. Tychicus! Onesimus! two shadows that once were men! and as they are, so we shall be."

---

1. See: A. T. Robertson, *Paul and the Intellectuals* (rev. ed.; Nashville: Broadman Press, 1959), p. 10.

49

1 and 2 Thessalonians: Jesus Is Coming Again

1 Thessalonians

The church at Thessalonica was founded by Paul on his second missionary journey (Acts 17:1-9). Although some Jews believed, the majority of the Christians were Gentiles, and these were mostly slaves and members of the working class (4:11-12). Paul's brief but amazingly fruitful ministry at Thessalonica was abruptly terminated by unbelieving Jews who incited a riot, obliging Paul to move on. Paul and his companions then journeyed on to Berea. Driven out of Berea by persecution, Paul went on to Athens, leaving Timothy and Silas behind. At Athens Paul sent word for his companions to follow him speedily, but from 1 Thessalonians 3:1-2 it seems he sent Timothy back to Thessalonica to inquire after the welfare of the infant church there. In time, Timothy returned to Paul (now at Corinth), bringing a glowing account of the Thessalonian church (3:6). This prompted Paul to write his first letter to them.

The theme of 1 Thessalonians is the second coming of Christ and its effect upon believers. Each of the five chapters ends on the note of the second coming. Interestingly enough, there is not a single Old Testament quotation in the epistle, although there are Old Testament allusions (5:1 ff).

Analysis of 1 Thessalonians

    I. THE LORD'S COMING—A SAVING TRUTH (1)
       A. How the Thessalonians Have Continued with the Lord (1:1-4)
       B. How the Thessalonians First Came to the Lord (1:5-10)
    II. THE LORD'S COMING—A STIMULATING TRUTH (2)
       A. The Totality of Paul's Committal (2:1-2)
       B. The Transparency of Paul's Conduct (2:3-12)
       C. The Triumph of Paul's Converts (2:13-14)
       D. The Tragedy of Paul's Countrymen (2:15-16)
       E. The Tangibility of Paul's Crown (2:17-20)
    III. THE LORD'S COMING—A STABILIZING TRUTH (3)
       A. Paul's Concern (3:1-5)
       B. Paul's Comfort (3:6-11)
       C. Paul's Call (3:12-13)
    IV. THE LORD'S COMING—A STRENGTHENING TRUTH (4)
       A. Our Mighty Potential (4:1-2)
       B. Our Moral Purity (4:3-8)
       C. Our Measured Progress (4:9-10)
       D. Our Manifest Purpose (4:11-12)
       E. Our Magnificent Prospects (4:13-18)
    V. THE LORD'S COMING—A SANCTIFYING TRUTH (5)
       A. A Word of Explanation (5:1-13)
         1. For the Sons of Men (5:1-3)
         2. For the Saints of God (5:4-13)
       B. A Word of Exhortation (5:14-28)
         1. Walk Virtuously (5:14-15)
         2. Walk Victoriously (5:16-28)

Paul was held in tender regard by the Thessalonian believers, so he felt no need to assert his apostolic authority. The only other epistles from which he excluded his title of apostle are 2 Thessalonians, Philippians, and Philemon. Paul began by recalling the conversion of his Thessalonian friends, reminding them how they "turned to God from idols to serve the living and true God; and to wait for his Son from heaven" (1:9-10).

Next Paul reminded them how careful he was when among them to behave himself in an exemplary way. He told of his joy that the Thessalonians unhesitatingly accepted God's Word at its face value. Although he had been driven out of their city by Jewish trouble-makers, Paul was stimulated by the thought that these very Thessalonian believers would comprise his hope, his joy, and his crown of rejoicing at the Lord's coming.

Repeatedly Paul told the Thessalonians of his desire to see them again. He recounted the comfort he received from Timothy's report and told how he ceaselessly prayed that he might have an opportunity to visit Thessalonica again and perfect that which was lacking in their faith (3:10). He fixed their attention again on the Lord's coming as a purifying hope, one which could give them real stability in their Christian lives.

Next Paul reminded them that they were to remember the charges he left with them and live as became saints. He then discussed the thrilling hope of the rapture awaiting all believers, living or dead, at the Lord's coming. This truth was to be a source of comfort and satisfaction to all.

Paul refreshed their minds on the "times and seasons" connected with the Lord's return and reminded them that His coming would be a time of disaster for those left behind. Believers are "not appointed to wrath" (5:9), but this does not mean they can live loosely. They are to live lives of practical sanctification so that their "whole spirit and soul and body be preserved blameless unto the coming of our Lord Jesus Christ" (5:23). Far from being an abstract theological idea, the truth of the Lord's coming is one of the most practical truths found in the New Testament.

2 Thessalonians

After writing his first letter to the Thessalonians, Paul received further news to the effect that the believers were being shaken in their faith on the matter of the Lord's return. Someone, it appears, had caused them to be troubled as to their relation to "the day of the Lord." Paul reminded the Thessalonians that he had already told them about these things (2:5), yet some had taken up the belief that that day had already begun (2:2). Paul told them that two things must happen before the Day of the Lord begins: there must be an apostasy and the Man of Sin must appear on the earth.

Paul's two Thessalonian letters have much in common. The first has to do mainly with the church, and the second mainly with the world; the first tells of Christ's appearing in the air, and the second tells of His advent to the earth; the first has to do chiefly with "the day of Christ," and the second chiefly with "the day of the Lord." Both contain important passages on the Lord's coming (1 Thessalonians 4:13-18; 2 Thessalonians 2:1-12).

Analysis of 2 Thessalonians

I. INTRODUCTION (1:1-2)
II. PAUL'S WORD OF ADMIRATION (1:3-12)

A. A Word of Undiluted Praise (1:3-4)
B. A Word of Undisputed Promise (1:5-10)
C. A Word of Undefeated Prayer (1:11-12)
III. PAUL'S WORD OF ADMONITION (2–3)
A. The Greatness of the Coming Lie (2:1-12)
1. The Immediate Deception Paul Fought (2:1-2)
2. The Immense Deception Paul Foresaw (2:3-12)
B. The Greatness of the Christian Life (2:13–3:15)
1. The Believer Is Chosen (2:13-14)
2. The Believer Is Challenged (2:15–3:5)
a. To Trust (2:15-17)
b. To Travail (3:1-2)
c. To Triumph (3:3-5)
3. The Believer Is Charged (3:6-15)
a. The Need for Discipline (3:6-11)
b. The Nature of Discipline (3:12-15)
IV. CONCLUSION (3:16-18)

Paul began his second letter by consoling the Thessalonians in their sufferings for the cause of Christ and by assuring them that the coming of Christ would bring them ample compensation as well as bringing a full measure of retribution on the world.

Next Paul turned his attention to the great falling away which will climax in the appearing of the Man of Sin and in the final consummation of the age. The last dispensation ended in the rejection of the true Christ; the present dispensation will end in the world's acceptance of the Antichrist. Paul assured the Thessalonians that finally the Restrainer (2:7) would be removed so that wickedness might come to its final bloom and be dealt with in judgment.

As in the first letter, the Apostle closed with practical admonitions. Some believers had become so convinced that the Lord's return was to take place immediately that they had given up working for a living and were thereby bringing the faith into disrepute. Paul told them plainly that the Lord's coming was not to be immediate and commanded them to get back to work. Waiting and working were to go hand in hand.

50

1 and 2 Timothy:
Pastoral Epistles

T imothy was the son of a Gentile father and a Jewish mother
(Acts 16:1, 3), reared in a knowledge of the Scriptures (2 Timothy 1:5; 3:14-15), and led to the Lord possibly by Paul himself
(1 Timothy 1:2). On his second missionary journey Paul found Timothy at Lystra. Timothy was well spoken of by the brethren of Lystra
and Iconium, and Paul determined to take him along as a member of
the missionary party. He became one of Paul's closest companions,
and to him Paul addressed two of his three pastoral letters. Paul's
second letter to Timothy was the last of which we have a record. Paul
gave Timothy the earliest instructions for the orderly arrangement of
the local church, and these instructions were of a simple nature. The
qualifications of a church leader, for example, are ethical and not
hierarchical in nature. From the various references in the New Testament, Timothy appears as a tactful young man of a nervous temperament
and a degree of physical weakness. He was a faithful and conscientious
worker, very dear to the Apostle and, indeed, the man Paul wanted with
him at the very end. Paul called him a "man of God," a high tribute indeed.

Outline of 1 Timothy

I. INTRODUCTION (1:1-2)
II. CHALLENGES MAINLY TO THE CHURCH (1:3–3:15)

A. As to Its Doctrine (1:3-20)
  1. The Loss of Truth (1:3-4)
  2. The Law of God (1:5-11)
  3. The Love of Christ (1:12-17)
  4. The Life of Faith (1:18-20)
B. As to Its Devotions (2:1-15)
  1. The Practice of Worship in the Church (2:1-8)
    a. Telling God about Men (2:1-3)
    b. Telling Men about God (2:4-8)
  2. The Place of Women in the Church (2:9-15)
    a. To Live in Sobriety (2:9-10)
    b. To Learn in Silence (2:11-15)
C. As to Its Duties (3:1-15)
  1. The Duties Discussed (3:1-13)
    a. Elders (3:1-7)
    b. Deacons (3:8-13)
  2. The Duties Displayed (3:14-15)
III. CHALLENGES MAINLY TO THE CHRISTIAN (3:16–6:19)
A. To Walk with God (3:16–4:16)
  1. The Mystery of Godliness Discussed (3:16–4:7a)
    a. Displayed in Christ (3:16)
    b. Denied by Satan (4:1-7a)
  2. The Manifestation of Godliness Discussed (4:7b-16)
    a. By Personal Exercise (4:7b-11)
    b. By Public Example (4:12-16)
B. To Witness for God (5:1–6:19)
  1. To the People of God (5:1–6:2)
    a. Fellowship for Saints (5:1-2)
    b. Fairness for Widows (5:3-16)
    c. Faithfulness to Elders (5:17-25)
    d. Firmness to Servants (6:1-2)
  2. To the Peril of Gold (6:3-19)
    a. The Deceitfulness of Riches (6:3-10)
    b. The Denial of Riches (6:11-14)
    c. The Dedication of Riches (6:15-19)
IV. CONCLUSION (6:20-21)

Paul's first letter to Timothy contains much practical advice for a young Christian worker faced with problems in the local church and conscious of personal limitations. Paul was most concerned that Timothy take a firm stand against false doctrine. He warned that false teaching in many forms was abroad. He gave instruction as to the vitality and scope of prayer and insisted that a woman's place in the

225

local church was not that of a teacher but that of an ornament of truth. The qualifications of elders and deacons were next set forth. The standards of the Spirit of God for those who take a place of leadership in the church are high indeed.

In all things Timothy was to be an example, and was not to allow his youth to be a hindrance to him. Paul touched on the coming apostasy, briefly outlining its spirit and form. Within the local church, order, love, and exercise of spiritual gifts were to be practiced. Widows that were "widows indeed" were to be supported by the church, but those having relatives, or those young enough to support themselves, were not to expect charity from other believers. Elders were to be given the respect that belonged to them, and servants were to faithfully discharge their duties to their masters, especially if they were fortunate enough to have believing masters.

In conclusion Paul touched on the perils of "supposing that gain is godliness" and of desiring to be rich. "The love of money," he said, "is the root of all evil." He enjoined those who were rich to invest their wealth for eternity.

What an encouragement this letter must have been to Timothy. And what an encouragement it has been to Christian leaders ever since. As that apostasy which the Apostle foresaw draws ever closer, we need more than ever to take heed to Paul's clarion call!

2 Timothy

When Paul came to write his second letter to Timothy, Nero was on the rampage. It was a dangerous thing to confess Christ, and many had forsaken Paul. He was now in a damp, cold dungeon under sentence of death, or at least expecting that sentence any day. His light imprisonment of previous years was a thing of the past, and his imprisonment now could well have been in the Tullianum, known as "the sepulcher" because many in it were eaten alive by rats.

Outline of 2 Timothy

I. INTRODUCTION (1:1-2)
II. PRESENT TESTINGS (1:3–2:26)
    A. Timothy's Personal Responsibilities (1:3-18)
       1. To Develop His Faith (1:3-6)
       2. To Dispel His Fears (1:7-18)
          a. The Exhortation (1:7-11)
            (1) Remember God's Spirit (1:7)
            (2) Remember God's Son (1:8-10)

Paul reminded Timothy of his great spiritual heritage in the faith of both his mother Eunice and his grandmother Lois. He was to develop his faith in view of this heritage and also in view of the fact that he had been called and commissioned and gifted to be a leader of the Church. He was to take courage and lay aside his fears. "Be not thou therefore ashamed," said Paul (1:8). "I am not ashamed" (1:12). "Onesiphorus . . . was not ashamed" (1:16). Paul felt very keenly his abandonment by "all . . . which are in Asia" (1: 15) and by Demas (4:10) and others. To keep his beloved Timothy's responsibilities before him, Paul drew a number of brief pen pictures. Timothy was to be a steward, a soldier, an athlete, a husbandman, a sufferer, a student, a servant.

In 2 Timothy, Paul elaborated on the coming apostasy and sought to fortify the Lord's servants for times of fierce testing to come. He urged a more thorough grasp of the Scriptures (3:15-17) and a faithful discharge of duties despite the inevitable turning away from the truth. In closing he talked about himself, giving a picture of a lonely man abandoned by his friends, cold, longing for warmer clothing, wishing he had his books, and wanting some human hand to reach him in friendship and fellowship in the hour of his trial. Yet, withal, Paul triumphed and looked forward to his crown! May the Lord challenge us to seek as abundant an entry into glory as awaited Paul at the end.

The letters of Paul to Timothy, together with his letter to Titus, are commonly called "pastoral epistles." Paul had a true shepherd's heart for the flock of God and he considered it his responsibility to train others in this important work of caring for the spiritual needs of God's people. Nowhere else in the Bible do we find so many instructions for the pastoral care of the churches. The important matters taken up in these letters are not regarded from the point of view of the congregation, as is so often the case in other epistles. They are taken up from the viewpoint of the overseer. These pastoral epistles, then, are especially the handbooks of all those who seek the shepherd's crown in the crowning day that's coming by and by.

51

Titus:
Letter to a Young Man

itus was converted at a comparatively early period in Paul's
ministry, for he accompanied Paul and Barnabas as part of the
Antioch delegation to Jerusalem to settle the matter of Gentile
freedom from the ceremonial law (Galatians 2:1-4). Like Timothy he
was young and gifted and intimate with Paul; but whereas Timothy
was half Jew and had been circumcised by Paul, Titus was wholly
Gentile and uncircumcised. Paul entrusted both these young men with
difficult missions, sending Timothy to Corinth and Ephesus, and Titus
to Corinth and Crete.

Crete, an island southeast of Greece, was a mountainous but
populous place boasting an ancient civilization. The Cretans were
great sailors and famous bowmen but had a very bad moral reputation. We have no information on the founding of the church at Crete,
although we do know that Cretans were present at Jerusalem on the
day of Pentecost (Acts 2:11). After Paul's release from his first Roman
imprisonment, he and Titus journeyed to Crete (1:5, 11, 13). Paul
left Titus there to "set in order the things that are wanting, and
ordain elders in every city." Later, Paul asked him to come to Nicop-
olis (3:12) and probably from there he went on to Dalamatia (2
Timothy 4:10).

Analysis of Titus

I. INTRODUCTION (1:1-4)
II. THE NAMING OF ELDERS IN THE LOCAL CHURCH (1:5-9)
Elders are to be:
A. Family Men (1:5-6)
B. Faultless Men (1:7)
C. Friendly Men (1:8)
D. Faithful Men (1:9)
III. THE NATURE OF ERROR IN THE LOCAL CHURCH (1:10-16)
A. The Motives of False Teachers (1:10-11)
B. The Menace of False Teachers (1:12-13)
C. The Message of False Teachers (1:14)
D. The Morals of False Teachers (1:15-16)
IV. THE NEED OF EXERCISE IN THE LOCAL CHURCH (2:1–3:11)
A. Personal Exercise (2:1-15)
1. About Behavior (2:1-10)
2. About Beliefs (2:11-15)
a. In View of Present Grace (2:11-12)
b. In View of Promised Glory (2:13-15)
B. Practical Exercise (3:1-11)
1. As Subjects of the Land (3:1-2)
2. As Saints of the Lord (3:3-11)
a. Remembering What We Were (3:3-8)
b. Remaining Where We Are (3:9-11)
V. CONCLUSION (3:12-15)

The first chapter has to do with the appointment of elders over some local churches on the island of Crete. As in his letter to Timothy, Paul spelled out carefully what Titus should look for in those set to rule over the house of God. One important qualification was that of teaching ability, since false teachers had to be exposed and expelled from the fellowship.

The remaining two chapters deal with the conduct and convictions expected of those who were members of the local church. The return of the Lord was again mentioned by Paul as being a most practical truth and a spur to holy living. The Apostle also gave a brief summary of the impact true conversion was bound to have upon the individual (3:3-8). As in so many of Paul's epistles, his letter to Titus closed with reference to other believers to whom he sent greetings and instructions. "Maintain good works" was Paul's parting exhortation, reminding us that our beliefs must affect our behavior. Good works are not the basis for salvation, but they are certainly the evidence of it.

52

Philemon:
Brief Note from Paul

This brief note was written at the same time as the epistle to the
Colossians and sent to the same town by the hand of the same
man. The Phrygian city of Colossae was located a few miles from
Laodicea on the great trade route between Ephesus and the Euphrates.
The church at Colossae was not founded by Paul nor is there any
evidence that he ever preached in any of the cities in the Lycus Valley.
The city was probably evangelized from Ephesus (Acts 19:10). Among
its prominent church members were Epaphras, Philemon, Apphia,
Archippus and later, the slave Onesimus. The letter to Philemon
concerns him. Philemon was a close friend of the Apostle's and had
probably been led to Christ by him (Philemon 19-20). Philemon was a
slave owner and probably well-to-do and of the upper class. Apphia
appears to have been his wife, and Archippus, well spoken of by Paul,
seems to have been his son. Onesimus was one of his slaves who had
fled from his master, stealing money to make his getaway and sinking
himself at last in the great anonymous throngs of Rome. There he
came under the influence of Paul, was converted and sent back to
Philemon under cover of a brief note in which Paul bared his heart and
struck a blow at slavery. As a runaway slave, Onesimus could expect
scourging, mutilation, and either crucifixion or the arena, under
Roman law. But Paul urged Philemon to exercise grace and treat his
returned slave rather as "a brother beloved."

Analysis of Philemon

    I. INTRODUCTION (1-3)
    II. THE PRAISE OF PHILEMON (4-7)
    III. THE PLEA FOR ONESIMUS (8-17)
    IV. THE PLEDGE OF PAUL (18-22)
    V. CONCLUSION (23-25)

Paul played on the name "Onesimus," which means "profitable" (11). Having sincerely commended Philemon for his love and practical kindness to him in times past, Paul entreated Philemon to forego the claims of the law against his slave and receive him back as a brother. Note Paul's "I owe you" and his "You owe me" (18-19). He promised to stand good for all the loss incurred by Philemon because of the bad behavior of Onesimus in the past. He closed by telling Philemon he was confident he would do more than Paul suggested, and he said he expected to be liberated himself soon and hoped to visit him. The letter is a model of tact and beautifully portrays the gospel of reconciliation.

53

Hebrews:
Outside the Camp

T here is considerable divergence of opinion concerning the author of the book of Hebrews. Luke, Barnabas, Clement of Rome, Apollos, and the Apostle Paul have all been suggested. The arguments for a Pauline authorship are weighty enough despite the objections made. It is claimed that Paul could not have been the author of Hebrews because the language, the style, the arguments are not Pauline. Moreover the epistle is anonymous whereas Paul's other epistles all bear his signature. Against this it can be argued that whatever differences in style and language Hebrews may contain as compared with the known Pauline epistles, the thoughts and the reasonings are very much like Paul's. Moreover all of Paul's other epistles were addressed to Gentiles whereas Hebrews was written for Jews. But it should not be forgotten that Paul could describe himself as "a Hebrew of the Hebrews" (Philippians 3:5). The suspicion with which the Jews regarded Paul and their deep hatred of him would in itself be ample reason for his withholding his name from any general epistle addressed to them. The closing verses of the epistle could well have come from Paul (13:18-19). And the reference made to "my bonds" (10:34) and to Timothy (13:23), and the characteristically Pauline "Grace be with you all" (13:25), suggest that the epistle may not be so anonymous as is sometimes claimed.

One reason why no human name is appended to Hebrews meets us in the first verse, for this is the only epistle which begins with the divine name in its opening sentence. How authoritative and commanding and important this letter must be. And how right and proper it is that all human authors should sink from sight before that name above all names.

Romans and Hebrews

Hebrews and Romans have certain similarities profitable to bear in mind. Romans heads the list of the Pauline epistles, and Hebrews heads the list of the general epistles.

Romans expounds and explains the believer's relationship to the moral law, and Hebrews expounds and explains the believer's relationship to the ceremonial law. Romans moves from law to grace, and Hebrews, from shadow to substance.

Analysis of Hebrews

I. THE SUPERIOR PERSON OF CHRIST (1:1–8:5)
    A. Superior in His Majesty (1:1–2:18)
        1. To the Prophets (1:1-3)
        2. To the Angels (1:4–2:18)
    B. Superior in His Ministry (3:1–8:5)
        1. His Practical Ministry (3:1–4:13)
            a. Compared with Moses (3:1-19)
            b. Compared with Joshua (4:1-13)
        2. His Priestly Ministry (4:14–8:5)
            a. Compared with Aaron (4:14–5:4)
            b. Compared with Melchizedek (5:5–8:5)
II. THE SUPERIOR PROVISIONS OF CALVARY (8:6–10:39)
    A. We Have a Better Security (8:6-13).
        The old covenant provided only a temporary security.
    B. We Have a Better Sanctuary (9:1-10).
        The tabernacle provided only a transient sanctuary.
    C. We Have a Better Sacrifice (9:11–10:39).
        The offerings provided only a typical sacrifice.
III. THE SUPERIOR PRINCIPLES OF CONDUCT (11–13)
    A. The Powerful Working of Faith (11)
    B. The Patient Waiting of Hope (12)
    C. The Perfect Willingness of Love (13)

To understand the primary emphasis of Hebrews it should be remembered that it was written to recently converted Jews in the very early days of Christianity. Upon these new Jewish believers the old religious customs of Judaism still exerted a powerful force. The Jewish *temple,* for example, was still standing, crowning the summit of Mount Moriah with magnificent splendor. With all its gorgeous rituals and its elaborate system of sacrifices it beckoned the Jewish convert to Christ to come back to its fold. Jewish *traditions,* born and bred into the Jewish believer's heart, still powerfully called him to come back to Judaism. The grandest names in history were associated with that religion. Traditions hoary with antiquity pulled upon all the pious emotions, national sentiments, and even religious superstitions of the Jewish believer. The temptation to go back must have been great indeed. Jewish *ties* of family, friendship, and fellowship were very strong. These ties had enabled the Jew to overcome persecution and resist assimilation for centuries. Now, by his conversion to Christ they were all threatened with severance. During Christ's life on earth the Pharisees had opposed the gospel. And now, during the period covered by the book of Acts, the Sadducees resisted the gospel. Jewish opposition commenced with the persecution of Peter and climaxed in the persecution of Paul. It began in Jerusalem and spread far and wide throughout the Dispersion. Moreover the Church was becoming increasingly Gentile in composition and this was an added problem to the Jewish convert. Then Jewish *teachings* were hard to renounce. Hot and fierce were the debates against Christianity in those early days. How dare these Jewish Christians set aside the law of Moses, the Aaronic priesthood, the solemn rites and rituals of the sacrificial system? So all in all the new convert from Judaism to Christianity had many problems to face, all of which the epistle to the Hebrews was designed to answer.

Summary of Hebrews

One of the key words in Hebrews is *better* (1:4; 6:9; 7:7; 7:19, 22; 8:6; 9:23; 10:34; 11:16, 35, 40; 12:24). The writer wanted his fellow Jewish believers to see that in Christ they had gained much more than they had renounced in Judaism. Christ is better than the prophets and the angels, superior to Moses and to Joshua, and has a priestly ministry far superior to that of Aaron. The Christian has better promises, a better sanctuary, a better covenant, a better country, and a better resurrection. It is far better to worship in the true heavenly tabernacle than in a man-made temple on earth. The sacrifice of Calvary renders obsolete all the ceremonial washings and offerings required under the Mosaic law.

The writer of Hebrews repeatedly emphasized the word *heavens* and often employed the adjective *heavenly* (1:10; 3:1; 4:14; 6:4; 7:26; 8:1, 5; 9:23, 24; 10:34; 11:16; 12:22, 23, 25, 26). His purpose was to show that, in contrast with Judaism which is earthly and concerned with physical ceremonies, Christianity is heavenly and spiritual. Another vital truth is connected with the word *once* and the thought "once for all" (6:4; 7:27; 9:12, 26, 28; 10:2, 10; 12:26, 27) intended to convey the truth of the absolute finality of the Christian revelation. It can readily be seen how these truths would encourage Jewish Christians who, for Christ's sake, had gone "outside the camp, bearing his reproach" (13:13).

Warning passages are prominent in the book. In 2:1-4 we are warned not to drift, in 3:7–4:13 we are told not to disbelieve, in 5:11–6:20 we are exhorted not to degenerate, in 10:26-39 we are urged not to despise, and in 12:15-29 we are commanded not to depart.

The epistle ends with strong emphasis on faith, hope, and love and with urgent exhortation to live out practically on earth all that is implied in our position in the heavenlies.

54

James: Belief That Behaves

Controversy has been waged about the author of the book of James. The writer calls himself "James, a servant of God and of the Lord Jesus Christ." The traditional view is that he was "the Lord's brother" (Galatians 1:19) who was prominent in the Jerusalem church and who took a leading part in the Council of Jerusalem (Acts 15. See also Matthew 13:55; Galatians 2:9). During the Lord's earthly life James was not a believer, but the Lord appeared to him after His resurrection (1 Corinthians 15:7).

The epistle is addressed to "the twelve tribes scattered abroad" but it is evident from its contents that it is primarily addressed to Jewish Christians. It is generally agreed that the epistle was written before the fall of Jerusalem and probably even before the Council of Jerusalem. Some maintain that it is the earliest of all the New Testament documents. It could well have been written to those who had been present in Jerusalem on the day of Pentecost and who had carried away with them the barest essentials of Christianity—in fact little more than the Messiahship of Jesus. James wrote in the style of an Old Testament prophet. His language was vivid and picturesque. He covered a wide range of subjects and drew repeatedly on the Old Testament, even the Apocrypha. It has been pointed out that, more than any other book of the New Testament, the book of James reflects the language of the Sermon on the Mount. The book is quite evidently not intended to be a theological treatise but rather a moral appeal.

Analysis of James

I. INTRODUCTION (1:1)
II. THE CHRISTIAN AND HIS BATTLES (1:2-16)
   A. The Testings of Christians (1:2-12)
      1. The Ppurpose of Testings (1:2-11)
         a. Our Enlargement (1:2-4)
         b. Our Enlightenment (1:5-8)
         c. Our Ennoblement (1:9-11)
      2. The Profit of Testings (1:12)
   B. The Temptations of Christians (1:13-16)
      1. The Source of Temptations (1:13-14)
      2. The Course of Temptations (1:15-16)
III. THE CHRISTIAN AND HIS BIBLE (1:17-27)
   A. The Bible Likened to a Gift (1:17-18)
      1. It Brings Divine Light (1:17)
      2. It Brings Divine Life (1:18)
   B. The Bible Likened to a Graft (1:19-22)
      1. It Will Change the Fruit of Our Lips (1:19-20)
      2. It Will Change the Fruit of Our Lives (1:21-22)
   C. The Bible Likened to a Glass (1:23-27)
      1. In Which We Look to Be Challenged (1:23-24)
      2. In Which We Look to Be Changed (1:25-27)
IV. THE CHRISTIAN AND HIS BRETHREN (2:1-13)
   Partiality is a sin against:
   A. The Lord (2:1-7)
   B. The Law (2:8-13)
V. THE CHRISTIAN AND HIS BELIEFS (2:14-26)
   The truth that "faith without works is dead" is:
   A. Emphatically Declared (2:14-17)
   B. Energetically Debated (2:18-20)
   C. Eternally Decided (2:21-26)
VI. THE CHRISTIAN AND HIS BEHAVIOR (3:1–4:12)
   A. Sin in the Life Must Be Revealed (3:1–4:4)
      1. In the Mouth (3:1-12)
      2. In the Mind (3:13-18)
      3. In the Members (4:1)
      4. In the Motives (4:2-4)
   B. Sin in the Life Must Be Resisted (4:5-10)
      1. Admit (4:5)
      2. Submit (4:6-7)
      3. Commit (4:8-10)
   C. Sin in the Life Must Be Repudiated (4:11-12)

VII. THE CHRISTIAN AND HIS BOASTING (4:13–5:6)
    It is wrong for the Christian to boast about:
    A. His Plans (4:13-17)
    B. His Prosperity (5:1-6)
VIII. THE CHRISTIAN AND HIS BURDENS (5:7-20)
    A. The Burden of Poverty (5:7-11)
    B. The Burden of Proof (5:12)
    C. The Burden of Prayer (5:13-18)
    D. The Burden for People (5:19-20)

The epistle of James is very practical, for James insists throughout on "a belief that behaves." Are testings and temptations being faced? Then the believer must see to it that he profits from the one and wins through to victory in the other. God may test but He does not tempt. The believer must distinguish between the two forms of experience. Is the believer reading his Bible? Then he must be sure to put its precepts into practice. Is there a temptation to show partiality to the rich and unkindness to the poor? This does not make much sense in the light of the way rich men usually behave. Does a man say he has faith? Then let him prove it by his works, as did Abraham and Rahab of old.

What is the test of a perfect man? The ability to hold his tongue, for of all the members the tongue is the most unruly. Why do some Christians seem to get no answers to prayer? Either because they do not pray or because they have lustful motives when they do pray. How can a Christian make even the devil flee? Simply by submitting himself to God. What will be the reward of the grasping rich? In the last days the working class will rise and demand its rights. If a Christian is happy, how should he express his joy? In singing psalms. If a Christian is sick what should he do? Call for the elders of the church and get right with God.

Who can read an epistle like this without coming under conviction of personal failure and shortcoming? James has great skill in getting at the conscience and translating Christianity into the practical everyday thing it is intended to be. This is a book by which we might well measure our lives.

Martin Luther's famous comment on James to the effect that it was "a veritable Epistle of straw" is based, of course, on the assumption that James contradicts Paul's doctrine of justification, by faith alone. But this is not so. Actually we are justified by faith in the sight of God and by works in the sight of man. The New Testament teaches that we are justified by grace, by blood, by faith, by works and by God.

55

1 and 2 Peter:
Salvation and Behavior

T he writer of the first epistle is unquestionably Peter, the great
apostle of the Gospels and of the book of Acts. This first epistle
of Peter was written from Babylon (5:13) and was addressed to
"the strangers scattered abroad throughout Pontus, Galatia,
Cappadocia, Asia, and Bithynia," regions forever associated with the
ministry of the Apostle Paul. From the emphasis on suffering in the
epistle it appears that the Jewish believers who were especially on
Peter's heart were in the midst of persecution for their faith in Christ.
Peter showed that Christ is our Example in suffering and the certainty
of our hope of glory. The latter part of the seventh decade of the first
century A.D. was certainly one of terrible persecution.

Outline of 1 Peter

    I. INTRODUCTION (1:1-2)
    II. THE QUESTION OF SALVATION (1:3-9)
    III. THE QUESTION OF SCRIPTURE (1:10-12)
    IV. THE QUESTION OF SANCTIFICATION (1:13-25)
    V. THE QUESTION OF SEPARATION (2:1-12)
    VI. THE QUESTION OF SUBMISSION (2:13–3:13)

Our salvation includes three elements: an expectant hope (1:3-4), an experiential faith (1:5-7), and an expressive love (1:8-9). So, come what may, the end is bound to be "joy unspeakable and full of glory." Persecution should not deter us, for did not the prophets of old diligently inquire into the Scriptures that came from their pens, seeking to understand "the sufferings of Christ and the glory that should follow"? Moreover the angels desire to gaze into these things of which believers have become partakers. Therefore the child of God must be holy. Peter contrasted "the former lusts" (1:14) with the family likeness (1:15) and went on to show that believers are "born again, not of corruptible seed, but of incorruptible, by the word of God, which liveth and abideth for ever" (1:23). Separation is essential to live a holy life. As newborn babes we are separated from the past habits of sin by *birth* (2:1-3), as living stones we are separated by *belief* from past habits of sin (2:4-10), and as strangers and pilgrims we are separated by *behavior* from past habits of sin (2:11).

Submission is an essential ingredient in the Christian life whether it be as subjects of the State, servants of a master, or saints of the Lord. We should submit even if suffering is entailed, for "Christ also suffered for us, leaving us an example, that ye should follow his steps" (2:21). An important section of the epistle deals specifically with the whole question of suffering. Peter showed that it will be experienced (3:14-17), for being a Christian does not exempt one from suffering. This was exemplified at Calvary (3:18-22). The Christ who allows us to suffer has Himself suffered and carried the whole experience right through to victory at God's right hand. Suffering indeed is to be expected (4:1-2), but it has an explanation (4:3-6) and can be exploited (4:7-11). Indeed, suffering was actually exalted by Peter, for he showed it to be a means of winning glory (4:12-14). Finally, Peter examined suffering and gave various reasons for it (4:15-19) .

Peter closed his epistle with exhortations to the shepherds of the flock and with warnings about Satan. The twin themes of suffering and glory run throughout the epistle, Peter describing himself as "a witness of the sufferings of Christ, and also a partaker of the glory" (5:1). In contrast with Peter, Paul was a witness of the glory and a partaker of the sufferings. In some measure every believer is called to share with Christ in both.

2 Peter

Controversy has raged around the authorship of this epistle but, despite the difference of tone between this one and 1 Peter, there are still good reasons for holding to the view that both these letters were Peter's. There is, of course, the direct claim of the epistle to be from Peter (1:1). The writer claims to be an apostle (1:1), claims to have been on the Mount of Transfiguration (1:16-18), claims to have been told by the Lord that he would die (1:13-15; John 21:18-19); and knew of Paul's epistles (3:15-16). Moreover there is a close resemblance between the two epistles, and the writer of 2 Peter claims to have written to his readers before (3:1).

In his second letter, Peter continues the practical teaching so characteristic of his first one and goes on to speak forcefully of the Lord's second coming. Peter knew he was to die. It is presumed that the second epistle was written soon after the first, probably before the fall of Jerusalem in A.D. 70. Peter's martyrdom took place about A.D. 68. Second Peter and Second Timothy have much in common, both writers being aware that martyrdom was near (2 Timothy 4:6; 2 Peter 1:14). Both warn of apostasy and both reflect the joyful spirit of the writers.

Outline of 2 Peter

I. THE CONVICTIONS OF THE FAITH (1)
  A. As to the Walk with God (1:1-15)
    1. The Secret of Commencing Well (1:1-4)
    2. The Secret of Continuing Well (1:5-9)
    3. The Secret of Completing Well (1:10-15)
  B. As to the Word of God (1:16-21)
II. THE CONTENTION FOR THE FAITH (2)
  A. The Doctrine of the Heretics (2:1-3a)
  B. The Doom of the Heretics (2:3b-9)
    1. The Nearness of That Doom (2:3b)
    2. The Nature of That Doom (2:4-9)
  C. The Deeds of the Heretics (2:10-22)
    1. Their Conduct Is Exposed (2:10-14)
    2. Their Claims Are Exposed (2:15-19)
    3. Their Converts Are Exposed (2:20-22)
III. THE CONSUMMATION OF THE FAITH (3)
  A. Peter Exposes the Scoffers (3:1-13)
    1. Their Insistent Denial of the Promise (3:1-4)
    2. Their Ignorant Denial of the Promise (3:5-13)
  B. Peter Exhorts the Saints (3:14-18)

It is one thing to start well in the Christian faith; it is something else to finish well. This was Peter's burden in the first chapter. Having reminded the saints that they had become "partakers of the divine nature," he went on to show that the Christian life thereafter was largely a matter of addition (1:5-7). Peter coveted for believers an "abundant entrance" into the everlasting kingdom and cited himself as an example of one who, with but a short time to live, was still faithful in serving his Lord. He urged the saints to rest their faith squarely on the Word of God.

Chapter 2 was devoted to an exposure of heresy which was already making its inroads into the assemblies of God's people. Peter reminded his readers that heresies were not something new; they had characterized the Old Testament era and had been duly punished by God. The error against which Peter warned was accompanied by immoral tendencies, pride, and covetousness, and would certainly meet with the judgment of God.

Finally Peter reminded his readers that the last days would see the coming of a generation of scoffers mocking advent truth. The patience of God and His longsuffering would, however, one day be exhausted and a fearful catastrophe of fire would overtake the globe.

Peter's remarkable prophecy concerning the day of the Lord (3:10-11) is well worth careful study. The words he uses are most accurate and descriptive. The word for "elements" translates the Greek word *stoicheia* which carries the meaning of the letters of the alphabet. Greek scholars, such as Liddell and Scott tell us that it conveys the thought of "the components into which matter is ultimately divided." In modern language, the word would simply mean "atoms."

The word for "dissolved" literally means to break up, destroy or melt. It is translated "unloose" in several places in the New Testament.

The phrase "a great noise" signifies, according to W. E. Vine, "with rushing sound as of roaring flames." The same authority tells us that "with fervent heat" signifies a fever. Peter's is the only known use of the expression in connection with inanimate objects.

Thus Peter, an ignorant and unlearned fisherman, under the inspiration of the Holy Spirit, has accurately described for us, in non-technical language, something that has been reserved for the twentieth century to really appreciate. Many are convinced that the dawn of the atomic age has brought the world to the threshold of "that great and terrible day of the Lord."

Peter's second epistle is a timely one for today. Since God will one day make all things new we are urged to live godly lives, giving heed to all the Scriptures.

56

The Epistles of John: Letters from a Very Old Man

John's writings are dated near the end of the first century, between A.D. 85 and 95. John was a very old man when he wrote and had had ample time to weigh and ponder his early experiences with the Lord and the rise and spread of Christianity. In his day heresy had already made deep inroads. John's epistles are characterized by sharp tones of black and white with no shades of gray between. Things are either right or wrong, true or false, good or evil. It is either salvation or damnation, Christ or Antichrist, with no middle or neutral ground.

Westcott was of the opinion that 1 John was the last book of the New Testament to be written. Supposing this to be so then what a contrast there is between the way the Bible begins and the way it ends! It begins with the words "In the beginning God" (Genesis 1:1) and ends, if Westcott be correct, with the words "Little children, keep yourself from idols" (1 John 5:2).

1 John

John gave his reasons for writing (1:4; 2:1, 7-8, 12-14, 21, 26; 5:13). He assumed on the part of his readers a mature experience with God. John did not argue but stated truth at its face value and left it at that.

Outline of 1 John

I. EXPERIENCING THE LIGHT OF GOD (1–2)
  A. The Communion with God Observed (1:1–2:2)
  B. The Commandments of God Obeyed (2:3-11)
  C. The Commendation of God Obtained (2:12-29)
II. EXPERIENCING THE LOVE OF GOD (3–4)
  A. Love That Is Pure (3:1-9)
  B. Love That Is Practical (3:10-24)
  C. Love That Is Perfect (4:1-21)
III. EXPERIENCING THE LIFE OF GOD (5)
  A. The Life Received (5:1-5)
  B. The Life Recorded (5:6-12)
  C. The Life Revealed (5:13-21)

While Paul's characteristic words are *faith, hope,* and *love,* John's are *light, life,* and *love.* These three words are woven into both his Gospel and his epistle.

The first two chapters expose us to the light of God, contrasting the dazzling purity of His nature (1:5-6) with the dreadful pollution of ours (1:7–2:2). God's commandments are to be kept, and they are all summed up in the one word *love.* The test as to whether or not we dwell in the light is whether or not we love our brethren. Victory over the world and over the spirit of Antichrist is possible for every believer through the Word of God and the Spirit of God.

The next two chapters dwell largely on the theme of God's love. That love has brought us into His family and ensures that every child of God will one day wear the family likeness. Yet the truth of God's love is a practical one: "Hereby perceive we the love of God, because he laid down his life for us: and we ought to lay down our lives for the brethren" (3:16). It is nonsense to claim that the love of God dwells in our hearts when we refuse to help those of our brethren in less fortunate circumstances than ourselves. John's first letter shows that love is not only a practical *truth* of Christianity but also a practical *test* of Christianity. The perfection of love is revealed in chapter 4, for it not only exposes falsehood (4:1-6) but it exemplifies faithfulness (4:7-21). In this section we find that great verse, "Herein is our love made perfect, that we may have boldness in the day of judgment: because as he is, so are we in this world" (4:17). Those last nine monosyllables beautifully sum up the Christian life.

The last chapter of the epistle deals primarily with the life of God. We receive that life through the miracle of the new birth (5:1-5). This life is recorded and there are two witnesses to this: the Spirit of God

(5:6-8) and the Son of God (5:9-12). God expects men to believe the record He has given in His Word concerning His Son. "And this is the record, that God hath given unto us eternal life, and this life is in his Son. He that hath the Son hath life; and he that hath not the Son of God hath not life" (5:11-12). The life is revealed in those who have accepted Christ in confidence (5:14) and in conquest (5:18-21).

In his Gospel, John records the Lord's words to Nicodemus, "Ye must be born again." In his first epistle he takes up this theme and gives us five tests whereby we can know that the new birth has actually taken place in our experience. There is the test of spiritual *desire* (3:9), the test of spiritual *disposition* (4:7), the test of spiritual *discernment* (5:1), the test of spiritual *dynamic* (5:4) and the test of spiritual *deliverance* (5:18). Look up these references and put yourself to the test!

2 John

The second epistle of John is addressed to "the elect lady and her children." Some have contended that this refers to a local church or to a church universal. The simpler view is that it refers to an unknown lady, possibly a widow. It would seem from a comparison of the first and last verses that the aged apostle had met this lady's children when they were on a visit to their cousins and that he was impressed by their devotion to the things of God (4).

Outline of 2 John

> I. JOHN COMMENDS THE LADY (1-4)
> II. JOHN COMMANDS THE LADY (5-6)
> III. JOHN CAUTIONS THE LADY (7-13)

John began by commending this lady for the testimony of her children whom he found "walking in the truth." The "truth" appears to be the whole body of Christian teaching later called by John "the doctrine of Christ" (9). Next John reminded the lady of the great commandment which embraces all other commandments, the commandment to love one another. Finally he gave her a word of caution against false teachers and told her to look out for those who would come purveying false doctrine. It is no act of Christian love to receive into one's home those who deliberately deny Christ. On the contrary, for truth's sake, they are to be refused admission. It is false charity to open the door to false teaching. This is very practical advice we need to take to heart in these days of widespread heresy which all too often is spread "from house to house."

3 John

John's second epistle was addressed to a woman; his third was addressed to a man, Gaius by name. Three people in the New Testament bear the name of Gaius: Gaius of Corinth (Romans 16:23; 1 Corinthians 1:14), Gaius of Macedonia (Acts 19:29), and Gaius of Derbe (Acts 20:4-5). The Gaius addressed by John may well have been one of these. The little note concerns three people, Gaius, Diotrephes, and Demetrius.

Outline of 3 John

I. THE PROSPERITY OF GAIUS (1-8)
   A. This Prosperity Is Declared (1-2)
   B. This Prosperity Is Demonstrated (3-8)
      1. In His Character (3)
      2. In His Children (4)
      3. In His Charity (5-8)
II. THE PRIDE OF DIOTREPHES (9-11)
   A. How This Pride Was Revealed (9)
   B. How This Pride Was Rebuked (10-11)
III. THE PRAISE OF DEMETRIUS (12)
IV. CONCLUSION (13-14)

Gaius was a faithful man whose reputation for practical goodness was well known. John desired that he might prosper and be in health "even as thy soul prospereth." That might be a good test for us to apply to ourselves! He was faithful in his family and in his fellowship, many of the Lord's servants having been helped by him.

Diotrephes was a pompous elder in the church who had assumed such power that he could even repudiate the aged Apostle John and keep from the saints a letter he had sent them. John warned Diotrephes that he would deal with him if he came that way. It is interesting to compare Paul's "if I come" (2 Corinthians 13:2) with John's "if I come" (3 John 10). John, as it were, held the rod over Diotrephes but did not say what he would do to him. The coming of Paul and the coming of John perhaps illustrate the coming of the Lord, when all will get what they deserve. John urged his friend Gaius not to be influenced by the spirit of Diotrephes.

Little is known about Demetrius except his "good report." It would indeed be a blessed thing if that alone were to be remembered of us.

57

Jude:
Apostasy Unmasked

T he epistle of Jude was written by the "brother of James," so the
writer was probably the Lord's half brother. We know nothing
more of him save that he is mentioned in Matthew 13:55 and Mark
6:3. The intense Jewish character of the book strongly intimates that
it was written for Hebrew Christians. It bears a strong similarity to
parts of 2 Peter.

Analysis of Jude

I. HIS EXPLANATION (1-4)
   A. His Salutation (1-2)
   B. His Subject (3-4)
      1. Chosen (3a)
      2. Changed (3b-4)
II. HIS EXPOSITION (5-16)
   A. Past Analogy (5-7)
      1. The Lost Power of Israel (5)
      2. The Lost Position of the Angels (6)
      3. The Lost Purity of Sodom (7)
   B. Present Analysis (8-13)
      1. Presumption (8-10)

2. Perversion (11)
  a. Rebellion against the Way to God—Cain
  b. Rebellion against the Walk with God—Balaam
  c. Rebellion against the Worship of God—Korah
3. Pretension (12-13)
C. Prophetic Announcement (14-16)
  1. The Undoing of Apostates (14-15a)
  2. The Ungodliness of Apostates (15b)
  3. The Unrighteousness of Apostates (16)
III. HIS EXHORTATION (17-25)
A. His Practical Theology (17-23)
  1. The Word of God (17-19)
  2. The Word with God (20-21)
  3. The Word for God (22-23)
B. His Practical Doxology (24-25)

Jude intended to write to his readers of "the common salvation" but because of an alarming growth in apostasy felt urged instead to write unmasking "the acts of the apostates." His main argument was based on analogies from the past, a careful analysis of the current outbreak of apostasy, and a consideration of an ancient prophetic announcement concerning latter-day departure from the faith.

Jude's three examples from the past dealt with Israel, the fallen angels, and the city of Sodom. Each instance was intended as a warning and was chosen to show that vengeance always follows apostasy. Analyzing the apostasy which was creeping into the Church, Jude showed first of all that it was characterized by presumption. While so great a dignity as the Archangel Michael refrained from railing against the devil in a dispute over the body of Moses, the apostates had no such scruples. Filthy themselves, they did not hesitate to besmirch and blaspheme others far greater than themselves. Furthermore, the apostasy was characterized by perversion, the same type of perverse rebellion against God as had been shown by three men of the past, Cain, Balaam, and Korah. Cain founded a new religion based on works and furthered by violence. Balaam prostituted a divine gift for material gain. And Korah led a rebellion against the spiritual leadership of Moses and Aaron.

Enoch, living in the days which preceded the flood and on the very verge of a fearful apostasy, actually foresaw that the Lord's coming at the end of the age would be preceded by a fearful apostasy from the true faith. Enoch faithfully warned against this apostasy. Enoch's prophecy is remarkable, for it is recorded nowhere else in the Bible. This prophecy appears to have been drawn from the Apocryphal book of Enoch, which is supposed to have been written a century or more before the birth of Christ.

Jude, in drawing his urgent little note to an end, exhorted his readers. He pointed to the Word of God as the sure source of information on all apostasy. God had not been taken by surprise by the rise of false teachers, for in the Scriptures He had plainly warned that they would appear in the last days. Jude urged the believers to keep themselves in the love of God, to be built up in the faith and to pray in the Holy Ghost. Jude told them to have compassion on some who had fallen into apostasy but to "make a difference" and to be careful not to become contaminated. He concluded with one of the most magnificent doxologies in the New Testament, a doxology which guarantees to the true believer that he will be presented faultless in the coming day.

On every hand today the great apostasy so frequently mentioned in the New Testament is making its advance. Every believer needs to know what God has to say about this subject. Hence, as a textbook the book of Jude is unsurpassed.

58

Revelation: The Future Unveiled

T he book of Revelation is given its divine title in the first verse: "the Revelation of Jesus Christ." The language of the book is Greek, but its thoughts and idioms are Hebrew and it is saturated with Old Testament language. There are about 550 references to Old Testament passages in the book. It is closely related to the book of Daniel, to which it forms a sequel. Also, many interesting comparisons and contrasts can be made between Genesis and Revelation. Genesis tells of Paradise lost, Revelation speaks of Paradise regained. The Garden of Eden in Genesis gives way in Revelation to the City of God. The tree of life in Genesis is seen again in Revelation. The serpent appears in Genesis and meets his doom in Revelation. Sin, sorrow, tears, the curse—all begin in Genesis and all vanish in Revelation. The book of Revelation naturally completes the circle of revealed truth begun in Genesis.

There are four main schools of interpretation of this book. The *preterists* maintain that the greatest part of the book has already been fulfilled in the early history of the Church. The *historicists* claim that the book of Revelation covers the whole period of history from the apostolic period to the present time. The *idealists* spiritualize the teaching of the book and say that it does not set forth actual events at all but that its symbols depict spiritual realities. The *futurists* believe that the major part of the book has to do with what is still future.

Outline of Revelation

I. INTRODUCTION (1:1-3)
II. VISIONS OF GRACE (1:4–3:22)
   A. The Vision John Had of the Christ (1:4-20)
      1. His Position (1:4-6)
      2. His Purpose (1:7-8)
      3. His Providence (1:9-11)
      4. His Person (1:12-16)
      5. His Power (1:17-20)
   B. The Views Jesus Has of the Church (2:1–3:22)
      1. The Practical View
         a. Conditions That Were Present Then
         b. Conditions That Are Persistent Still
      2. The Prophetical View
III. VISIONS OF GOVERNMENT (4–20)
   A. The Beginning of Sorrows (4–11)
      1. The Throne of Power in Heaven (4–5)
      2. The Throes of Power on Earth (6–11)
         a. The Breaking of the Seals (6–8)
            (1) Details Given Particularly
            (2) Design Given Parenthetically
         b. The Blowing of the Trumpets (9–11)
            (1) Details Given Particularly
            (2) Design Given Parenthetically
   B. The Beasts of Earth (12–18)
      1. A Preview of Their Kingdom (12)
      (the maturity of the plan) .
         a. The Extermination of Saints
         b. The Exaltation of Satan
      2. An Overview of Their Kingdom (13–16)
      (the malignity of the period)
         a. The Demands of the Beast
         b. The Designs of the Beast
         c. The Doom of the Beast
      3. A Review of Their Kingdom (17–18)
      (the mystery of the prince)
         a. Religious Monopoly (17:1-6)
         b. Personal Mystery (17:7-13)
         c. Political Monarchy (17:14-18)
         d. Economic Mastery (18:1-24)
   C. The Battle of Armageddon (19–20)
      1. Festive Joy in Heaven (19:1-10)

The scenes in the book of Revelation alternate between Heaven and earth with a precise regularity. We are given a scene in Heaven in which God's will is declared, and this is followed by a scene on earth wherein God's will is done. Thus this book shows us the full and final answer to that petition the Lord taught the disciples to make: "Thy will be done on earth as it is in heaven."

The first of John's visions was of the glorified Lord Himself. John saw Him in a threefold aspect: Godward, as the One "which is, and which was, and which is to come" (1:4); Selfward, as "the faithful witness, and the first begotten of the dead, and the prince of the kings of the earth" (1:5); Manward, as the One "that loved us, and washed us from our sins in his own blood, and hath made us kings and priests unto God" (1:5-6). John described Him: His garment, His hair, His eyes, His feet, His voice, His hand, His mouth, and His countenance. So terrific was the vision that John fell at His feet as dead (1:17). There is an interesting progression to be observed in this vision. John said, "I heard" (1:10), "I turned" (1:12), "I saw" (1:12), and "I fell" (1:17). It was the same beloved Lord upon whose breast he had leaned in former times, but now He was glorified and awesome. Yet, in grace, He ministered to the fears of His servant. John said, "And he laid his right hand upon me, saying unto me, Fear not; . . ." (1:17).

The Seven Churches

There are at least three different ways of studying the letters to the seven churches of Asia. Some see in them admonitions to seven literal churches in Asia Minor existing in John's day. Others see in them practical injunctions to churches in all ages of the Church era, the seven churches addressed typifying conditions which constantly reappear in various local gatherings of God's people. Yet another view takes the seven churches as being prophetical and symbolizing the entire history of the Church on earth. According to this view *Ephesus* depicts the postapostolic era with the gradual falling away of the church from its first love. *Smyrna* sets forth the era of the persecuting Caesars. *Pergamos* focuses attention on the day when Christianity became the state religion of the Roman empire. *Thyatira* covers the Papal era. *Sardis* deals with the growth of Protestantism. *Philadelphia* draws attention to the religious revivals and the new emphasis on missions that would come toward the end. And *Laodicea* brings down the curtain on the worldliness of the church at last.

The Government of God

The greater part of the book of Revelation deals with the judgments of God which harden the hearts of men, making possible the coming of the Beast, the Antichrist, the Man of Sin. After showing us that "God is still on the throne" (chapters 4–5), John showed how the seals and trumpets usher in appalling conditions on earth. It has been suggested that under the seals *man* is seen bringing trouble on the earth but that under the trumpets it is *Satan* who is the prime actor. The last three trumpet judgments have additional horrors in the form of woes (8:13; 12:12).

When the trumpet judgments have run their course, the scene is set for the appearing of the devil's false Messiah. This person is called the Beast in Revelation 13 and is given his power by Satan. Chapter 17, which looks back upon the coming of this Beast, tells us he will be a resurrected man and will be hand in glove with a world apostate religious system. The Beast will be ably seconded in his schemes by a second beast who will persuade the peoples of the earth to worship the first beast's image. Signs and lying wonders will be performed by this pair to awe the world and bring all peoples under their influence. Those who refuse to wear the Beast's "mark" will be slain. Two prophets, appearing in the spirit and power of Moses and Elijah, will spearhead the resistance of the faithful, but eventually the two will be slain in Jerusalem and their death will become the occasion for universal jubilation. This Satan-inspired joy will be short-lived because the slain prophets will be publicly restored to life by God. To consolidate his power, the Antichrist will use his allies to overthrow the apostate religious system which had helped him in the early days of his rise to dominion. The Beast's kingdom will at first give every promise of prosperity, as chapter 18 depicts, but when he shows his true colors and insists that all men wear his mark, God will intervene. As the Beast's tyranny increases God will begin to pour out His vials of wrath against him. The final act in the drama will take place when the armies of the world are summoned to Armageddon to fight against the Lord Himself. The Lord will descend from Heaven on a white horse and sweep the field. The two beasts will be cast into the lake of fire, and the devil will be chained for a thousand years. At the end of the millennium period Satan will again be loosed and lead the last rebellion against the Lord. Fiery judgment will sweep the globe, and then all the dead of all the ages (all those who have had no share in the first resurrection) will be summoned to appear before the great white throne. At this last dread trial men will be judged by their works and doomed accordingly.

Glory

The book of Revelation concludes with a view of the celestial City, from which are excluded forever all those who have resisted God and refused His claims. Three times before the last amen is written we have the Lord's proclamation of His certain coming again. Every redeemed heart must echo the last prayer of Holy Writ, "Even so, come, Lord Jesus."

The Sevens of Revelation

	1	2	3	4	5	6	7
INTRODUCTION	THE SEVEN CHURCHES						
THE HEAVENLY VISION	1	2	3	4	5	6	7
THE SEVEN SEALS	1	2	3	4	5	6 THOSE SAVED DURING THE GREAT TRIBULATION	7
THE SEVEN TRUMPETS	1	2	3	4	5 WOE	6 WOE THE LITTLE BOOK / THE TWO WITNESSES	7 WOE
THE SEVEN PERSONAGES	1	2	3	4	5	6	7 THE THREE ANGELS / HARVEST VINTAGE
THE SEVEN VIALS	1	2	3	4	5	6 THE THREE FROGS	7
THE SEVEN DOOMS	1	2	3	4 THE MILLENNIUM	5	6	7 NEW HEAVEN AND NEW EARTH